London's Underground Spaces

Edinburgh Critical Studies in Victorian Culture

Series Editor: Julian Wolfreys

Volumes available in the series:

In Lady Audley's Shadow: Mary Elizabeth Braddon and Victorian Literary Genres
Saverio Tomaiuolo
978 0 7486 4115 4 Hbk

Blasted Literature: Victorian Political Fiction and the Shock of Modernism
Deaglán Ó Donghaile
978 0 7486 4067 6 Hbk

William Morris and the Idea of Community: Romance, History and Propaganda, 1880–1914
Anna Vaninskaya
978 0 7486 4149 9 Hbk

1895: Drama, Disaster and Disgrace in Late Victorian Britain
Nicholas Freeman
978 0 7486 4056 0 Hbk

Determined Spirits: Eugenics, Heredity and Racial Regeneration in Anglo-American Spiritualist Writing, 1848–1930
Christine Ferguson
978 0 7486 3965 6 Hbk

Dickens's London: Perception, Subjectivity and Phenomenal Urban Multiplicity
Julian Wolfreys
978 0 7486 4040 9 Hbk

Re-Imagining the 'Dark Continent' in fin de siècle *Literature*
Robbie McLaughlan
978 0 7486 4715 6 Hbk

Roomscape: Women Readers in the British Museum from George Eliot to Virginia Woolf
Susan David Bernstein
978 0 7486 4065 2 Hbk

Walter Pater: Individualism and Aesthetic Philosophy
Kate Hext
978 0 7486 4625 8 Hbk

London's Underground Spaces: Representing the Victorian City, 1840–1915
Hwang Haewon
978 0 7486 7607 1 Hbk

Moving Images: Nineteenth-Century Reading and Screen Practices
Helen Groth
978 0 7486 6948 6 Hbk

Jane Morris: The Burden of History
Wendy Parkins
978 0 7486 4127 7 Hbk

Thomas Hardy's Legal Fictions
Trish Ferguson
978 0 7486 7324 7 Hbk

Forthcoming volumes:

Her Father's Name: Gender, Theatricality and Spiritualism in Florence Marryat's Fiction
Tatiana Kontou
978 0 7486 4007 2 Hbk

British India and Victorian Culture
Máire ni Fhlathúin
978 0 7486 4068 3 Hbk

Women and the Railway, 1850–1915
Anna Despotopoulou
978 0 7486 7694 1 Hbk

Visit the Edinburgh Critical Studies in Victorian Culture web page at www.euppublishing.com/series/ecve

Also Available:
Victoriographies – A Journal of Nineteenth-Century Writing, 1790–1914, edited by Julian Wolfreys.
ISSN: 2044-2416
www.eupjournals.com/vic

London's Underground Spaces

Representing the Victorian City, 1840–1915

Haewon Hwang

EDINBURGH
University Press

Edinburgh University Press Ltd
22 George Square, Edinburgh EH8 9LF

www.euppublishing.com

Typeset in 10.5/13 Sabon by
Servis Filmsetting Ltd, Stockport, Cheshire,
and printed and bound in Great Britain by
CPI Group (UK) Ltd, Croydon CR0 4YY

A CIP record for this book is available from the British Library

ISBN 978 0 7486 7607 1 (hardback)
ISBN 978 0 7486 7608 8 (webready PDF)
ISBN 978 0 7486 7609 5 (epub)

Contents

List of Illustrations

Series Editor's Preface

'Victorian' is a term, at once indicative of a strongly determined concept and an often notoriously vague notion, emptied of all meaningful content by the many journalistic misconceptions that persist about the inhabitants and cultures of the British Isles and Victoria's Empire in the nineteenth century. As such, it has become a by-word for the assumption of various, often contradictory habits of thought, belief, behaviour and perceptions. Victorian studies and studies in nineteenth-century literature and culture have, from their institutional inception, questioned narrowness of presumption, pushed at the limits of the nominal definition, and have sought to question the very grounds on which the unreflective perception of the so-called Victorian has been built; and so they continue to do. Victorian and nineteenth-century studies of literature and culture maintain a breadth and diversity of interest, of focus and inquiry, in an interrogative and intellectually open-minded and challenging manner, which are equal to the exploration and inquisitiveness of its subjects. Many of the questions asked by scholars and researchers of the innumerable productions of nineteenth-century society actively put into suspension the clichés and stereotypes of 'Victorianism', whether the approach has been sustained by historical, scientific, philosophical, empirical, ideological or theoretical concerns; indeed, it would be incorrect to assume that each of these approaches to the idea of the Victorian has been, or has remained, in the main exclusive, sealed off from the interests and engagements of other approaches. A vital interdisciplinarity has been pursued and embraced, for the most part, even as there has been contest and debate amongst Victorianists, pursued with as much fervour as the affirmative exploration between different disciplines and differing epistemologies put to work in the service of reading the nineteenth century.

Edinburgh Critical Studies in Victorian Culture aims to take up both the debates and the inventive approaches and departures from convention that studies in the nineteenth century have witnessed for the last half century at least. Aiming to maintain a 'Victorian' (in the most positive sense of that motif) spirit of inquiry, the series' purpose is to continue and augment the cross-fertilisation of interdisciplinary approaches, and to offer, in addition, a number of timely and untimely revisions of Victorian literature, culture, history and identity. At the same time, the series will ask questions concerning what has been missed or improperly received, misread, or not read at all, in order to present a multi-faceted and heterogeneous kaleidoscope of representations. Drawing on the most provocative, thoughtful and original research, the series will seek to prod at the notion of the 'Victorian', and in so doing, principally through theoretically and epistemologically sophisticated close readings of the historicity of literature and culture in the nineteenth century, to offer the reader provocative insights into a world that is at once overly familiar, and irreducibly different, other and strange. Working from original sources, primary documents and recent inter-disciplinary theoretical models, Edinburgh Critical Studies in Victorian Culture seeks not simply to push at the boundaries of research in the nineteenth century, but also to inaugurate the persistent erasure and provisional, strategic redrawing of those borders.

Julian Wolfreys

Acknowledgements

As I come up for air, I am indebted to many institutions and individuals for their generous support and guidance through this subterranean journey. First and foremost, I am grateful to the English Department at King's College London, in particular Mark Turner, who first inspired me to read the city in an 'uncommercial' way and continued to lend his critical insight and urban expertise in shaping this project into a book. Within the department, a special thanks goes to Max Saunders and Anna Snaith for their helpful comments, support and friendship, Josephine McDonagh for her timely feedback, John Stokes for his warmth and sense of humour, as well as Lizzie Eger and Clare Brant for their encouragement and empathy. My colleagues during my time at King's, especially Jane Darcy, Richard Maguire and Laurence Scott made this project all the more worthwhile, and postgraduate life would have been infinitely duller without Sarah Strachan, Susan Lowndes-Marques and Hope Wolf. I am also enormously thankful for the administrative, editorial and technological assistance of Dot Pearce, Helene Hokland, Kristin Jenson, Jonny Williams and Andria McGrath who all helped see this work to fruition.

Other scholars in the field, in particular, David L. Pike and Paul Dobraszczyk, inspired me to continue digging, even when I feared all had been excavated. My readers Laura Marcus and Ana Parejo Vadillo also illuminated various ways this work can fit into a larger discursive field, while William Todd III and Andreas Schönle opened my eyes to the depths of narratology and Dostoevsky in an earlier part of my academic life. Many of the sections received critical input from the participants of various London and 'Underground' conferences, hosted by the Institute of Historical Studies, University of Greenwich, University of Cambridge and City University of New York. I am also enormously thankful to Julian Wolfreys whose work I admired from an early stage and whose spectral observations 'punctuate' my own study in a re-ghosting of the

Victorian landscape. Furthermore, I would like to give special thanks to Jackie Jones and Jenny Daly at Edinburgh University Press for taking on this project with Julian and for seeing the potential for its inclusion in the series.

On the funding side, I am grateful to the AHRC, Roberts Funds, Inglis Studentship, and King's Postgraduate Teaching Fellowship for financially supporting my research and for the wonderful teaching opportunities at King's College London. Various museums, libraries and individuals also opened their doors generously and procured the materials and images I needed for this work, including The British Library (especially the staff at Rare Books), Senate House Library, The University of Hong Kong Library, Manchester City Galleries, Birmingham Central Library, University of Reading Library, Tate Britain, Victoria and Albert Museum, Bridgeman Art Gallery, London Transport Museum, The Museum of London, Imperial War Museum, Punch Limited, Hywel Williams, and Ministère de la Culture – Médiathèque du Patrimoine, Dist. RMN-Grand Palais / Imaginechina. Thames Water also deserves special thanks for allowing me to take my first foray into Bazalgette's sewers.

As this research spanned many cities and travelled across continents with me, I also wish to express my gratitude to everyone who made my transition from London to Hong Kong a smooth one. At The University of Hong Kong, I am extremely grateful to Julia Kuehn for welcoming me into the department and for the support I received from the faculty, especially from Paul Smethurst, Wendy Gan and Otto Heim. My students also deserve a special note of thanks for indulging my Derridean meanderings during lectures and seminars. I also found a welcome audience at The Chinese University of Hong Kong, where David Parker and Simon Haines graciously invited me to speak in their seminar series. Melissa Lee was instrumental in facilitating contact with the university and in introducing me to the visual culture of Hong Kong. Furthermore, I would like to thank Elaine Chan, Marvin Arellano, Eileen Estorninos, Anna Herminanda, and Emielin Aldea for giving me the greatest gift of time so that I could focus on this project over the years.

On a final and personal note, I would like to express my gratitude to my family who, despite the distance, carried me through the process. Special thanks to my mother Kyung Bun Min for instilling the love of language, literature and poetry, my sisters Haesin Jung and Haera Lee for their protection and encouragement through the years, their partners Stanley Jung and Edward Lee for their balanced outlook, their children; Tristan, Erin, Cameron, Chloe, Claire and Ethan for their boundless imagination and irrepressible spirit, Rod and Dot Taylor for their breadth and depth of artistic knowledge, Nick Taylor for never taking continental philosophers too seriously, and finally, to my children Kairo and Karina Taylor who were born between chapters and managed to breathe new life into them. This book is dedicated to the memory of my father, Jong Chon Hwang, who was a postal worker, union leader, photographer, newspaper editor, drycleaner and a champion of Korean-American immigrants in his all-too-brief lifetime.

Introduction

Qui si convien lasciare ogni sospetto; ogni viltà conviene qui sia morta.
Here must all hesitation be left behind; here every cowardice must meet its
death.

Dante Alighieri, 'Inferno' in *The Divine Comedy* (1321)

The dark and ominous warning that marks the threshold into Dante's
underworld, as well as the preface to Karl Marx's philosophical tract
Capital: A Critique of Political Economy, reveals the complex intersection of physical, metaphorical and metaphysical appropriations
of underground space from antiquity to modernity. Classical themes
of *katabasis*, or the meta-narrative of descent that dominated images of
heroic journeys, articulated a poetics of the underground that embraced
eschatological themes of death, redemption and renewal. Although
these associations remained critical in apprehending the underground
in earlier representations, it was not until the eighteenth century that
scientific discourse of geological explorations infused the rhetoric with
more rational and technical sensibilities, ultimately leading to such distinctions as the 'organic' and the 'inorganic' environment later defined
by the urban critic Lewis Mumford.[1] The space below ground, once
unknowable and unseen, was readily available to the naked eye, and
the contradictions between the concrete 'place' and the imagined 'space'
created anxieties on the surface of modern life, especially as subterranean networks began to proliferate in the nineteenth century, most
spectacularly in the cities of London and Paris.

This book's inquiry into the underground spaces of modernity
begins with the basic premise that the development of the subterranean
environment cannot be extricated from the social, cultural and political discourses shaping urban consciousness in Victorian London. As
population density, industrialisation and social fragmentation created
fissures on the surface of the city, technology and engineering developed
ways to control these anxieties by firmly burying them, literally and

figuratively, underground. The drilling, mining and excavations that allowed the urban eye to witness the depths of the earth and the space into which their fears and hopes were to be (dis)placed led to an eruption of underground sensibilities that permeated linguistic, artistic and literary representations of the lower depths. The pervasiveness of this theme is reiterated by Wendy Lesser, who argues that

> ... the underground is itself an excellent metaphor for metaphor. It is on the one hand, a real place in the world, and on the other hand it is an idea or a feeling: the physical place seems inherently suggestive of the spiritual or literary connotations, and those connotations in turn enrich our experience of the material object.[2]

In its fluidity, the underground becomes a shifting spatial locus that engages in a dialectical relationship with some of the crucial discourses emerging from the metropolis in the nineteenth century. By exploring the material infrastructures underneath the streets and analysing the points of intersection between the built environment and the urban imaginary, this study privileges the subterranean consciousness as the prevalent mode of mapping, experiencing and reinventing the city, one that persists in interrogating surface modes of existence in the contemporary world.

However, the concept of the 'underground' encompasses a vast array of spatial and sensorial experiences that are paradoxically subterranean and aboveground. Countless numbers of utility pipes, tunnels and wires compete for underground space, but there are also private cellars, vaults and bunkers as well as arcades, prisons and factories that imitate subterranean dwellings. The underworld is peopled by convicts, prostitutes, the homeless and revolutionaries, while real or imagined rats and alligators roam the conduits, terrorising the urban imagination. Recent studies on the underground also attest to the endless fascination and horror of what lies beneath the streets. In the most comprehensive historical text, *London under London* (1984), Richard Trench and Ellis Hillman guide the reader through the construction and consummation of various subterranean infrastructures, highlighting the struggles and the technological achievements of the first city to dig its way to expansion. Meanwhile, Stephen Smith's *Underground London: Travels Beneath the Streets* (2004) maintains a more anecdotal, dreamlike quality that clearly draws on Iain Sinclair's collections of the ruins and runes of London's underground past. The most recent contribution, Peter Ackroyd's *London Under* (2011), firmly puts the underground on the literary map as an enduring site of fascination, as he plumbs the murkier depths of London for '[f]orgotten things, discarded things, secret things'.[3] However, most work on this topic remains historical, focusing on engineering feats or disused spaces that become the stuff of myth for subterranean enthusiasts such as *Subterranea Britannica*, an organisation dedicated to meticulously discovering, recording and preserving underground spaces in the whole of the United Kingdom.[4] Other major studies on the underground cover individual infrastructure in minute detail; just on the history of the underground railway, there are volumes on its material development and impact on the city in such comprehensive works as T. C. Barker and Michael Robbins's two-volume *A History of London Transport* (1974) and Stephen Halliday's *Underground to Everywhere* (2001), which stand amidst the endless shelves of books in the London Transport Museum in Covent Garden. Furthermore, books on advertising and poetry on the Underground also provide coffee table dressing and popular reading materials for tourist consumption.

Due to the scope of available material, there was some expectation that finding representations of the underground in Victorian visual and literary works would be plentiful and provocative, especially as London was the first city in the world to lay down the new infrastructure. Although there was a great deal of historical information regarding the engineering and architectural significance of various structures, literary traces were almost as invisible as the spaces underneath. There were numerous, oblique references, perhaps a scene that mentioned a brief ride in an underground carriage, or an allusion to the sewers, but for the most part, the underground was not given any direct or sustained treatment in any novel, poetry or work of art that captured London's imaginary engagement with the space. It was only in later *fin-de-siècle* science-fiction novels that the underground emerges as an abstract, tech-nological space that coincides with the introduction of electrification and other scientific advancements that 'cleaned up' the underground, but for the most part, all that was left was a messy montage of subter-ranean clues that expressed the consciousness of the world below, but an unconscious avoidance with what should remain invisible from the surface of modern life. This glaring absence shifted the focus to two main concerns of this book. How do we conceptualise the underground in urban space, and how do we deal with what is unseen, intangible and inarticulable?

Among various theoretical approaches, there are two distinct yet complementary methodologies that are frequently utilised in the appre-hension of underground space. The first method is to paradoxically trace the underground through narratives and discourses aboveground, using Freud's strategies to uncover repressed anxieties about the world below.

The second approach evokes a Marxist reading of the divisions of classes through the layers of the underground that relegates the labouring classes to the lowest stratum of the economic hierarchy. In *Capital*, Marx reiterates this vertical axis by describing labour as the 'hidden abode of production' that sustains the upper world of visual commodities and capitalist consumption.[5] As Rosalind Williams confirms, 'Both Marx and Freud depend so much upon subterranean imagery that it is now virtually impossible to read a text about the underworld without filtering it through a Marxist or Freudian interpretation – without reading the buried world as the subconscious, or the working class, or both.'[6]

Although this study builds on these critical foundations, it also extends this trajectory by focusing on the *disappearance* of the underground as another significant way of reading spaces of *différance* in the city, relying on Jacques Derrida's work on deconstruction and spectrality to reveal a textual haunting of the underground in the Victorian imagination. His concept of 'hauntology', expressed most forcefully in *Specters of Marx* (1994), embodies two concepts, 'haunting' and 'ontology', which attempts to describe

> . . . an unnameable or almost unnameable thing: something, between something and someone, anyone or anything, something 'this thing' . . . that looks at us, that concerns us [qui nous regarde] . . . It is still nothing that can be seen when one speaks of it.[7]

'This thing' that lies beyond the realm of language is also embodied in the spectral traces of the underground, the existence of which radically destabilises the ways of understanding the modern metropolis. In literature, poetry and in the arts, the underground appears and reappears in fleeting images that resonate with some of the most critical debates on social progress and reform, allowing a critique of the system in oblique and circuitous ways. It is this idea of 'justice' that Derrida associates so strongly with spectres, the seemingly threatening nature of their appearance/reappearance, but the unassuming way in which they lay bare the apparatus by which institutions exercise control. Thus, this book not only examines the extent to which underground spaces were represented or under-represented, but it also uses the concept of looking below the surface as a textual practice in tracing the shadow of the underground in narratives that never explicitly refer to the space, but whose presence continues to radically destabilise the city.

As such, this book is also an extension of many of the critical works on Victorian haunting and spectrality that continue to challenge the contours of urban representation, in particular Julian Wolfreys' *Writing*

London: Materiality, Memory, Spectrality (2004). Tracing the trajectory of London writing from the *fin de siècle* to the twentieth century, Wolfreys demonstrates the city as a constant site of construction and erasure, relying on textual traces of urban experience that spectrally interpenetrate each other spatially and temporally:

> [T]he true city text, the true act of writing the city, allows for the production of the text that, in its formation is analogous with the city, and is thus a performative text inasmuch as it never merely represents or speaks of the city, but enacts the city's assemblage through the assemblage of traces, ruins and remainders that write the city in ruins, though never as such.[8]

The assemblage of underground traces also 'write' the city, and by placing these fragments alongside their material history, this study reveals how these images cohere or disintegrate, and what this might mean to the way we read Victorian London and indeed, literature as a whole.

In contributing most significantly to the transformation of London, three underground structures stand out as the main arteries and spaces through which the urban environment was reshaped and re-imagined, namely the sewers, the underground railway, and cemeteries. Because all of these spaces participated in the discourse of social reform, the final chapter also explores underground revolutionary organisations as a natural and metaphorical extension of the spatial practice of urban contestation. Although the material history of each infrastructure reveals a relatively sanitised picture of order and progress, other Victorian artefacts such as maps, cartoons, guidebooks and advertisements supplement this vision with the complexities and contradictions inherent in the underground. As a subject that might not have met the standards of the more conservative publishing houses, there were serious challenges in conceptualising such a space for writers. However, despite such difficulties conforming to a conservative middle-class readership, writers still managed to incorporate the material in innovative, almost impressionistic ways, embedding subterranean images within the realist, Gothic and modernist traditions. To this end, this book explores the ghostly presence of the underground in works of fiction written by more established authors such as Charles Dickens, Bram Stoker and Mary Elizabeth Braddon, but also finds a more sustained treatment of underground themes in their lesser-known short stories. Other less canonical authors, such as Sheridan LeFanu, Edward Bulwer-Lytton, and Emmuska Orczy also engage with the space in their short fiction and novellas, whose Gothic, science fiction, and detective mystery forms allow for the *frisson* with the underworld to emerge more fully.

The focus on the period 1840–1915 frames this argument, as the timeline coincides not only with the excavation and proliferation of subterranean conduits in London, but also with the modernisation that made the underground more streamlined and accessible, allowing for more imaginary engagement with the space at the turn of the century. What the underground, then, portended for modernism was the future, a future abruptly disrupted by the onset of World War I. This book traces this arc in the constant appearance, disappearance, and re-appearance of the underground space that shadowed some of the most critical moments or fissures in London's literary and cultural history. Although Paris figures largely in my analysis, this study does not attempt to draw a comparison between the two cities; rather, Paris brings into relief some of the more distinct features of London's underground landscape, as both cities clearly influenced each other in the formation of underground sensibilities. Their legacy, or as Derrida would term the 'inheritance', of Victorian substructures and subcultures will be touched upon in the conclusion, as other global cities appropriate the underground as a site of political struggle and dissidence in the fractured climate of the twenty-first century.

Amidst the increasing academic interest in underground spaces, this study is a product and an extension of two seminal works that have greatly expanded the potential for underground research beyond its historical realm. Rosalind Williams's *Notes on the Underground* (1990) is one of the first studies to analyse the significant relationship between literature, science and technology as they informed one another in the representation of the underground. She begins with the significance of mining in the early 1800s and characterises the underground as the first wholly technical, man-made space that disrupted the notion of surface and depth. In her elegant dissection, she observes that 'sublime images dominated the first industrial revolution, while fantastic ones characterized the second industrial revolution', and continues to ground her analysis in historical and temporal terms.[9] Although she covers a broad spectrum of underground spaces, from Milton's satanic underworld to World War II underground shelters, my focus is on the development of the underground in London from the Victorian era to the early twentieth century, as this crucial period cemented the foundation for all future representations. Furthermore, this study goes beyond material representations and excavates the types of discourses the underground engaged with on the surface of the city. For example, how did the design of the first interceptory sewers in the 1860s superimpose a new social and sanitary map onto the streets of London? How did the image of tunnels infested with rats become conflated with the image of the lower classes, prostitutes and foreigners? What psychic messes were contained underground that threatened Victorian categories of order and disorder?

In examining these questions, my book departs from the neatness of Williams's historically segmented approach to reveal how different visions of the subterranean space interpenetrated one another and created more contradictions in the modern city. Although she relies mostly on the impact of science on the underground, this study argues that the technological incursion into the subterranean space always jostled with the mythical notions embedded in the urban psyche, creating a form of ambivalence inherent in its conflicting representations. Thus, the 'sublime' cannot be divorced from the 'fantastical' in any clear manner in the discourse of the underground, just as one cannot extricate the 'mythical' from any 'technological' subterranean journey, as they are always superimposed by real and imagined associations from the past and present. Although the chapters are divided by individual underground infrastructure, the argument remains that the discourses of one always overlapped with others and that the social, cultural and political map of the underground has always been a struggle: a series of palimpsestic traces rather than the holistic, teleological cartography envisioned by Williams.

The second major work on the underground that informs this study is David Pike's *Subterranean Cities: The World beneath Paris and London* (2005).[10] His in-depth, encyclopaedic excavations of subterranean representations in literature, history and film have remapped the underground landscape and unearthed a dizzying array of subterranean images and metaphors, illuminating the vertical city from above and below. However, this book departs from his project in three significant ways. Firstly, the pervasiveness of what I term 'underground consciousness' is not based on the *abundance* of subterranean representations, which is the basis of Pike's argument, but an *absence* of any consistent or significant images that reveal how the underground impacted the urban imagination. This is precisely where Jacques Derrida's theory of 'spectrality' and 'non-presence' is instrumental in deconstructing the representation of subterranean spaces. Derrida's work provides the subtext for the methodology, which not only focuses on the moment when the underground appears, but also when it disappears. Such 'haunting' can be observed in *Our Mutual Friend* (1865), where Charles Dickens never explicitly mentions the sewer, though it is the ultimate novel of the sewer, as powerful as Victor Hugo's *Les Misérables* (1862) in its cloacal incantation and incarnation. When subterranean structures do appear in texts, they are often flickering, passing glimpses and not a major set piece for the novel; however, they remain a crucial nexus for encounters with the past, the subconscious and the unknown. Thus, the underground is ubiquitous, yet never fully articulated in the Victorian imagination; rather, it is represented in fragments and fleeting references that reveal the ephemerality and contingency of modern underground sensibilities.

Relying on this theoretical argument, the second point of divergence from David Pike's work is on his interpretation of the differences between Paris and London undergrounds, one that tends to privilege Paris as the locus of aesthetic and literary innovation with an affinity towards subterranean impulses. Both cities were epicentres of underground activity in the mid-nineteenth century. London, under the leadership of sanitary reformer Edwin Chadwick, expedited the development of underground sewers as well as new cemeteries *ex urbis* to counter the spread of infectious diseases. Simultaneously in Paris, Georges Haussmann pressed for *tout à l'égout*, while eradicating slums from the city centre and realigning the streets into the pristine squares and radial projections that attempted to clean up the messy *boues* of Paris. Both cities vied for international recognition for their technological achievements, but it was Paris that opened up its public works to the world. It offered guided tours through the vast corridors of skulls and bones in the Catacombs as well as boat trips through the sewers, whose novelty was touted in tourist brochures. Although Pike argues that the Parisian underworld was 'rendered as a spectacle' while London 'repressed', 'eliminated' and 'flushed out of sight whatever was defined as dirt', this book argues that London's mediation of underground spaces was equally present, though primarily through structural absences, allusive metaphors and Derridean 'hauntings' that sought to circumvent direct confrontation with the material subject for a more metaphorical conceptualisation of subterranean infrastructure.[11]

Finally, this work hopes to extend the research on the underground by shedding more light on feminine appropriations of underground space. All too often, the urban underground, as a technological space, is rendered in masculine terms, from the navvies digging the foundations of the earth to the engineers who designed the architecture and executed the design. Even the materials utilised in the construction – steel, glass and iron – evoke a rationalised, masculine subterranean environment with little room for the emotive, uncontrollable powers associated with the Victorian feminine. Although Pike briefly touches on women of the underworld, they are either grouped together with other marginalised sections of the urban populace – ragpickers, revolutionaries and slum dwellers – or seen as middle-class women who delight in the novelty of the new public transport or sewer boat tours. However, this study analyses the extent to which women reappropriated the underground and the subterranean metaphor to forge and create new identities in the rapidly expanding city. Through encounters in the underground or by 'going underground' and pursuing a secret existence, the subterranean descent helps us to rethink the way women occupied and refashioned their identities in the city. Although previous studies have made the inextricable link between sewers and prostitutes, this work will broaden the scope to see how other structures, most notably underground transport and cemeteries, also became gendered sites for issues relating to movement for women, as well as the women's movement.

Spatial Practices and Realignments

> A whole history remains to be written of *spaces* – which would at the same time be the history of *powers* . . . from the great strategies of geopolitics to the little tactics of the habitat.
>
> Michel Foucault, *Power/Knowledge* (1972–7)

In this intersection of urban and cultural studies, there are a number of theorists and critics whose work locates the underground as a fluid, discursive space that tells the history of powers through the history of the disempowered. In addition to Derrida, whose criticism helps to trace the haunting nature of underground spaces, a range of frameworks also contribute to the understanding of these layers and how to deal with the problem of invisibility.

One of the most critical philosophers who looms largely in this study is Michel Foucault, whose observations of surveillance, spatiality and discourse ground my research through its examination of social institutions and their distribution of knowledge and power. The underground, previously unseen and ungoverned, becomes another site of discipline and rationalisation as the space becomes co-opted by transportation authorities and capitalist enterprises in the development of public works and private advertising. As Foucault maintains in *Discipline and Punish* (1977), 'visibility is a trap', and the Panopticon above attempts to extend its gaze beneath the surface of the city to shed light on the underworld, from convicts and criminals to prostitutes and the poor. The drains and tunnels also remap the surface of the city, as loci of power remain the dominant nodes of intersection for waste removal and urban transport. However, the underground manages to resist the all-seeing 'eye' and sustains its darkness, mystery and mythic power through individual spatial practices. Such democratising possibilities are articulated in Foucault's 'Of Other Spaces' (1967), which begins to sketch the outline of an alternative city through his vision of a 'heterotopia' that actively resists hegemonic, institutional forces. Primarily as a space of 'otherness', it always embodies dual meanings, subject to individual appropriations of the dominant space. In this sense, the underground railway can be seen as a collective, timetabled, utilitarian machine on the one hand, while in the Victorian imagination, it was also depicted as a private, time-less capsule of intimate itineraries and more transgressive encounters. In Foucault's spaces of difference, cemeteries and sewers also stand as resisting structures, or 'heterotopias of deviation', where individuals, whether through infection or sedition, remain outside the realm of the visible world of commodification and codification.

The second major theorist who informs my work is Henri Lefebvre, whose spatial observations also liberate urban spaces to the practices of individuals. Such interventions are elaborated in his critical work, *The Production of Space* (1974), which identifies the social relations that create and recreate spatial existence through everyday movements and practices. In defining his spatial triad, Lefebvre breaks down space into three components: perceived, conceived and lived. While 'perceived space' is governed by physical movements of the body and 'conceived space' born of social order and ideological imperatives, it is 'lived space' or 'representational space' that is produced by social interactions, 'embodying complex symbolisms, sometimes coded, sometimes not, linked to the *clandestine* or the *underground* side of social life, as also to art'.[12] The first two spaces are easier to identify within the material history of subterranean structures; however, it is the third space, the 'representational space' that eludes direct literary and aesthetic engage-ment that acts as a crucial structuring absence in the Victorian imagina-tion. Lefebvre's view that 'space is never empty: it always embodies a meaning' draws on Marxist ideas of production, where all spaces carry traces of individual experience that may be invisible but is critical to the visual economy or the spectacle of the city.[13] It is within this socio-spatial dialectic that the underground serves as the 'representational' space of the city, a fluid, 'clandestine' side of modern life that resists categorisation but reveals the contradictions inherent in the world above.

Aesthetic and sensorial responses are also crucial in defining the underground space as a powerful demarcator of high and low cultural forms, repulsion and desire, cleanliness and filth. In the apprehension of subterranean space, Mary Douglas's anthropological work *Purity and Danger* (1966) serves as the foundation for understanding how these categories are created and disrupted in the development of underground sensibilities. Her theory of dirt as 'a matter out of place', which has been used frequently in feminist and cultural studies, reveals that ideas of filth and purity arise out of a cultural system which allows society to order the world.[14] Thus, pollution, rather than an absolute phenomenon, is the result of ambiguities in classification and systematic separation. The development of subterranean infrastructure then seeks to reinforce these boundaries, bodily and otherwise, to define modern civilisation as one that can dispose of dirt in all its material and metaphorical forms. Sewers and cemeteries bury bodily excretions and rotting corpses, while institutions and censors define what is pornography and art. However, the prevalence of filth in a multitude of forms, from 'dust' and mud to prostitution and poverty, attests to an explosion of discourses on filth that could not be contained underneath the city's surface. As Foucault explains in *The History of Sexuality* (1977), efforts to contain and codify sexuality led to an eruption of discourses on a topic considered taboo, which flooded medical journals, sensational novels, magazines and the arts. In the same manner, the underground became a locus of transgression and fascination, a liminal space that threatened the order of things above and illuminated the very inconsistencies of surface existence.

The development of olfactory senses is also crucial in defining high and low sensibilities, as the *eradication* of smell becomes a Victorian project that sought to counter such debilitating phenomena as the 'The Great Stink of London' in 1858. Alain Corbin's *The Foul and the Fragrant* (1986) is helpful in locating the nineteenth century as the era in which sanitary reformers used tactics to separate the 'deodorized bourgeoisie from the foul-smelling masses'.[15] This not only initiated massive works underneath the city, but also extended its rhetoric of hygiene to bodily regimens, from daily ablutions to the advent of perfumes in a new aesthetic of urban and bodily cleanliness. However, the most conceptual representation of disgust in its relationship to the underground appears in Winfried Menninghaus's *Disgust* (1999), which argues that this repulsive sensation is what lies below the surface of beauty and is a necessary 'other' of the beautiful in aesthetic discourse. He further maintains that disgust can be an imaginary sensation, but one that continues to threaten the classical ideal of bodily beauty. This counter-distinction is crucial in the way it informs one method of understanding Victorian associations of the underground space as a filthy, foul-smelling den of thieves and prostitutes in opposition to the ordered, sanitised and *propre* upper strata in a new spatial assessment of society and civilisation. Thus, sewers, cemeteries and even underground trains were seen as civilising agents to bury all that was seen as threatening and pollutive, thereby mapping the aesthetic discourse of the bodily strata onto the corpus of the city. Many of the illustrations used in this book are representative of this oscillation between attraction and repulsion, filth and cleanliness that emerged as a result of these discourses.

From the aesthetic and sensorial realm, Julia Kristeva takes the concept of disgust into psychoanalytical discourse in her study *Powers of Horror* (1982), which combines many of the discourses on filth and disgust to articulate a new power dynamic in the formation of underground sensibilities. Drawing on Freud and Lacan, she associates the 'abject' with bodily fluids and orifices, especially that of the maternal figure, which the subject must renounce in order to embrace the symbolic order.[16] The violation and horror arising from the separation from the mother resides in the subject's unconscious until it is invoked through corporeal and cultural transgressions, which point to the ways that society condemns the feminine as filthy. However, Kristeva notes that this act inevitably endows the maternal with great power. The insistence of the feminine reveals how the abject allows one to critique the paternal symbolic order through the moments in which the abject erupts from the buried conscious to the horror of the subject's association with it. Such encounters are rife in Victorian narratives, where the underground becomes the maternal-female space and the sudden awakening to its presence in everyday life becomes an uncanny presence that haunts the text in horrific ways. Violations, such as bodysnatching or even the common trope of a clandestine extramarital affair, raise the spectre of the 'abject' and often infantilises or incarcerates the subject in its wake. The discourse of disgust, then, is the ultimate discourse of the underground, in which the attending reactions of revolt and horror reveal an aesthetics of power and primordial impulses that challenge the psychic structure on which society relies.

Digging through the Layers

> The underground, the underground, the poet of the underground! The feuilleton writers repeat this as though there were something degrading in it for me. Fools, this is my glory, because truth is here.
> Fyodor Dostoevsky, *Notebooks for Notes from Underground* (1863)

In the proliferation of underground discourses, various subterranean infrastructures allude to the tunnelling metaphor in rich and suggestive ways. The completion of Marc Brunel's Thames Tunnel in 1843, the first underwater pathway in London, serves as a departing point, as it opened the Victorian imagination to the once-impossible concept of travelling and inhabiting the underworld. The chapters are divided into three main subterranean structures that were critical to urban expansion and which were the most provocative in their visual and literary apprehension of the underground: the sewers, the underground railway and cemeteries. Each chapter will raise specific questions about the underground's material *representation* and its conceptual *realisation* in the constant production and consumption of subterranean images and metaphors. The guiding principle underpinning construction was the concept of 'circulation' to counter various forms of blockages on the city streets; however, subterranean structures also gestured towards 'civilisation' that Victorians attempted to codify at the height of their imperial powers.

The first chapter on sewers argues that the material history and the literary representation of sewers were at odds with each other. Historically, the development of the underground drainage system that coincided with sanitary discourses concerning the spread of infectious diseases were widely reported and circulated. Parliamentary reports, combined with medical and scientific journals, argued for 'circulation versus stagnation', justifying the first system of underground sewers to distance human waste, bury the source of contamination out of sight and remove it from the centre of the city in an outward, centrifugal movement. However, the material and psychic space remained invisible in literary representations, as novelists circumvented the topic of bodily excrement for a wider discursive subject of filth, from mud and fog to 'dust' and slums. However, even in these surface manifestations, the metaphor of the sewer was prevalent, as the Thames came to represent the crisis of representation in its embodiment of both a sewer and a purifying agent, while moral filth flowed through rookeries and alleyways, personified by criminals, deviants, prostitutes and other 'lower orders'. The individual body had to be deodorised, while the body of the city had to be protected from miasmatic pollutants in its myriad forms.

In the conceptualisation of sewer, three segments of the urban populace were strongly associated with refuse and its removal: the poor, prostitutes and foreigners. Through the sketches of realism in Charles Dickens, George Gissing and Zola, this section reveals the connection between sewers and embodiment of the 'lower classes' in their social, moral and biological manifestations. Although sewers are never explicitly mentioned, their haunting presence consigns the working classes to a dark, subterranean realm, as fear of degeneration also permeated the discourse of filth. Another oblique representation of the sewers is made through its metaphoric affiliation with prostitutes, who were also seen as a force of moral and syphilitic contamination. It is only later in the nineteenth century that the tragic heroine is supplanted by a more sexual and socially ambiguous image in the novels of Zola, Gissing and Henry James, as they emerge from the underground to occupy more public areas of the city. Finally, I consider filth and sewers in relation to foreigners, who posed a threat to the distinct idea of 'Englishness' and raised middle-class anxieties about the potential of racial degeneration and contamination from abroad. This fear manifests itself in such texts as Bram Stoker's Gothic representations of 'otherness' and Arthur Conan Doyle's detective stories that attempt to remove foreign impurities in the city. Again, the discourse of the sewer and filth extends itself metaphorically beyond its material networks to ask broader political questions of national identity and power.

The second chapter on the underground railway builds on the themes of repulsion, attraction and circulation encountered in the sewers, but highlights the ways in which the subterranean space was eventually assimilated to the rhythms of everyday life. In the beginning, the ease and affordability of riding the underground train in the nineteenth century were always overshadowed by a spectre of disaster. While homes and buildings were destroyed in the construction of the railway, a series of explosions and railroad disasters caused shock and trauma for many of its commuters. Medical reports into poor ventilation and underground accidents uncovered the psychological stresses of the subterranean traveller, which were also represented in works by Dickens and Trollope, where the tension between man and technology manifests itself in ghostly preoccupations with death and destruction. Despite its negative connotations, the Underground ultimately became the acceptable mode of travel for working-class and middle-class commuters, and the section argues for a more redemptive reading of the underground through its speed and democratisation of movement in the metropolis.

The literary representation of the underground railway, however, also appears as Derridean traces haunting the lives of urban dwellers, especially women, as they began to explore the city through this new medium. As Derrida notes, 'Modern technology, contrary to appearances, although it is scientific, increases tenfold the power of ghosts. The future belongs to ghosts.'[17] Indeed journeys underground in the new technology of the metropolis were riddled with uncanny encounters, ghostly preoccupations and a return of violent memories. It was not until the electrification of train cars at the turn of the century that the underground railway sheds its image as a dangerous vehicle of steam and asphyxiation and is transformed into a utopian model of urban travel, whisking away individuals to the pictures or the promise of fresh air in the verdant 'Metroland' of the garden suburbs. In all its manifestations, the underground railway appears as a space of contradiction and paradoxes, as well as psychic displacement and oneiric possibilities, represented in the works of Gissing, Wells, Orczy and Pound.

From tunnels and transport networks that intimately connected urban dwellers, the next subterranean structure that radically reconfigures the socio-spatial dynamics of the city is the urban cemetery. Movement and circulation were still the guiding urban rationale in the spatial organisation of the necropolis, from the displacement of the dead *ex urbis* to the removal of burial grounds like St Pancras to build a major underground station. This chapter explores how the Victorians reconciled these utilitarian methods in treating the dead with the psychological trauma of death itself. The removal of graveyards from churches away from the city centre replaced the traditional notions of a Christian afterlife with a Derridean 'revenance' that lingers in the interstices of life and death in a perennial haunting of the Victorian imagination. The 'revenant', which Derrida describes as 'that which comes back', articulates a new form of mourning in which spirits and apparitions of the dead become very much a part of the present:

> It is something that one does not know, precisely, and one does not know if precisely it is, if it exists, if it responds to a name and corresponds to an essence. One does not know: not out of ignorance, but because this non-object, this non-present present, this being-there of an absent or departed one no longer belongs to knowledge.[18]

In confrontations with these spectres, all that lies outside the realm of language and knowledge returns to haunt the city in multifarious ways, gesturing towards the inability of the underground to contain corpses or anxieties about death.

Unlike the sewers and the underground railway, cemeteries and graveyards appear more frequently in imaginary works of fiction, but they become the site of haunting itself. The underground burial spaces reveal an absence of bodies, but an increasing presence of spirits or spectres that raise some of the crucial metaphysical questions of modern life. Dickens, again, confirms himself as the voice of the underworld as he boldly confronts the themes of death and resurrection in his novels and his 'Christmas Stories'. Meanwhile, Robert Louis Stevenson explores the dark life of resurrectionists, or body snatchers, whose recycling of corpses for medical purposes and financial gain ultimately reduced the dead body to a commodity, as well as a free-floating signifier for all that was abject and unspeakable in the discourse of death. As the belief in a Christian afterlife waned at the turn of the century, poets such as Thomas Hardy often explored death and mourning by assimilating the dead amongst the living, while Wilkie Collins and Mary Elizabeth

Braddon envisaged the tomb as a site of reinvention, particularly for women, though not without grave consequences. In the invocation and conjuration of spirits from the underground, London, then, becomes the surface manifestation of the graveyard itself in its final transformation as the city of the dead, anticipating the imagery of T. S. Eliot's wasteland at the turn of the century.

As material substructures are subsumed by metaphorical reappropriations, I focus on the most conceptual use of the 'underground' in Chapter 4 on revolutionary activities that divorced the term from direct spatial connotations. In this ideological framework, Marxism, nationalism and terrorism all converge in the network of subversive subterranean activities, which extended beyond the borders of London to Russia, Ireland, continental Europe and the Americas. Although socialist gatherings and political meetings were often spatialised in underground terms as a place that was hidden, secret and covert, the rhetoric of political movements was pervasive and contagious on the surface of the city, as demonstrations and dynamite targets, both below and aboveground, terrorised the urban imagination. The threats to overthrow monarchies on the continent, the assassination of President James A. Garfield and the murder of Tsar Alexander II in the 1880s all contributed to the sense of impending violence from an indistinguishable group of Marxists, nihilists and anarchists, whose motivations and actions overlapped in their depictions in literature and the popular press.

However, the majority of the attacks on London were plots by Fenian 'dynamitards' who were the first terrorists to plant bombs in underground railway stations and national monuments in their political offensive to establish an independent Irish Republic. Despite such visible forms of attack, the media and literature often elided the 'Irish Question' in favour of a more localised form of defiance, embodied in home-grown socialists. Although some sensational stories do recount the story of Irish defiance, many novels harboured the ghost of terrorism through more solipsistic and existential examinations of individual consciousness, rooted in Fyodor Dostoevsky's *Notes from Underground* (1864) that portrays the individual's struggle to extricate oneself from the social and political frameworks that define him. Through actions and words that no longer signify, this chapter examines the *absence* of terrorism in literary works by Henry James, Joseph Conrad, Robert Louis Stevenson, and G. K. Chesterton. Instead, the spectre of violence pervades the novel in private and domestic ways, while language also breaks down in the narrative of underground rebellion, as the staccato militancy of manifestos gives way to fragmentation, incoherence and even silence in literary representation. The insignificance of words and the impossibility of individual action become a recurring theme, echoing the restlessness and the preoccupation with the fate of humanity before the onset of World War I. In these texts, every event and speech act, rather than being a mimesis of terror, is a *mimicry* of that potential, as the underground as a space and as a metaphor for subversion wanes at the turn of the century.

Which Way to the Underground?

All that is solid melts into air, all that is holy is profaned, and man is at last compelled to face with sober senses, his real conditions of life, and his relations with his kind.

Karl Marx, *The Communist Manifesto* (1848)

The underground as a material repository of dreams, fears and subversion does not completely disappear at the turn of the twentieth century. Although the final section of the book focuses on the extent to which the built environment concedes to a more metaphorical space whose symbolic power decreases with each reappropriation, the underground, as a physical space, does not exactly 'melt into [the] air' of modernity. By engaging with some of the crucial discourses of the nineteenth century, the underground looks forward to a revival and re-scrutiny in the twenty-first century, as global subterranean spaces return to re-politicise the lower depths and renegotiate the antinomies of existence. However, the recurring themes that have their roots in Victorian London reveal an enduring preoccupation with the space that intermittently and unexpectedly resurfaces to engage the public consciousness with all that is unsaid and unseen in the urban environment.

Although many of the nineteenth-century tropes of the underground appear as clichés later in contemporary films and popular representations, I attempt to contextualise the subterranean space in its historical vivacity and audacity, locating it as one of the primary features of modernity that dislocated the individual's sense of time and space, while opening up new ways of apprehending urban life. While this book is not a comprehensive history of underground infrastructure, it attempts to highlight the significance of its history in the way the meaning of the 'underground' opened up new linguistic, aesthetic and literary modes of representation. Sewers, the underground railway and cemeteries were the first substructures to open up the imagination to the possibilities below, but their material presence was often substituted and *supplemented* by the Gothic impulse in Derridean hauntings. In deconstructing the underground, tracing its presence as well as its absence, I resist defining the underground in any fixed terms; rather, I suggest that the fluidity of the underground is where it derives its greatest power to radically challenge the vertical and visible aspects of the modern city that paradoxically sets itself against, yet relies on, this critical space of alterity to define itself.

Notes

1. See Mumford, *Technics and Civilization*, p. 69.
2. Lesser, *The Life Below Ground*, p. 3.
3. Ackroyd, *London Under*, p. 13.
4. For more details, see <www.subbrit.org.uk> (accessed 4 September 2007).
5. Marx, *Capital*, p. 279.
6. Williams, *Notes on the Underground*, p. 48.
7. Derrida, *Specters of Marx*, p. 6.
8. Wolfreys, *Writing London*, p. 217.
9. Williams, *Notes on the Underground*, p. 17.
10. Pike's most recent work, *Metropolis on the Styx*, also delves into the undergrounds of Paris and London, but focuses more on the image of hell in its urban manifestations.
11. Pike, 'Sewage Treatments: Vertical Space and Waste in Nineteenth-Century Paris and London', in Cohen and Johnson (eds), *Filth*, p. 55.
12. Lefebvre, *The Production of Space*, p. 33. Italics are my own.
13. Ibid. p. 154.
14. Douglas, *Purity and Danger*, p. 44.
15. Corbin, *The Foul and the Fragrant*, p. 55.
16. Kristeva, *Powers of Horror*.
17. Interview with Jacques Derrida and Bernard Stiegler [1993], *Echographies of Television*, p. 115.
18. Derrida, *Specters of Marx*, p. 6.

Chapter 1

The Incontinent City:
Sewers, Disgust and Liminality

Like the human body, London hides its organisms within it. There are arteries bearing the body's fluids, lungs enabling it to breathe, bones giving it support, muscles endowing it with strength, nerves carrying signals, and bowels disposing wastes.

Richard Trench and Ellis Hillman, *London under London* (1984)

Of all the corporeal functions that underground infrastructures support, the sewers and the removal of waste remain the most 'invisible' and unrecognised in the representation of the modern city. Perhaps the relegation of this most essential system speaks more of contemporary society's approach to human excrement: something to be forgotten with the first flush, an object to be eliminated from the home and diverted to the outskirts of the city, a solid that should be sublimated in some state-sponsored plant as we wash our hands clean of it. However, in all these elisions, the underlying rhetoric that permeates excremental (non)discourse is clear; the effective removal of filth and waste from the body of the city is essential in forging and maintaining social, psychological and cultural boundaries. As Alain Corbin maintains, 'The urban physiology of excretion constitutes one of the privileged means of access to social mentalities.'[1] By privileging the sewers and following the flow of their rationalisation in nineteenth-century London, this chapter attempts to unearth the links between the development of the underground sewer and its seeping impact on the surface of the city, from the spatial reorganisation of the urban landscape to the cultural formation of the sewer in the social and literary imagination. The sewer, as a conduit for urban refuse, becomes synonymous with all that is pollutive in the city, mapping a new flow of urban movement to cleanse the city of its material and metaphorical associations.

Before embarking on this journey, a history of the construction of the Victorian sewers sheds light on the context in which such representations surfaced. Despite the relatively 'clean' language that is associated with contemporary modes of waste disposal, the 'sewerage question' in the 1840s and 1850s was fraught with filthier implications. In discussing the state of the working classes, Steven Marcus argues that there was a significant shift in middle-class consciousness during this period, primarily because 'millions of English men, women and children were living in shit'.[2] Human excreta piled up in basement sewers, ran on surface drainages and emptied into the Thames, which in turn supplied London with approximately fifty per cent of the city's drinking water. A scathing *Punch* cartoon in 1849 alludes to the circulatory nature of sewage, as it traces the path of 'the water that John drinks' from 'the sewer . . . cesspool and sink', and gestures at the recycling of human waste into capital as it winks at the 'vested int'rests' of the government, which profited from its ostensible removal (Fig. 1.1). However, most of the waste remained stagnant in underground cesspits, as noxious odours permeated the floorboards above, releasing toxic gases throughout the building, with little or no ventilation. A description of a Westminster workhouse in 1851 elaborates on the abject state of affairs:

> A chamber is reached about 30 feet in length, from the roof of which hangings of putrid matter like stalactites descend three feet in length . . . The deposits have been found to comprise all the ingredients from breweries, gasworks, and the several chemical and mineral factories; dead dogs, cats, kittens, and rats: offal from the slaughter houses . . . On 12th January we were nearly losing a whole party by choke damp, the last man being dragged out on his back . . . in a state of insensibility.[3]

Thus, sewage was never solely an excremental affair; it involved carcasses, industrial waste, natural and unnatural residues of modern life that reflected the amalgam of changes occurring in the city above. The inescapability of filth both disgusted and fascinated the Victorians, who began to construct in their minds an image of an unseen, all-pervasive pestilence that hovered in the air and threatened to invade their bodies and their homes. Most notably, the river, as the source and mouth of all things foul, provided fecund material for *Punch* satirists, who repeatedly questioned the potential composition of 'Sewer Thames', capturing the disease-ridden state of the environment and fuelling public anxiety of contagion and death across the entire city.[4] As the ultimate symbol of the sewer, the Thames continued to haunt the public imagination with contaminating, deathly associations, as filth, at first, did not discriminate; it flooded every gully, alley and rookery, from the working classes to the middle classes, from the cesspit to the drawing room.

Medical reports also contributed to the widening public discourse on pollution and pressed the matter of sanitary reform to the forefront of

THE WATER THAT JOHN DRINKS.

THIS is the water that JOHN drinks.

This is the Thames with its cento of stink,
That supplies the water that JOHN drinks.

These are the fish that float in the ink-
-y stream of the Thames with its cento of stink,
That supplies the water that JOHN drinks.

This is the sewer, from cesspool and sink,
That feeds the fish that float in the ink-
-y stream of the Thames with its cento of stink,
That supplies the water that JOHN drinks.

These are vested int'rests, that fill to the brink,
The network of sewers from cesspool and sink,
That feed the fish that float in the ink-
-y stream of the Thames, with its cento of stink,
That supplies the water that JOHN drinks.

This is the price that we pay to wink
At the vested int'rests that fill to the brink,
The network of sewers from cesspool and sink,
That feed the fish that float in the ink-
-y stream of the Thames with its cento of stink,
That supplies the water that JOHN drinks.

Figure 1.1 'The Water That John Drinks', *Punch,* 6 October 1849. Punch Limited.

urban consciousness. The major epidemics that swept through London in the mid-nineteenth century, including typhoid, typhus, tuberculosis and the dreaded cholera, debilitated the city and firmly put the word 'fever' on everyone's lips as the ultimate death knell.[5] Medical journals such as *The Lancet* and newspapers, most notably *The Times*, published hundreds of articles speculating on the pathology of these deadly diseases, but the most prevalent belief during this period was the 'miasmatic' or 'atmospheric' theory that inhalation of putrid substances in the air spread the infection.[6] Thus, proximity to sewers, overcrowding and lack of ventilation were all culprits of the contagion. In 1859, Edward H. Greenhow, a medical investigator, published a survey in the Second Report to the Privy Council, which concluded that the high rates of mortality from diarrhoeal diseases had a tendency

> to prevail in places where human excrement is allowed to accumulate in cesspools and privies. The facts of the case are so striking . . . that it is impossible not to admit the relationship as one of cause and effect . . .[7]

Another medical investigator, William Budd, also made direct links between typhoid outbreaks to 'putrid emanations' and extended the metaphor connecting the bowels of the city and the human digestive system when he proclaimed in *The Lancet*, 'The sewer may be looked upon, in fact, as a *direct continuation of the diseased intestine*.'[8] This corporeal association becomes symbolically embedded in the Victorian imagination, as Erin O'Connor suggests:

> In the minds of physicians and social commentators alike, the choleraic body and the city were coextensive . . . Shooting out gallons of fluid that, like the London water supply, was clouded with foreign matter, the choleraic body in turn became a signifier for faulty sewerage.[9]

In conflating dirt, excrement and disease, medical and scientific discourse contributed to the prevailing notion that the urban body needed to be flushed of its miasmatic pollutants, a belief that was to have far greater ramifications in the projection of filth onto various segments of the urban populace. From a pervasive aspect of everyday life, the presence of waste became a signifier for all that was dangerous and threatening, casting those in close proximity to it in the same light.

In the face of a looming catastrophe, the government set out to make sanitary reform a priority, and under the banner of Benjamin Disraeli's slogan *Sanitas Sanitatum*, the Metropolitan Consolidated Commission of Sewers was created in 1847 with the responsibility of cleaning up the 'cesspool city'. Inspections and surveys overground and underground created an enormous body of work, captured in Statistical Surveys and Parliamentary Papers, but the numbers all pointed to the capital's 200,000 cesspits and 369 sewers as the source of the pressing problem. In his report to the Parliamentary Committee, leading Victorian reformer Edwin Chadwick declared, 'All smell is, if it be intense, immediate acute disease: and eventually we may say that by depressing the system and rendering it susceptible to the action of all causes, *all smell is disease*.'[10] However, even Chadwick could not portend the biggest smell to take over London on a hot summer's day in 1858, when the Thames sent a revolting message to the Houses of Parliament in the form of 'The Great Stink':

> For the first time in the history of man, the sewage of nearly three millions of people had been brought to seethe and ferment under a burning sun, in one vast open cloaca lying in their midst. The result we all know. Stench so foul, we may well believe, had never before ascended to pollute this lower air. Never before, at least, had a stink risen to the height of an historic event.[11]

The overwhelming stench forced the Parliament to adjourn the meeting, but more importantly, the crisis expedited the approval of a construction project to rebuild the antiquated sewers, an enormous task entrusted to an enterprising and fastidious engineer, Sir Joseph Bazalgette.

As the Chief Engineer to the Metropolitan Board of Works, Bazalgette designed and built the extraordinary system of interceptory sewers, pumping stations and treatment plants that are still very much in use today. When the grand scheme began in 1859, *The Builder* commented, 'For good or for evil, the metropolis has entered upon a work of no common magnitude', and when the work was completed six years later, the plumbing triumph became the blueprint for the rest of the world.[12] Although remembered only by a modest bust of him next to Hungerford Bridge, Bazalgette is often credited with purifying the Thames of its pestilence, and by ridding the city of water-borne diseases, the 'seer of sewage' is also regarded as having 'saved more lives than any single Victorian public official'.[13] Furthermore, he reorganised the physical contours of the city when he constructed the Victoria, Albert and Chelsea Embankments in order to support the sewage system below, but more significantly, he shifted the social topography of the city when he made excrement, refuse and dirt firmly underground and invisible.

The 'Great Unwashed' and the Incontinent City

'A ghastly deafening, sickening sight it was. Go, scented Belgravian! And see what London is!'

Charles Kingsley, *Alton Locke* (1850)

In the creation of the sewers, class distinctions became more prominent in the vertical representation of the city. One painting that exemplifies the delicate balance between the various strata of society is Ford Madox Brown's *Work* (1852–65), in which the muscular navvies are vigorously digging a hole in the middle of a crowded street, while strollers of all classes remain in the margins, oblivious to the massive underground

Figure 1.2   Ford Madox Brown, *Work* (1852–65). Oil on canvas. Manchester City Galleries.

project at hand (Fig. 1.2). Although different classes of society are represented in this work, from the street sellers and the idle rich, to the intellectuals, Thomas Carlyle and F. D. Maurice, the excavators 'provide the foundation that sustains all other ranks'.[14] Despite the heroic representation of labour and the central position it takes in the painting, work gained a much more negative image in its association with the underground in the formation of the sewers. As the ground was being dug up to lay down the new infrastructure of the metropolis, there were also ruptures in the social order so harmoniously depicted in Brown's vision. The sewer inevitably became the extension of the working classes, separating them from the other classes in a chasmic divide that attempted to banish labour from sight.

In the early nineteenth century, the term 'the lower class' was loosely organised around various social types, from the urban worker to criminals to rural peasants. The term 'working class' emerged around 1815, but it was in the 1840s, at the height of the industrial revolution, that a specific urban working class was identified and differentiated from the privileged land-owning class, ultimately creating the concept of 'two Englands', one above the surface, the other deeply entrenched underground.[15] In the *Punch* cartoon 'Capital and Labour', the two distinct

CARTOON, N⁰. V.

CAPITAL AND LABOUR.

Figure 1.3   'Capital and Labour', *Punch*, 29 July 1843. Punch Limited.

layers are portrayed with trademark sarcasm and a caption that reads, 'The works being performed wholly underground, ought never to have been intruded upon the notice of the public' (Fig. 1.3).[16] The division between the huddled masses in the mine below and the rich being served by servants above not only reveals the stark contrast between the rich and the poor, but also exposes the invisibility of the labouring classes on which the wealth of the upper world relies. Thus, the subterranean space of the labouring poor became, in Marxist terms, 'the hidden abode of production' where 'we shall see, not only how capital produces, but how capital is itself produced'.[17] In creating this substructure, the rhetoric of the sewer, with its binary oppositions of clean and unclean, foul and fragrant, rich and the poor, contributed significantly to the widening of this socio-economic divide.

The cleaning up of the sewers coincided with the efforts of many Victorian reformers who contributed to the gulf by reporting on the state of the slums in an attempt to appeal to the compassion of the authorities as well as the bourgeoisie. Numerous authors contributed to the 'Condition-of-England' realist tradition, which paradoxically provided a discourse of social protest against the conditions of the poor *and* the alienation of its working-class subjects. From Thomas Carlyle, who coined the term, to Charles Kingsley, Elizabeth Gaskell and William Booth, novels and investigative reporting about the poor elicited sympathy as well as sensationalism in detailing the living habits and habitations of the lower classes.[18] This dual-edged nature was captured in the imagination of the middle-class readers, as Peter Stallybrass and Allon White argue: 'It was in the reforming text as much as in the novel that the nineteenth century was produced as the locus of fear, disgust, and fascination.'[19] Even in *The Condition of the Working Class in England* (1844), Friedrich Engels links the disenfranchised with the image of sewerage, as the poor are often festering behind respectable fronts of bourgeoisie streets and shops. He observes an old man in a cowshed, 'who earned a living by removing manure and garbage with his handcart. Pools of filth lay close to his shed'. In another hidden court, Engels discovers that 'the privy is so dirty that the inhabitants can only enter or leave the court if they are prepared to wade through puddles of stale urine and excrement'.[20] Key sanitary reformer Edwin Chadwick also observes the deplorable conditions of the lower classes through a scatological lens in his famous report, *The Report on the Sanitary Conditions of the Labouring Population of Great Britain* (1842), but he connects filth to a larger view of the human condition when he argues that the 'fever nests and seats of physical depravity are also the seats of moral depravity, disorder, and crime with which the police have the most to do'.[21] Thus, dirt, disease, and moral degradation were conflated in the discourse of the poor and social reform.

Perhaps the strongest moral judgment came from Henry Mayhew's *London Labour and the London Poor* (1862), in which he reduces the poor to a species from another country, mapping the slums through the eyes of a colonial anthropologist. Beginning with a chapter on 'wandering tribes', Mayhew may as well be describing an indigenous population in the remotest part of the world rather than the labouring class from the East End:

> The nomad then is distinguished from the civilized man by his repugnance to regular and continuous labour – by his want of providence in laying up store for the future . . . – by his passion for stupefying herbs and roots, and, when possible, for intoxicating fermented liquors . . . – by the absence of chastity among his women, and his disregard of female honour – and lastly, by his vague sense of religion.[22]

Critic Gertrude Himmelfarb, who dissects Mayhew's motives to shock and entertain, criticises him for focusing 'almost entirely with street-folk' and 'those that will not work', while omitting other hardworking labourers such as 'tailors, weavers, carpenters, or dressmakers'.[23] Furthermore, historian Anthony Wohl comments:

[Mayhew] also portrays them as a race apart 'human rats' and 'refuse population', they 'skulk' or 'huddle together' in 'sewer-like' courts and alleys or 'burrow' in 'holes and corners' . . . They are portrayed as 'oozing out on to the pavements and into the gutters' like so much human excrement – literally the 'residuum.'[24]

From all of these primitive, animalistic and Darwinian connotations, it is not surprising that the metonymic association between sewage and slum-dwellers was supplanted by a more metaphoric language in which the words 'poor' and 'filth' became inextricable and interchangeable. As Elizabeth Wilson suggests:

> For the Victorians, excrement became a metaphor for and a symbol for moral filth, perhaps even for the working class itself, and when they spoke and wrote of the cleansing of the city of filth, refuse, and dung, they may really have longed to rid the cities of the labouring poor altogether.[25]

In the conflation of dirt and the lower classes, the bourgeoisie attempted to guard themselves against the contagion of 'moral miasma' in their midst. As filth traversed social, moral and psychic boundaries, the underground space of sewers became a site of cultural panic as social tensions became magnified and distorted through the gaze of middle-class anxiety.

Contributing to this fear and disorder was the 'olfactory revolution' in which sanitary reforms sweeping through the city extended to the deodorisation of the body. In the same way that Mary Douglas explains dirt as 'matter out of place'[26] that can only offend when it threatens cultural classifications, Alain Corbin also contends that '[a]bhorrence of smells produces its own form of social power. Foul smelling rubbish appears to threaten the social order, whereas the reassuring victory of the hygienic and the fragrant promises to buttress its stability'.[27] Whereas previously, olfactory distinctions between the classes did not exist, the advent of sewers and sanitary tactics made a clear separation between the deodorised middle class and the foulness of the 'Great Unwashed', a term that emerged in the hygienic discourse of the 1830s. As Corbin asserts, 'the *absence* of intrusive odour enabled the individual to distinguish himself from the putrid masses, stinking like death, like sin, and at the same time implicitly to justify the treatment meted out to them'.[28] The significance of smell is also emphasised in Freud's *Civilisation and Its Discontents*, which locates it as the convergence of disgust and desire, while attributing the 'diminution of the olfactory stimuli' as an inevitable outcome of civilisation.[29] With the removal of excremental odours, the stench of the poor became at once recognised and reviled, further resigning the lower classes to the liminal spaces of urban modernity.

The theory of circulation was also a critical factor that informed the sanitary movement in its efforts to rid the city of offensive sights and smells. On the surface of the streets with its teeming masses and underneath the city in the blocked sewer passages, the stagnation of solids and other matter, as well as the commingling of classes, all contributed to a perceived state of disease and degeneration at mid-century. In a speech to the Sanitary Congress in Brussels in 1856, F. O. Ward, a key urban reformer, summed up the solution to the incontinent city:

> Continuous circulation is the fundamental principle of English sanitary reformers. According to their theory, the conveyance of pure water by mains into towns and its distribution into houses, as well as the removal of foul water by drains from the houses and from the streets into the fields for agricultural production, should go on without cessation and without stagnation either in the houses or the streets.[30]

In line with this principle, urban planners and sanitary reformers rebuilt the arteries of the city in accordance with the view that 'what was stagnant had to be put into circulation'.[31] As underground sewers and water mains were being constructed to facilitate the flow of filth, streets on the surface were also widened and cleaned up in order to remove unhealthy congestion and ease traffic. However, in conjunction with the material reorganisation of the city, sanitary reformers extended the valuation of filth to other urban phenomena in a new linguistic appropriation of filth and cleanliness. For example, James Winter notes that the term 'street' was 'lowered in value, linked to loss of innocence in conjunction with walker, woman, language . . .'.[32] With the new flow of urban circulation, all efforts were focused on the removal of vulgar or obscene traces in the public realm, including prostitutes, pornography and poverty, all which had to be made invisible or 'underground' in order to institute a new ritualised sense of cleanliness and order on the surface of the city.

In purifying and circulating what was once stagnant, Victorian hygienists turned their surveillance to the problem of overcrowding in slums, which were seen the most acutely as a site of corruption, danger and disease. Once again, the vocabulary of pestilence and the poor went hand in hand, enlarging the scope of circulatory functions from the flow of excrement to the 'ventilation' of working-class districts. The removal of the poor to the outskirts of the city and garden suburbs, supported by a new infrastructure of urban transport, allowed for what Didier Gille describes as a 'centrifugal movement', which cleansed the city by propelling the working classes out into the urban periphery.[33] This social and psychic displacement in London was also mirrored in Paris under the massive urbanisation of the Second Empire, which created what T. J.

Clark terms the 'melancholic banlieue', a suburban sprawl of new slums and *faubourgs*.[34] Even in the vocabulary of the sewer, the concept of movement and flow became embedded in its usage:

> The terms 'sewer' (*égout*) and 'cloaca' (*cloaque*) had been used interchange-ably during the Old Regime and the first decades of the nineteenth century . . . Only gradually was a clear distinction drawn between a sewer, defined as a place where 'the water and the refuse have an outflow' and a cloaca, defined as a site where 'the water is stagnant and putrid.' Use of the word cloaca carried with it the zoological connotation of a common intestinal, urinary, and generative canal . . . By the Second Empire, the fact that the term sewer denoted a social construction, not an anatomical borrowing, had taken on significance . . . less a natural organ than a natural form subordinated to man's use.[35]

Thus, the taming of the sewer carried with it far greater social connota-tions, from disseminating the urban poor to a teleological theory of technical advancement. The body of the city was to be regulated and controlled, and the efforts to subordinate filth and excrement to man's use even extended to the manufacturing of fertiliser in a continuous recycling of the city's organic capital. In such a seismic shift in sensorial, geographic and economic redistribution of the metropolis, it is hardly surprising that authors of the mid to late nineteenth century had a central preoccupation with, and a healthy scepticism of, underground spaces that portended both progress and destruction. The literature of the underground reflected a complex and tenuous relationship between the surface world and its subterranean counterpart, reinforcing the dichotomy growing in the social strata as well as introducing a new layer of imaginary worlds that offered alternative, and often times more dangerous, possibilities of confrontation and co-existence.

Literature of Filth/Visions of the Sublime

> If you look for the working classes in fiction and especially English fiction, all you find is a hole.
>
> George Orwell, *Inside the Whale* (1940)

Despite the significant shifts in the social and political topography of the city that accompanied the construction of the sewers, there was a marked *absence* in the representation of the structure that elicited such fascination and disgust. In comparing the material and conceptual representations of modern sewers in Paris and London, it becomes clear that both cities engaged in the discourses of contagion, circulation and civilisation, but articulated these anxieties in varying degrees in their literary, cultural and aesthetic production. David Pike argues that Paris confronted sewer matter more boldly, while London tended to elide the topic in favour of a more sanitised urban landscape:

> The Parisian underworld was rendered as a spectacle, the *frisson* of otherness was mild . . . What could be enjoyed by all in the context of Paris must quickly be flushed out of the space of London . . . unlike in Paris, neither sewage nor prostitution was ever given extended, explicit treatment in Victorian fiction of any literary pretension (although crime certainly was).[36]

Although Pike points to the plethora of literary and artistic examples in Paris and the dearth of sewer narratives in London, both cities had complex responses to filth, and while Paris's integration of filth privileged more direct representations, London's mediation of filth was equally present through suggestive metaphors, indirect allusions and Derridean 'hauntings'. Invisible yet pervasively tangible, London's spatial representation of filth and sewers favoured a more surface allusion to the River Thames, the dusty alleyways and mud-caked streets that commingled all the end products of the human body and the city in a collective representation of urban refuse. As a pollutive and a productive force, filth represented the ambivalence London felt towards the new infrastructure that redefined its perception of what it meant to be 'underground'.

In Paris, the sewer had already been the locus of political activity, most notably in the French Revolution at the end of the eighteenth century, where it had been a site of numerous seditious activities, associated with escaped convicts, criminals, gunpowder plots and revolutionaries.[37] The traces of the struggle persisted into the nineteenth century, where it regained momentum in a new and more virulent state of social unrest. Rupert Christiansen, in his study of the Second Empire, notes:

> Paris in 1848 was volatile and anarchic, almost what sociologists today would call a 'virus city', expanding and responding with wanton unpredictability, beyond rational administration. Eight times within twenty years denizens of the working-class areas had thrown up barricades and shouted for revolution; epidemics of cholera had killed tens of thousands and the death rate was higher than that of London; crime spread in waves of comparably destructive effect . . .[38]

In this counterpart to London's Babylon, Parisian sewers ensconced the city's thieves, street urchins, convicts and revolutionaries, while serving as a potent cultural symbol of moral disintegration and political disorder. In the circulatory metaphor that dominated the image of the subterranean conduits, the criminal underworld represented the social refuse of the city and the residuum of a new order.

The most powerful and enduring novel to capture the subversive role of the sewers is Victor Hugo's *Les Misérables* (1862), which capitalised on their revolutionary history to reclaim the subterranean space as a necessary locus of social and political interrogation. In the chapter 'Intestine of the Leviathan', Hugo describes the limitless possibilities of the sewers and ardently declares:

> The history of men is reflected in the history of sewers . . . Crime, intelligence, social protest, freedom of conscience, thought, theft, all that human laws prosecuted or have prosecuted, was hidden in this pit . . .[39]

As the central conduit through which convicts and revolutionaries escape, the underground arteries provide both a material haven from authorities as well as a metaphorical space of personal reinvention and redemption. Although the most famous underground scene follows the chase between police chief Javert and the main hero, Jean Valjean, as he carries Marius through the sewers, the central thesis of the text rests on the transformative potential of Jean Valjean. Hugo emphasises the regenerative power of the underground, which only matched his passionate belief in the recycling potential of sewage as fertiliser. Thus Valjean's descent into the sewers embraces the same recycling motif, as he is baptismally cleansed of his 'filthy' identity and re-emerges as the purified voice of the revolution. For Hugo, waste was a necessary corollary of urban life, in the same manner that the sewers held a mirror to the inequities of the world above. In his social vision, the pollutive and productive elements of filth were to be embraced and integrated into the landscape of Paris. As Richard Maxwell observes about the text, 'The sewer is the realm of argot: slang as crime . . . where the energies of urban speech and urban writing in all their varieties combine at last.'[40] This integrationist vision between the above world and the underworld then reiterates the holistic approach of Paris in its explicit image of the sewers in communication and in communion with the surface order.

Contending with this representation was the design by Georges Haussmann and chief engineer Eugène Belgrand to physically and metaphorically clean out the drains of Paris by reconstructing the sewers in a complete overhaul of the city in the 1850s. Defying Hugo's vision of an alternative, underground city, the new subterranean network was co-opted as a national symbol of engineering triumph, opening itself up to the naked eye in public tours of 'un second Paris souterrain' in the World Exposition of 1867. Guidebooks advertised the novelty of the boat tour of the sewers 'in which ladies need have no hesitation in taking part', while critic Maxime du Camp noted in 1870 that 'it has become a sort of a pleasure trip to visit the sewers'.[41] In this reinvention and reappropriation of the sewers, the underground became less of a transgressive space than a reassurance that the bourgeois order reigned below. Hugo's underground battleground for revolutionary change and truth became another spectacle for middle-class consumption and capitalist enterprise, and although the subversive power of the sewers waned, they remained an icon of the city's history and an enduring influence on Paris's cultural identity.

In London's visual and literary imagination, the sewers did not receive central treatment, as did its Parisian counterpart, but its ghostly traces were equally palpable in the portrayal of waste and its affiliation with criminality and the lower classes. On one hand, the construction of Bazalgette's sewers was captured in meticulous detail in the press, especially in *The Illustrated London News*, that celebrated it as an engineering feat. As Paul Dobraszczyk notes, the wood engravings, although historical in nature, had many features of the sublime, opening up the underground to multiple, shifting aesthetic interpretations.[42] However, the underground space was, for the most part, elided in literature in favour of a more metaphorical depiction of the sewer that haunted the city in a myriad of guises. Perhaps the most prolific writer of the underground, who never explicitly mentions the subterranean space, is Charles Dickens, aptly described by P. J. Keating as 'an excavator who makes a vertical cut into society'.[43] Digging through the social depths of London, Dickens makes it impossible for the reader to avoid the filthy reality that surrounds his characters. In *Little Dorrit* (1855–7), his vision of London captures the essence of stagnation and suffocation so feared by the Victorians as he projects these anxieties onto the Thames: 'Through the heart of the town a deadly sewer ebbed and flowed, in the place of a fine river', while in 'fifty thousand lairs . . . the inhabitants gasped for air'.[44] The opening pages of *Bleak House* (1852–3) also bury the city in a tide of excremental mud that seems as pervasive as the 'fog everywhere':

> Dogs, indistinguishable in mire. Horses scarcely better; splashed to their very blinkers. Foot passengers, jostling one another's umbrellas, in a general infection of ill temper, and losing their foot-hold at street corners, where ten of thousands of other foot passengers have been slipping and sliding since the day broke (if this day ever broke), adding new deposits to the crust upon crust of mud.[45]

In the mélange of filth and dirt, characters emerge from the bituminous underworld to disrupt categories and oppositions that underscore society's most cherished notions of order and cleanliness. Miasmatic pollutants spread from the filthy alleys of Tom All-Alone's to physically and morally infect the wealthy Dedlocks in Chesney Wold in a circulatory map of social relations. The blockages at Chancery court that protract the *Jarndyce vs. Jarndyce* case further reinforce the sewer imagery in the depiction of a constipated legal system that impedes social movement and narrative progression.

As John Forster describes in *Life of Dickens*, Dickens maintained a profound 'attraction of repulsion' towards 'almshouses', 'dust-heaps' and 'dock-leaves', sketching the bowels of the metropolis, from the criminal underworld in Fleet and Newgate prisons to the abject squalor in the rookeries of St Giles and the Seven Dials.[46] In his novels, particularly *The Pickwick Papers* (1836–7), *Oliver Twist* (1837–9) and *Nicholas Nickleby* (1838–9), refuse from the sewers seems to literally flow out onto the streets in the images of 'pale and pinched-up faces . . . hungry eyes, half-naked shivering figures'.[47] Like the fog, filth emerges as the medium that 'creeps', 'defiles' and 'pollutes', and the poor, as the symbolic descendants of the sewers, become the subject of both compassion and revulsion in their new manifestation. Elaborating on Freud's psychoanalytic relationship between waste and repression, Michael Steig, in his essay 'Dickens's Excremental Vision', further notes 'the imagery of anality, and its structural ramifications in the multiple progressions from blockage to actual or potential explosion, represents a level of unity deeper than any previously brought to light'.[48] In *Bleak House*, filthy blockages in their physical and moral manifestation manage to infect everyone in their path, but it is in *Our Mutual Friend* (1864–5) where Freud's vision of anal repression is most vividly realised.

In Freud's essays on the theory of sexuality, he links human waste with the desire for money in a sublimation of an individual's attachment to his own faeces. As the child is forced to reject his own excrement and learns to feel disgusted by it, his libidinal desires are transferred to a subconscious longing for a form of financial sustenance in which 'excrement is aliment'.[49] This impulse is seen in actual historical examples, from Chadwick to Haussmann, who attempted to transform human waste into a profitable enterprise in many of their commercial ventures in sewage farming. In *Our Mutual Friend*, Dickens also employs this transformative, recycling metaphor through his repressive use of 'dust', which is simultaneously everywhere, yet nowhere. As Ellen Handy notes, while Mr Boffin's wealth derived from the euphemistic 'dust', 'other substances are certainly implied'.[50] From ashes and street sweepings to 'night soil' or human excrement, 'dust' blurs all distinctions between dry and wet waste and becomes the pervasive metaphor and allusion to the sewage that Dickens does not explicitly articulate. It is this repressed, sublimated form of human detritus that transforms the bumbling Mr Boffin into the Golden Dustman, while resurrecting John

Harmon's dead body into the figure of John Rokesmith, only to restore John Harmon back to life in a re-evaluation and revaluation of his identity.

Furthermore, the image of the sewer becomes displaced onto the River Thames, which plays a crucial role throughout the novel as a conduit that both defiles and transforms individuals in a baptismal reawakening. The haunting, opening scene of Gaffer Hexam and his daughter Lizzie rowing through the Thames in search of corpses and valuables anoints the river as a sinister sewer swallowing the excesses and wastes of the city. The subterranean overtones further align the waterman with the filth and mud of the sewers, as well as with ferryman Charon in a remy-thologisation of the underworld:

> Allied to the bottom of the river rather than the surface, by reason of the slime and ooze with which it was covered, and its sodden state, this boat and the two figures in it obviously were doing something that they often did, and were seeking what they often sought. Half savage as the man showed . . . with such dress as he wore seeming to be made out of the mud that begrimed his boat, still there was a business-like usage in his steady gaze. So with every lithe action of the girl, with every turn of her wrist, perhaps most of all with her look of dread or horror; they were things of usage.[51]

Usage and, more importantly, reusage become central tropes in the novel as John Harmon's body is washed up on the river, precipitating a redistribution of wealth and an overturning of social hierarchy. The river also becomes a sanitising force that redeems Eugene Wrayburn's purposeless life, as he decides to marry someone of lower social stand-ing in a sympathetic recasting of a weary London barrister. Like a Chadwickean sanitary map, Dickens's London reveals the circulation of waste, money and morality in which the city and the river offer possi-bilities of recovery and redemption. As Mrs Boffin states of the recycled Harmon inheritance, the 'money had turned bright again, after a long long rust in the dark, and was at last a beginning to sparkle in the sun-light'.[52] From repression to self-actualisation, filth becomes the medium through which individuals emerge from the muck of urban existence to a new sense of identity and authority, as it attempts to uncover the truth of human nature and buried desires. Although sewers are never explic-itly mentioned in the text, their role and function become the spectre and the subtext for the entire novel, rivalling Hugo's *oeuvre* in elevating the underground conduits to the level of myth.

Like Gaffer Hexam and Rogue Riderhood, the Victorian underworld was peopled by individuals who were quick to take advantage of the opportunities in the disposal of the city's waste.[53] The panorama of sewer explorers, whom I term the 'degraded *flâneur*', resembled the

Bakhtinian world of the 'carnivalesque', which resisted dominant social and cultural norms that reigned above. While the *flâneur* is generally understood, following Benjamin, as a detached, bourgeois observer who delights in the visual spectacle of the city, I think it is suggestive in thinking about the underside of *flanerie* in both class and spatial terms.[54] Like the *flâneur*, his underground counterpart had freedom of movement in the subterranean tunnels and relied heavily on the visual economy of the city, although in his world, it was the economy of waste and the recreation of its value. Amongst those who were drawn to filth and lucre were the 'flushers' who cleaned out blockages in the sewers, the 'toshers' who searched for coins or jewellery lost in the passages, the 'mudlarks' who searched for remnants along the Thames, as well as the 'pure-finders' who collected dog faeces. However, such a productive vision of the underworld was undercut by more pollutive representations of the subterranean space and working classes in the mid-to-late nineteenth century, most notably in the landscape of miners and factory workers, whose collectivity evoked fear rather than sympathy. Thus, the heterogeneity of underground life was supplanted by the faceless masses of the 'furnace, engine and the factory' that threatened the city with disorder and degeneration.[55]

In a new image of the working classes, the threat of a revolution from below often formed the basis for anxieties of a Marxist overthrow by the proletariat. In the glow of torches, the images of the abyss and the flow of factory workers that marched on endlessly, the underground depicted the social sublime of a vast subterranean path towards a bloody clash of social ideals. As Engels presciently declares:

> If the capitalist class is as mad as all that, and if they are so blinded by temporary success that they cannot understand the most obvious signs of the times – then we must indeed give up all hope of seeing a peaceful solution to the social question in England. The only possible outcome of this state of affairs is a great revolution and it is absolutely certain that such a rising will take place.[56]

Such fears of violence and social unrest are captured in novels across the century, from the industrial fiction of Elizabeth Gaskell to the social Darwinism of Zola. In Gaskell's *North and South* (1855), a mob of striking mill workers appear as subhuman, savage creatures whose primitivism threatens to devour the middle classes. 'As soon as they saw Mr. Thornton', Gaskell writes, 'they set up a yell, – to call it not human is nothing, – it was the demoniac desire of some terrible wild beast for the food that is withheld from his ravening.'[57] This Darwinian perspective is also echoed in Zola's *Germinal* (1885), where the underground mine is a hungry, 'voracious beast' (aptly called 'le Voreux') that threatens to consume the bourgeoisie. As the voices of striking miners crescendo outside his home, the manager of the mine expresses the gulf that divides the two classes and the desire to intermingle with the lower orders:

> Why couldn't he invite them to dinner and let them stuff their faces with his pheasant while he went off to fornicate in the bushes, screwing the girls without giving a damn about whoever had screwed them before? . . . Oh, to live like a wild animal, to have no possessions, to tumble in the hay with the ugliest, dirtiest tram girl, and be able to be happy with that![58]

Here, the underground, with all its filthy, devolutionary associations, becomes an object of fascination and longing, but Zola does not offer an easy solution to the social question. Rather, in the destruction of the mine, which ruins everyone's lives, and concluding with the hope for a 'germinal', or renewal, he sows the seeds of the *possibility* of redress in the vertical hierarchy of social relations. From the 1850s to the 1890s, the underground signified both the locus of the working classes as well as the potential for change, which were illustrated in oscillating depictions of social progress and destruction in literature, from the realist novel to the fantastic novel. The social issues in mines and factories were mirrored in the city, but the distinction between the upper and lower worlds became more indistinct as the vertical framework became more horizontal in a new capitalist space, where the lower classes became a more permanent fixture on the surface of the new industrial economy.

In contrast, London's underworld is devoid of hope or redemption as exemplified by George Gissing's *The Nether World* (1889) in which the *absence* of the physical underground space suggests resignation and futility. In this horizontal representation, factory workers and slum-dwellers haunt the claustrophobic alleys of Clerkenwell, resembling stagnant cesspools of waste and filth without an outlet. The opening scene of *The Nether World* begins with the unexpected appearance of John Snowdon seeking to bestow his newfound wealth on his grandchild, a familiar echo of *Great Expectations*, which tantalises the reader with some anticipation of social redress. However, Gissing subverts, if not degrades, the Dickensian landscape by denying every character the chance of a better life in the outside world. The plotline is cyclical if not static: money is offered and rescinded, lost and squandered, and in the end, the characters remain utterly unchanged by the course of events. Thus, Sidney Kirkwood, a character who could have seized an opportunity for personal happiness, resigns himself to an unloving marriage and a life of poverty. 'Who was he that he should look for pleasant things in his course through the world? "We are the lower orders; we are the working classes," he said bitterly to his friend, and that seemed the final answer to all his aspirations.'[59] As Stephen Gill notes in his introduction to the novel, *The Nether World* is marked by a striking absence of 'Christianity, philanthropy, reference to trades, unionism, or concerted action, and absence of romantic love'.[60] In this desiccated wasteland, the denizens live above ground, but choose of their own will to live a subterranean existence without any hope for mobility or salvation.

Although realist novels often depicted a stalemate in the ability of the lower orders to rise above their station in life, later fantastic novels envisaged an underworld that would bring down the upper world in its degenerative path. Again, the discourse of the sewers is elided here, but the technological feat of the subterranean infrastructure is one of the invisible guiding principles in the basis for a new vision of an alternative city. The spectre of the sewers and of Marx remained very much a part of the new imaginary underworld that questioned social divisions and the future of civilisation in a rapidly changing, industrialised society. As writers attempted to map out the evolutionary consequences of technology, progress and the ensuing social struggle, Edward Bulwer-Lytton's *The Coming Race* (1871) was one of the first texts to promote a utopian vision of the underworld. The narrator, a mining engineer, descends into a chasm and discovers an underworld 'of a wild and solemn beauty impossible to describe . . . so lovely, yet so awful' that recalls Edmund Burke's inquiry into the sublime and beautiful.[61] The dual-edged nature of this utopian paradise, tinged with horror, is echoed in the description of the new race of seraphim-like creatures whose discovery of 'vril', an alternative energy source, allows the new race to eliminate war, violence and poverty. However, despite their perfection, they cannot produce art or original ideas. Thus, Bulwer-Lytton alludes to the degenerative aspect of evolutionary determinism, explaining that such a society 'would be fatal to ourselves . . . it would be deadly to us, not from its vices but its society which we should find extremely dull, and in which the current equality would prohibit all greatness'.[62] While promoting modern ideas like socialism, feminism and democracy, Bulwer-Lytton also expresses his anxiety about the dilutive impact of technology on individual identity, a persistent theme in *fin-de-siècle* science fiction novels that portend the end of civilisation at the hands of 'the machine'.

The dual-edged nature of scientific progress is also reflected through various layers of society in H. G. Wells's dystopian tale, *The Time Machine* (1895), which contains the most explicit representation of the underground as both a site of progress and degeneration. A scientist known as 'The Time Traveller' visits the future and returns to relay his encounter with two species who will inhabit the surface and the lower depths: the childlike Eloi, who have inherited a pastoral utopia that resembles Bulwer-Lytton's paradise, and the Morlocks, a race of bestial but powerful creatures who live beneath the ground. Although at first the Eloi seem to live in a virtual utopia without poverty or crime, their degenerative traits are revealed when the protagonist encounters their underground counterpart. Reinforcing the subterranean imagery of the working class in industrial novels, the Morlocks control the machinery by which the upper world is supported, but they also devour the Eloi in a cannibalistic display of brute strength and mercilessness. The traveller equates this power structure in familiar Marxist and Darwinist terms:

> And this same widening gulf . . . will make that exchange between class and class, that promotion by intermarriage which at present retards the splitting of our species along lines of social stratification, less and less frequent. So, in the end, above ground you must have the Haves, pursuing pleasure, and comfort and beauty, and below ground the Have-nots; the Workers getting continually adapted to the conditions of their labour.[63]

His hypothesis rests on the socialist division between capital and labour, as well as social determinism, but Wells complicates this relationship by revealing a symbiotic degeneration of both worlds, where 'the Upperworld man had drifted toward his feeble pettiness, and the Underworld to mere mechanical industry'.[64] In the physical and moral deterioration of the two species, Wells paints an apocalyptic picture of society's dissolution under pressures of industrialisation and technological achievement in all layers of the social strata. Inverting, blurring and reinventing realities, Wells's vertical contradictions in society appear repetitively as a trope for his future science fiction works, such as *The War of the Worlds* (1898), *The Sleeper Awakes* (1910) and *The Shape of Things to Come* (1933), as the subterranean metaphor remains the basis of his cautionary tales that sought to unearth the pernicious effects of technological dominance.

Throughout the social explorations of the underground, Rosalind Williams suggests that one of the greatest projects of nineteenth-century literature was to reconcile sympathy and fear as the reader is guided though the lower depths of society.[65] The construction of the sewers, within sanitary and medical discourses and the rhetoric of filth and olfaction, served as the basis of these journeys, exposing the middle class to fascinating yet fearful portrayals of the working classes, who eventually became the faceless masses. Although references to the material sewers remained notably absent in literature, the social underworld was often seen through the medium of filth and dirt that served as indirect allusions to the drains that remapped the social body of the city. On the surface, however, these marginalised areas of poverty were always described in subterranean overtones. As H. G. Wells aptly observes, 'Even now, does not an East-end worker live in such artificial conditions as practically cut off from the natural surface of the earth?'[66] Throughout the nineteenth century, the subterranean metaphor shifted from the conscience of the city to the repression of middle-class anxieties, from a space of political revolutions to a site of degeneracy. Extending its association with the working classes, the sewer also becomes a potent personification of women in the intersection of social and gender hierarchy in Victorian society.

Tainted Love: Prostitutes and Sexual Contagion

Now had the watchman walk'd his second round;
When *Cloacina* hears the rumbling sound
Of her brown lover's cart, for well she knows
That pleasing thunder: swift the Goddess rose,
And through the streets pursu'd the distant noise,
Her bosom panting with expected joys.
John Gay, *Trivia: Or, the Art of Walking the Streets of London* (1716)

In response to the fears of contamination from prostitutes, the sewer also becomes an apt symbol of female orifices in the conflation of ordure, odour and disorder. Historically, however, its presence was always paradoxically pollutive *and* productive. The inextricable link between sewers and prostitutes dates back to the Middle Ages, when Augustine of Hippo declared that prostitution was a necessary evil: just as a well-ordered palace needed good sewers, so a well-ordered city needed brothels.[67] In Rome, Cloacina, the goddess of the sewers, presided over the Cloaca Maxima, which conferred her a higher, more exalted status, yet her identity was destabilised by the image of her as both the goddess of filth as well as purity. From these historical and mythological beginnings, the prostitute's body has been reinscribed over the centuries by multiple identities, but it was most notably in the wake of nineteenth-century sanitary and medical discourses that she was construed as a threat to the social order, conflated with pollution and disease. However, rather than trying to make them *invisible*, as the bourgeoisie attempted to do with the lower classes, there was a legal imperative to identify and locate them in the 'ocular economy' of the metropolis.[68] In the same manner that the Foucauldian Panopticon made visibility a deterrent to unlawful acts, the police engaged in the role of sanitary inspectors shedding light on and criminalising streetwalkers. Furthermore, under the Contagious Diseases Act of 1864, the police were allowed to detain prostitutes and record their medical histories in an accumulation of knowledge that was also used as a form of control. Thus, the prostitute's body became a site of 'abjection' that threatened to break down the distinction between subject and object, as well as the respectable matron and the fallen women. The prostitute, associated with bodily orifices and uncontainable sexuality, was a threat to the symbolic ordering of Victorian society and threatened the body of the city with syphilitic contamination and degeneration. However, efforts to control this symbolic underground occupation were ironically subverted by the laws themselves, reconfiguring the way women occupied the city streets. Although the River Thames remained a critical metaphor for the sewer, aligning 'fallen women' with the waste products of the city, the discourse of purity also elevated women from the lower depths to new circulatory practices that allowed them to participate more fully in the modern metropolis.

In the construction of the metaphoric relations between the sewer and the body of the prostitute, sanitary reformers were the key figures again in the framework that posited the whore as a residuum of industrial capitalism. Both Paris and London depicted her as a pollutive force in the city, but they departed in their assimilation of her ambiguous position as both a necessary commodity and a contagious moral hazard. Paris was more explicit in the representation of the prostitute as an economic necessity, while London painted a more tragic picture of the wayward woman, relying on subtle allusions to her underground identity and the need for her rehabilitation. French reformer Alexandre Parent-Duchâtelet, who was responsible for the construction of the modern Parisian sewer system, drew a direct parallel between the sewers and prostitutes in his survey *De la prostitution* in 1836:

> Prostitutes are as inevitable in an agglomeration of man as sewers, cesspits and garbage dumps; civil authority should conduct itself in the same manner in regard to the one as to the other: its duty is to survey them, to attenuate by every possible means the detriments inherent to them, and for that purpose to hide them, to relegate them to the most obscure corners, in a word to render their presence as inconspicuous as possible.[69]

Across the Channel, English physician William Acton was more philosophical in his attitude towards the prostitute, equating her as a natural extension of the working class, rather than an embodiment of all that was immoral and corrupt in the city. In his work, *Prostitution*, Acton claimed that prostitutes were 'spreading about a loathsome poison' but justified their presence by observing that 'prostitution is a transitory state through which untold number of British women are ever on their passage . . . multitudes are mothers before they become prostitutes, and others become mothers during their evil career'.[70] As an alternative to the hardships of factory life, prostitution offered a survival strategy for working-class women in the city. In this sliding representation of the prostitute as 'the great social evil' and a 'necessary evil', her identity created a crisis of category, or as Elizabeth Wilson describes, 'an irruption in the city, a symptom of disorder, and a problem: the Sphinx in the city'.[71]

The sense of smell continued to inform reformers as they attempted to distinguish the prostitute in the social and moral geography of the metropolis. Havelock Ellis originally analysed the disappearance of the strong female scent of 'musk and civet' in the olfactory revolution of the nineteenth century, as such perfumes accentuated the 'animal primitivism' that was such a sensorial component of sexual invitation. In creating 'the woman's atmosphere', new rituals were enforced that governed the ritual of the toilette, including 'cleanliness of hands, feet, armpits, groin, and genital organs'.[72] In 'Hygiene Projects', Baudelaire also wrote obsessively of how he organised his daily existence around 'Toilet/Prayer/Work', while his unfinished work *Mon coeur mis à nu* (1867) sketched the outlines of 'Un chapitre sur la toilette, moralité de la toilette et les bonheurs de la toilette'.[73] Given the new sanitary regime regarding the body, it is no coincidence that 'putain' or 'puta' derives from 'putrid', from the overwhelming stench of the sewer. Furthermore, Jacques Léonard's linguistic analyses of medical discourse of this period denote how frequently the terms *wretched, dirty, slovenly, stench* and *infect* were used together.[74] In the interchangeability of these terms, prostitutes, excrement and disease were thrown into the same filthy muck that threatened to contaminate the city. In demarcating new rituals of cleanliness, Georges Vigarello notes, it is 'the case of the body [which] involved a total reconstruction of the world above and below cities'.[75] The body of the prostitute who transgressed these boundaries was thus seen as a carrier of filth and a threat to the orderliness of the regime, both of the body and of the state.

In Alain Corbin's analysis of commercial sex in the nineteenth century, he summarises three key areas in which the aims of the government, hygienists and police converged. First was the need to preserve public morality and to maintain the innocence of young girls 'from the spectacle of vice'.[76] Second was the need to protect male lineage from becoming adulterated by unknown women of disreputable means. Finally, there was the need to defend the nation's health from the prostitute's potential transmission of disease. In the medical field, doctors often relied on the corpses of prostitutes from the morgue for dissection purposes, and the association they had with venereal diseases, such as syphilis and gonorrhoea, perpetuated miasmatic models of contagion.[77] Thus 'the more refined person' was to avoid even

> the slightest contact, so far as possible, with the bodies and garments of other people, in the knowledge that, even greater than the hygienic danger of contamination, there is always the danger of contact with the spiritually inferior and repugnant who at any moment can appear in our immediate vicinity, especially in the densely populated centres of the cities, like germs in an unhealthy body.[78]

This fear of contact then mapped a new flow of movement in the metropolis based on perceptions of areas that prostitutes frequented, creating certain nodes of infection that became in Lefebvrian terms, a 'conceived space', where meaning is institutionally prescribed by social norms. Public areas of the city to be avoided included slums, trains, theatres and fairs, which became the socially produced space of anxiety and contamination. The ambiguous state of the prostitute called for government intervention in identifying the source of the pollution through surveillance and containment. Such measures, however, were to create a bigger conundrum in the gender and class debates regarding urban street practices.

The Contagious Diseases Acts of 1864, 1866 and 1869 sought to prevent these social and moral collusions by allowing the police to arrest women, subject them to compulsory medical examinations and detain them in lock-hospitals if they were considered 'diseased'. Furthermore, the Acts explicitly stated that 'there is no comparison to be made between prostitutes and the men who consort with them', and thus, male morality was never questioned.[79] Recalling Michel Foucault's *Discipline and Punish*, in which he argues that accumulation of information becomes a form of social control, the Acts allowed for a level of surveillance that stigmatised prostitutes, who were ultimately seen as 'dirt out of place', in Douglas's terms. A Hudson's Soap advertisement from 1 December 1888 embodies this relationship as a policeman sheds light on a poster declaring 'Arrest all dirt and cleanse everything by using Hudson's Soap', while promising 'Purity, Health & Satisfaction' as its reward for daily usage (Fig. 1.4). Christopher Pittard notes that the advertisement gains new significance in the context of the Whitechapel murders of Jack the Ripper that occurred only weeks before, linking crime and vice in the social purity debate with the 'infected criminal'.[80] However, it also inveigles prostitutes in the unwitting image of infection

Figure 1.4   'Hudson's Extract of Soap', *The Graphic*, 1 August 1891. Courtesy of The University of Hong Kong Library.

and contamination, as they were the primary victims in the notorious murders in the East End. In purifying, cleaning and throwing light upon the dark underworld of prostitution, the female streetwalker was policed, apprehended and criminalised to ensure her 'permanent visibility' within the anonymous crowds of the city.

Even under such intense vigilance and scrutiny, prostitutes and women found ways to resist dominant ideological codes governing public spaces. One inadvertent way in which the Acts worked against their intended goals was by broadening the discourse of prostitutes to all women. In multiple cases of mistaken identity, innocent women merely walking through the streets unaccompanied were either arrested by the police or accosted by men on the streets. The infamous 'Cass Case' in 1887, involving the wrongful arrest of a respectable woman shopping on Regent Street, provoked furore and rallied middle-class women to fight for the right to walk unchaperoned through the city streets. Lynda Nead explains the difficulty of making distinctions between prostitutes and respectable women, as these two categories often overlapped in the visual culture of the city.

> London in the 1860s was governed by the principles of visual exchange; by the display of goods and advertisements, by the fashioning of self and society. The only way for conservative models of femininity to be maintained within this environment was to prove them resistant to the seductions of the city's visual culture. To place them in the city, but not on the city; on the streets, but withdraw from their specular exchange.[81]

However, in the emerging culture of consumption and exchange, women adopted new practices of seeing and being seen, demarcating specific routes through the city and codifying new zones of femininity and self-possession.[82] As the ongoing criticism regarding the shifting image of the *flâneur* attests, 'the power of the "male gaze" does not go unchallenged . . . it is met by the blunt frontal stare of prostitute'.[83] Furthermore, Judith Walkowitz and Elizabeth Wilson reveal the presence of more female walkers in the city, including shoppers, shopgirls, female entertainers, charity workers, cross-dressers and lesbians, who circulated freely around the city in search of pleasure and excitement.[84] In all of these exchanges, the efforts to contain, document and codify gender and sexuality had the very opposite effect: rather than containing sexual boundaries, the culture of purity only released the flood of resisting discourses about the place of men and women in the city, while exploding the notion of the streetwalker into a myriad of fluid and fluctuating identities.

Michel Foucault's *The History of Sexuality* (1984) is useful here in tracing the ways in which the discourse of sexuality emerged from the underground and proliferated as an acceptable form of dialogue and social inquiry within the dominant ideology. Defining it as a 'historical construct', Foucault argues that sexuality is:

> ... not just a furtive reality that is difficult to grasp, but a great *surface* network in which the stimulation of bodies, the intensification of pleasures, the incitement to discourse, the formation of special knowledges, the strengthening of controls and resistances, are linked to one another, in accordance with a few major strategies of knowledge and power.[85]

In attempting to control sexuality and women, institutional forces only faced more resistance, as the growing debate of women's rights culminated in a repeal of the Contagious Diseases Act under the leadership of Josephine Butler and the Ladies National Association (LNA). However, as Walkowitz observes, it was not only a struggle to protect prostitutes that instigated the movement. Amongst the issues facing legislature and policy makers were 'the double standard of sexual morality, the participation of women in political activity, the control of women by male doctors, and the role of the state in enforcing sexual and social morality of the poor'.[86] The repeal movement, under a larger discursive umbrella of women's rights, formed an alliance between working-class and middle-class feminists, forging a new empowering identity in the emergence of the 'New Woman' in the *fin-de-siècle* metropolis.

Reading the Body of the Prostitute

> As a heap of rubbish will ferment, so surely will a number of unvirtuous women deteriorate.
>
> William Acton, *Prostitution* (1857)

If the prostitute was born of the sewer, she was destined to remain in the sewer in the literary accounts of her fate in early Victorian representation. The image of the 'fallen woman' and the overused trope of the 'virgin/whore' revealed the vertical examination of women in their fall from respectability in the middle-class imagination. Although the Victorian era is often equated with institutional repression of sexuality, literary and visual representations of the wayward woman flooded bookshops in sensational novels and investigative journalism, even at a time of social crisis and moral panic amongst the middle classes. The prostitute had become so familiar that *Tait's Edinburgh Magazine* protested that 'the subject of the "Social Evil" has been overdone', echoing Foucault's observation that there was a 'discursive explosion' in the field of sexuality in the line of acceptable medical, scientific and criminal discourses.[87] However, the representation of the fallen woman was also matched by images of women re-occupying the streets as social debates regarding spatial freedom for all women rose to the forefront of urban consciousness. In juxtaposing the representation of London prostitutes to the Parisian courtesan, London also emerges as a subtler mediator of filth while gesturing at both cities to be productive intermediaries of women's prominence on the surface of the city.

In Paris, the 'dirty pictures' that flooded the salons of nineteenth-century Paris attest to the crucial role of filth in the aesthetic discourse of modernity. At the forefront was Édouard Manet with his sensational portrayal of prostitutes in *Le Déjeuner sur L'herbe* and *Olympia* (1863), where the prostitutes' nonchalant and confrontational gaze defied classical notions of flawless beauty and veiled nudity. In settings that evoked timeless allusions to the reclining nude and pastoral images of women bathing unseen, the discreet subject was transformed into a self-assured harlot, painted in broad impressionistic brushstrokes that defied traditional aesthetics of the body. Winfried Menninghaus's theory of disgust emphasises the classical obsession with the smooth surface of the body as the boundary between all that is acceptable and perverse. 'Disgust . . . is the dark and dangerous undercurrent, always threatening to break through from just below the classical surface, spoiling and soiling its beauty.'[88] As the paintings elicited disgust and furore from the critics, the topic of prostitutes also circulated freely amongst the bourgeoisie, questioning the role of realism in art, as well as how to define 'high' and 'low' art forms. In this vertical representation, the sewer metaphor of the prostitute and the orifices that threatened to devour men became assimilated into the aesthetic culture of Paris that ultimately elevated the lowly streetwalker into a powerful courtesan.

The novel that most vividly portrays the life of a courtesan is Émile Zola's *Nana* (1876), whose eponymous heroine is in full possession of her sexuality and threatens to ruin men with her physical and material appetite. Critics have often referred to Zola's works as *crapule*, driving Zola to complain, 'I heard my work treated as a puddle of mud and blood, as a sewer, as filth.'[89] Such excremental associations are not lost in Nana's characterisation as a 'golden fly' and the product of a 'dung-hill plant' that 'rotted the aristocracy' and 'entered the windows of palaces and poisoned men within by merely settling on them in her flight'.[90] In this metaphor of contagion, Nana is still a subject of moral disgust in the Freudian sense, as she symbolises the repression of unconscious sexual desires, embodied in the opening scene in which she unveils her naked body:

Nobody laughed any more . . . A wind seemed to have passed over the audience, a soft wind laden with hidden menace . . . the woman stood revealed,
a disturbing woman with all the impulsive madness of her sex, opening the
gates of the unknown world of desire.[91]

Characterising feminine sexuality, Jean-Paul Sartre describes the female
body as a mouth or a hole that 'gapes open', while Julia Kristeva, in
associating the feminine with the disruption of the symbolic ordering
of the world, further argues that the masculine does 'not seem to have
. . . sufficient strength to dam up the abject or demoniacal potential of
the feminine'.[92] In these psychoanalytic representations, the body of the
prostitute is represented by excess, surfeit and overindulgence, which
parallels Nana's personification of Paris herself, overflowing with waste
and overconsumption. The description of Nana's new home, where she
'devours' her men, articulates the engorged, bulimic body politic of the
prostitute and the city on the verge of a vomitous eruption:

Never had the eye beheld such a rage of expenditure. The great house seemed
to have been built over a gulf, in which men – their worldly possessions,
their fortunes, their very names – were swallowed up without leaving even a
handful of dust behind them . . . Yesterday's food was thrown into the gutter,
and the collection of provisions in the house was such that the servants grew
disgusted with it. The glass was all sticky with sugar, and the gas-burners
flared and flared till the rooms seemed ready to explode.[93]

In the stickiness and the revulsion towards excess, Zola equates disgust
with a violent physical reaction, akin to Sartre's *nausée* towards the
superfluousness of existence that threatens to overflow and swallow
up civilisation.[94] Nana's open and uncontrolled promiscuity cannot go
unpunished, as her life is cut brutally short by smallpox, which has been
interpreted by some critics as Zola's euphemism for syphilis. As she
dies, her wanton life is captured in her face, which 'assumed the greyish
hue of mud, and on that formless pulp, where the features had ceased
to be traceable, they already resembled some decaying damp from the
grave'.[95] From the filth of her femininity to the putrid excretions of her
body, Nana is the ultimate site of abjection that threatens the social and
economic foundations of the city with decadence and degeneration. In
this final representation, Nana ascends from the sewers only to return
to the sewer in a cyclical reincorporation of her being as a circulating
commodity and waste product.

Although London's visual and literary depictions of the prostitute
also aligned her with the sewer, there were more circumventions and
circumlocutions to avoid direct confrontation with the subject and her
disreputable career. In sentimental overtones, the prostitute was rarely

labelled a prostitute, but a 'social evil', a 'painted woman', a 'fallen woman' or a 'gay woman', recognised primarily by their perambulations in areas such as the Strand, Haymarket, or Hyde Park during certain hours of the day. One of the bolder encounters with prostitutes was detailed in Henry Mayhew's *London Labour and the London Poor* (1862), ironically enough in a section entitled 'Those That Will Not Work', in which Mayhew interviewed women who plied their trade in the arches and alleyways of London. In his revealing exposé, the subterranean caverns of the Adelphi Arches on the Strand became a mythical place of clandestine encounters and criminality, an image reinforced by its proximity to the river, which, like a sewer, collected the debris of the city and washed it upon the embankment. Although Mayhew portrays the prostitutes with some sympathy, his categorisation of the types of women who resort to this profession included 'park women', 'sailor's women', 'maid-servants' and 'female operatives', which included milliners, dress-makers and ballet girls.[96] In such an inclusive definition of an exclusive field, Mayhew was merely partaking in a discourse that was to have larger ramifications on an entire populace of women who became implicated in the regulation of streetwalking as a spatial practice.

Of all the allusions to prostitutes, however, the 'fallen woman' was the most common name given to women who fell from the height of virtue to the depths of depravity. In this vertical metaphor, women often fell twice: first in succumbing to her moral weakness, and second, by leaping from a bridge into the river, where her suicide expiated her sins. Thus, some form of moral redress was possible, although only in death. Thomas Hood immortalised this image in his poem 'The Bridge of Sighs' (1844), which became the inspiration for a number of paintings that merged the prostitute's 'muddy impurity' with the 'black flowing river'.[97] Again, the Thames was the incarnation of the sewer, which both polluted and purified women in its destabilising presence. John Everett Millais's illustration to Hood's poem (1858) captures the haunting presence of the river as the prostitute stares out into the void, while Gustave Doré's engraving *Glad to Death's Mystery, Swift to be Hurl'd* (1878) portrays London as a menacing city, as an angelic woman contemplates jumping into the underworld of Hades (Fig. 1.5). In both, the innocence of the prostitute is emphasised to reveal them as victims, rather than perpetrators of the crime. In the ensuing images of drowned women, from Augustus Leopold Egg's *Past and Present* (1858) to George Frederick Watts's *Found Drowned* (c. 1848–50), the notorious Adelphi Arches frame the paintings in semi-circles that closely resemble the bricked tunnels of the London sewers (Fig. 1.6). Through such indirect parallels and subtle allusions, the prostitute was both vilified and victimised in

Figure 1.5   Gustave Doré, *Glad to Death's Mystery, Swift to be Hurl'd* (1851).
Illustration for Thomas Hood's 'The Bridge of Sighs'. Watercolour and Indian Ink.
© Victoria and Albert Museum, London.

Figure 1.6   Augustus Leopold Egg, *Past and Present, No. 3* (1858). Oil on canvas. Tate Images/Digital Images. © Tate, London 2012.

subterranean overtones that relegated her to the liminal spaces of the modernity.

The river also offers images of sacrifice as well as salvation in literary depictions, particularly in the works of Dickens, that engage with the discourse of prostitution and purity through circuitous descriptions of fallen women. As the founder of Urania Cottage, an asylum for fallen women, Dickens was deeply involved with contemporary debates concerning the redeemability of prostitutes.[98] Despite his sympathy for the cause, however, his fictional characters fall into the same refuse of the river as the women before, albeit in portrayals of compassion and forgiveness. Nancy in *Oliver Twist* (1839) is declared 'a prostitute' in the first-edition introduction of the novel, but in the text, her career is only mentioned obliquely by a reference to her physical attributes and dress, which was common practice in discerning streetwalkers.

> They wore a good deal of hair, not very neatly turned up behind, and were rather untidy about the shoes and stockings. They were not exactly pretty, perhaps; but they had a great deal of colour in their faces, and looked quite

stout and healthy. Being remarkably free and easy with their manners, Oliver thought them to be very nice girls indeed. Which there is no doubt they were.[99]

In spite of her robust outward appearance, Nancy eventually succumbs to the life she has chosen for herself, contemplating suicide as the only way out of her wayward existence: 'Look at that dark water. How many times do you read of such as I who spring into the tide . . .'[100] Though tainted by her descent from respectability, Nancy is portrayed as a compassionate girl who dutifully gives up her own life to save Oliver from a life of depravity. In this vision of self-sacrifice, she is redeemed morally in the reader's eyes, but her life is unsalvageable as she is brutally murdered by her lover, Sikes.

Martha in *David Copperfield* (1850) almost follows the same violent fate but is saved only by being transported to the furthest reaches of Australia to begin her life anew. The Thames again plays a crucial role as a conduit for moral refuse as well as moral redemption. In the illustration of Martha at the threshold of the Thames, she is associated with 'the polluted stream' that 'the refuse . . . had cast out and left to corruption and decay'.[101] In attempting to merge with the river, she exclaims:

> I know it's like me . . . I know that I belong to it. I know that it's the natural company of such as I am! It comes from the country places, where there was once no harm in it – and it creeps through the dismal streets, defiled and miserable – and it goes away like my life to a great sea, that is always troubled – and I feel that I must go with it![102]

Despite her own wish to die, Martha is saved by the very river that pumps her out like sewage from the heart of London to distant Australia, where the chance for her moral restitution remains questionable but open to interpretation. As a carrier of filth that opens up to cleaner waters, the sewer is the spectre of demise and renewal for prostitutes in the Dickensian moral landscape.

As the discourse of prostitution emerged from the sewer to the forefront of feminist consciousness, the politics of movement and circulation of all women became a critical issue that complicated the notion of 'streetwalking'. With the advent of new jobs and better transport systems, many more women were able to participate socially and economically in the city, and as middle-class shoppers jostled with shopgirls, factory workers and potential prostitutes, the codes of physical and economic exchange shifted dramatically. Although Rachel Bowlby in *Just Looking* (1985) argues that shopgirls can be seen as a product of capitalist exploitation (as the prostitute was), these women also presented a powerful new presence in the circulatory map of the city.[103] The role of the *flâneuse* in relation to the development of the underground railways will be elaborated in Chapter 2; however, I also want to touch upon here the underground connections to female streetwalkers who, as Deborah Parsons notes in *Streetwalking the Metropolis* (2000), occupied the public realm as 'observing subjects in the city'.[104] Shopgirls in particular represented the transitional or liminal space between a prostitute and a potential *flâneuse* in the Victorian imagination, as novels presented them in full possession of their sexuality and the economic means to explore the city on their own terms.

In literary representations, shopgirls are not usually the central characters in the novel, but they tend to eclipse their male counterparts, who are often grappling with their own impotence in the face of such powerful women. Sally Ledger further notes that the shopgirl is 'a sexually suspect and socially disruptive figure, and this stems both from her association with modern commerce – a new and to some minds "vulgar" phenomenon – and from the difficulty of labelling her in class terms'.[105] In Henry James's novel *The Princess Casamassima* (1886), Millicent Henning exemplifies this ambiguity, as she overshadows the effete Hyacinth in her perambulations around the city. Described as 'larger than life', Millicent is 'a daughter of London, of the crowded streets and hustling traffic of the great city; she had drawn her health and strength from its dingy courts and foggy thoroughfares'.[106] A far cry from the pale, degenerative features of lower-class women, Millicent's robust appearance and sexuality allows her to have a sexual encounter with the powerful aristocrat Sholto without the attending shame and remorse that taints most Victorian heroines. Likewise in George Gissing's *The Odd Women* (1893), Monica, a former shopgirl, roams freely and becomes a visible figure in the city despite her husband's attempts to contain her in the countryside. In a marital dispute about her flagrant wanderings, Monica argues:

> 'Suppose the thought took you that you should go and walk about the city some afternoon, and you wished to go alone, just to be more at ease. Should I have a right to forbid you, or grumble at you? And yet you are very dissatisfied if I wish to go anywhere alone.'
> 'But here's the old confusion, I am a man; you are a woman.'
> 'A woman ought to go about just as freely as a man.'[107]

Such dialogues reflected the concerns and the discourse of the 'New Woman' that challenged male hierarchical norms about marriage, property and female independence. Although Monica is juxtaposed against two prototypes of the New Woman, embodied in Rhoda Nunn and Mary Barfoot, who run their own typing school for women, she is equally defiant in contesting male norms by occupying the streets of London rather than building an occupation on them.

From her association with filth and the sewer, the prostitute became the spectre from which definitions of women and their roles became enmeshed in the discourses of social reform. By shedding light on her underground identity in an attempt to contain her, institutional forces merely brought more issues of sexual equality and freedom of movement to the surface of urban consciousness. Although there were references to prostitutes in British literature, the oblique allusions to their nocturnal trade departed from the more direct Parisian model of the courtesan. The circuitous method by which their career was then invoked simultaneously enlarged the fate of prostitutes to the social and political rights of all women. In the debate, heavily influenced by biological and evolutionary discourses, the fate of civilisation rested on the women's sexual selection of men. As feminist Olive Schreiner argues:

> If the parasite woman on the couch, loaded with gew-gaws, the plaything and amusement of man, be the permanent and final manifestation of female human life on the globe, then that couch is also the death-bed of human evolution . . . beyond the little struggle of today, lies the longer struggle of the centuries, in which neither she alone nor her sex alone are concerned, but all mankind.[108]

Whether the woman was a streetwalking whore or a middle-class woman living off her husband's income, she was contributing to the deterioration of humanity in her parasitic indolence. Thus, the eugenics movement called for a new concept of values regarding morality and sexuality, one that would embrace what Angelique Richardson terms 'eugenic virtue' or a law of social selection through which 'the future of the British race be secured'.[109] Under the discursive fear of degeneration, the eugenics movement would also have far-reaching implications on the representation of foreigners, who were also associated with the contaminating touch of prostitutes.

Imperial Impurities/Foreign Filth

> It has been said that beasts of chase still roam in the verdant fastness of Grosvenor square, that there are undiscovered patches of primaeval forest in Hyde Park and that Hampstead sewers shelter a monstrous breed of black swine, which have propagated and run wild among the slimy feculence, and whose ferocious snouts will one day up-root Highgate archway, while they make Holloway intolerable with their grunting.
>
> *The Daily Telegraph*, 10 October 1859

In this mythical underground, the recognisable traces of the contemporary New York urban legend of the alligators in the sewer appear here in a slightly modified form: rather than a radioactive reptile lost in the labyrinth of the city, the myth here alludes to an organic 'matter out of place', embodied in the filthy black pig that threatens to rupture the peacefulness of the neighbourhood above. In *Mythologies*, Roland Barthes offers significant insight into the way myths function in society, from representation and circulation to its production of meaning as 'the foundation of a collective morality'.[110] Previous manifestations of sewers unveiled the polluting and infectious codifications of the poor and prostitutes; it seems only logical that the Victorians extended this repulsion to foreigners, who, in their real and imagined alterity, threatened to upturn the foundations of society and defile the very roots of a collective 'British' consciousness. As Christopher Prendergast suggests, 'the city acquired and retained identity in direct proportion to its success in ridding itself of "impure" matter, on a spectrum from excrement to revolutionaries, perverts, and foreigners'.[111] However, in an attempt to locate these alien blockages and pump the sewage out to distant colonial territories, England ultimately had to deal with the imperial detritus that circulated back to the heart of the Empire. The colonising impulse, combined with fear of foreign contamination, produced a double standard in the treatment of dirt within and dirt without. While trying to sanitise foreign filth on English soil, the desire to domesticate and create value out of filth on imperial shores created more disjunctures in the urban psyche, as the question of national identity also became submerged in excremental discourse.

By the 1840s the influx of immigrants and refugees was directly linked with vice and degradation in the Victorian imagination. Although the demographics ranged from the Chinese 'dens of iniquity' in Limehouse to Africans consigned to servitude in affluent homes, the greatest resentment was reserved for the Irish and the Jews, who posed a more visible threat in sheer numbers, as they populated the East End. Newspapers frequently circulated inflated figures for these populations, and *Punch* cartoonists regularly satirised immigrant populations as dangerous hordes whose proximity would defile the respectable middle classes. Such associations inevitably reinforced the image of foreigners as devolved, uncivilised masses, and writers often expressed horror that 'those people can exist – and even thrive – in an atmosphere and amid surroundings which to the more highly-developed Englishman and Englishwoman mean death and disease'.[112] It was particularly in this anti-foreigner context that the most vicious attacks on the Irish emerged.

As early as the seventeenth century, the Irish had been described as a race living 'beyond the pale', living in 'foul dunghil' and foraging for food 'like beasts out of ditches'.[113] This underground imagery persisted into the nineteenth century, but in more specifically animalistic terms, as the Irish were closely associated with the swineherd. Engels lends credibility to this image when he observes:

> the Irishman allows the pig to share his own living quarters. This new, abnormal method of rearing livestock in the large towns is entirely of the Irish origin . . . The Irishman lives and sleeps with the pig, the children play with the pig, ride on its back, and roll about in the filth with it.[114]

Although keeping pigs in town was a common English practice, through repeated metaphoric associations, the 'Irishman as pig' gained linguistic currency. In fact, the original 'swines in the sewers of Hampstead' myth that circulated during this time was often interpreted as the threat of an underground plot by the Irish to use the sewer systems to attack various government buildings in London.[115] As most of the sewers were built using Irish labour, the fear of the Irish was particularly resonant underground, as exemplified by Mayhew's interview with one worker who described the sewers as full of rats 'fighting and squawking . . . like a parcel of drunken Irishmen'.[116] In his visit to Ireland in 1860, Charles Kingsley degrades the Irish further down the degenerative chain when he opined:

> I am haunted by the human chimpanzees I saw along that hundred miles of horrible country . . . But to see white chimpanzees is dreadful; if they were black, one would not feel it so much, but their skins, except where tanned by exposure, are as white as ours.[117]

Ultimately, the pig, the rat and the monkey appear as repetitive evolutionary metaphors, as mediators of filth and as the embodiment of the 'other' in all of its transgressive and animalistic connotations.

In addition to the Irish, the Jews were equally vilified in their caricaturisation and association with filth, but in this case, with filthy lucre. In the 1880s, Jews fled to England, escaping pograms in Eastern Europe and seeking refuge in the East End, where they faced a different form of persecution as they developed their communities.[118] From such images as Fagin in *Oliver Twist* (1839) and *Punch* cartoons like 'The Dealer in Old Clothes' (1851) illustrating a corrupt Jew bribing young boys, to the villainous Svengali in *Trilby* (1894), the stereotype of the Jew as an opportunistic moneylender and a deceitful rogue persisted. Ultimately, the government responded with the Aliens Act of 1905, severely curtailing the immigration of foreigners into the country. However, the population of London by then had already diversified, and in its cosmopolitanism, Karl Baedeker famously noted that 'there were more Scotsmen in London than in Aberdeen, more Irishmen than in Dublin, more Jews than in Palestine, and more Roman Catholics than in Rome'.[119] However, the presence of such threats to the notion of racial purity and the concept of 'Englishness' elicited renewed efforts to protect the heart of the Empire from foreign impurities and the threat of contamination.

While dirt from foreigners infected London from within, there was more filth to conquer on distant shores, as the sewer imagery extended its conduits beyond the borders of the capital to the detritus of imperial colonies. The flushing of London's own criminal pollutants began with the migration of English convicts to Australia and America, which were perceived as sewage dumps for human refuse. However, other imperial colonies, especially India and Africa, promised more return on sanitary investment, as the Victorians attempted to superimpose their ideals of cleanliness with a view to expanding their mercantile economy. In his survey of the construction of the East, Edward Said argues that '[t]he European culture gained in strength and identity by setting itself against the Orient as a sort of surrogate and even underground self'.[120] Embedded in this demarcation is the conceptualisation of the 'other' as a darker version of oneself, and this insistence was prevalent in the British bifurcation of the colonial and colonised, especially in India and Africa, which were imagined as the darkest and the dirtiest of all territories.

The discourse of filth was particularly resonant in India, as it was referred to as the 'natural home of cholera', and the source of the disease was traced by John Snow to 'the alluvial swamps and malarious jungles of Asia, where it was first engendered amid miles of vapourous poisons, and still broods over wasted nations, the agents of innumerable death'.[121] Thus, like the miasmatic secretions of London slum-dwellers, the polluting effects of Indians were also to be avoided, as European residential quarters were built at a considerable distance from native areas. Vijay Prashad argues that India was endowed with a limited version of a 'colonial modernity' when the British set up a *cordon sanitaire* between themselves and the natives.[122] Meanwhile, Claude Lévi-Strauss justifies this segregation through a form of cultural relativism:

> Filth, chaos, promiscuity, congestion; ruins, huts, mud, dirt, dung, urine, pus, humours, secretions and running sores; all the things which we expect urban life to give us organised protection . . . all these by-products of cohabitation do not set any limitation on it in India. They are more like a natural environment which the Indian town needs in order to prosper . . . [T]his filth acquires a kind of domestic status through having been exuded, excreted, trampled on and handled by so many men.[123]

As Kristeva argues, horror arises from the confrontation with bodily fluids and secretions that disrupt 'the frailty of the symbolic order', and the proximity to Indians who blurred all boundaries between self and excretory practices justified the abrogation of any responsibility for the conditions of the native poor.[124] In a new system of waste management, the English physically separated themselves from what they perceived as abject matter, and like a pumping station, sanitised the products of the colony's labour to pass through the hygienic divide, only to filter back to England in their sanitised form.

In colonial Africa, the discourse of filth was also mapped onto the bodies of indigenous tribes, but the natives were exploited for more commercial and propagandistic purposes. One publication that provoked disgust and horror was John G. Bourke's 'Scatalogic Rites of All Nations' (1891), which described Zuni tribal customs of consuming great quantities of urine and excrement as a form of native ceremony. As Stephen Greenblatt explicates in 'Filthy Rites', the proper control of one's wastes demarcated the

> entrance into civility, an entrance that distinguishes not only the child from the adult, but the member of the privileged group from the vulgar, the upper classes from the lower, the courtly from the rustic, the civilized from the savage'.[125]

The denigration of Africans to a filthy, subhuman species justified a persistent and often violent subjugation of the community to the wheels of imperial progress. Furthermore, in the rhetoric of cleanliness that pervaded the English consciousness, the image of Africans as savage became central to the promotion of the single great purifier of Victorian invention: soap. In her analysis of imperial commercialism and fetishism, Anne McClintock argues, 'Soap advertising, in particular the Pears soap campaign, took its place at the vanguard of Britain's new commodity culture and its civilizing mission . . . From the outset, Victorian advertising took shape around the reinvention of racial difference.'[126] Such differences were stamped on the household commodity in images that ranged from a black child who turns white after a bath with Pears soap, to advertisements depicting monkeys to promote bathing as a deterrent to racial degeneration. In the intersection of biology and cultural production, Donna Haraway claims that, '[p]rimatology is a Western discourse . . . a political order that works by the negotiation of boundaries achieved through ordering differences . . . the primate body, as part of the body of nature, may be read as a map of power'.[127] Thus, this simian image became an acknowledged symbol of the lower, subaltern classes, promoting a racial iconography of evolutionary progress and reinforcing the hierarchical boundaries between the pure and impure, coloniser and colonised.

However, cleanliness and civilisation did not come without its residuum and discontents. The underside of the new commodity spectacle revealed more industrial pollution arising from 'the soap-works with their new smoke-vomiting chimneys' and more rubbish accumulated in the dustbins of modernity, composed of 'imperial desire, teas, biscuits, tobaccos, Bovril, tins of cocoa, and above all, soaps'.[128] In a further ironic twist, Pears soap was accused of pornography in its iconographic advertisements of near-naked children, and John Everett Millais became notorious after being accused of prostituting himself to the manufacturer by selling his painting of *Bubbles* (1886) for commercial purposes, the first artist in history to do so.[129] Thus, filth begets filth. This circulatory metaphor and the transformation of filth as it passes hands from the coloniser to the colonised, back to the rubbish heaps of the coloniser's own backyard, becomes a repetitive motif in the representation of repressed anxieties that underscored the guilt, shame and remorse in the Victorian psyche.

Embanking the Empire: Literature of Otherness

Sewage whether fluid or solid, mixed or unmixed, is very much like our convicts, everybody wants to get rid of it, and no one consents to have it.
John Hollingshead, *Underground London* (1862)

The foreigner who becomes an embodiment of sewage and an object of disgust and fascination is a fluid figure in the literature of modernity. Although the link between sewers and foreignness is never explicitly mentioned in literary representation, it is his ghostly 'otherness' that poses the greatest threat to the city, expressed in subterranean overtones. In his irreverent study of stercus, *History of Shit*, Dominique Laporte emphasises the power of the state in relation to sewers when he proclaims, 'Without a master, one cannot be cleaned. Purification, whether by fire or by the work, by baptism or by death, requires submission to the law.'[130] In this Hegelian master-and-servant dialectic, the subjugation of foreign filth was necessary in the development of the modern state, a repressive relationship that appears in multiple guises in the colonial fictional discourse of the late nineteenth century. As the concept of 'Englishness' was in danger of dilution and devolution, authors approached the subject of 'foreignness' indirectly in Gothic hauntings and detective stories that attempted to decode the identity of criminals, who were frequently linked to distant and exotic lands.

Although the sewer is never explicitly mentioned, it lingers as a spectral conduit through which the identity of foreigners is traced and eventually flushed out of the city. By examining some of the key works by Bram Stoker and Arthur Conan Doyle that confront this 'otherness', I reveal the extent to which filth refuses to submit to the power of the law, and how its insistence on assimilating into the metropolis reveals the regenerative power of filth in recreating one's identity.

In the British literary imaginary, some of the key themes of Irish and otherness, as well as filth and contamination, attest to this potential. At the most fundamental level, dirt has already been observed as something alien, a fearful presence that needs to be excluded and an inassimilable object that needs to be classified as unusable. Although Robert Louis Stevenson, Oscar Wilde and J. Sheridan Le Fanu confront this sense of alterity in their Gothic narratives, Bram Stoker's works most strongly reflect the anxieties of 'otherness' in his explorations of terror, repression and the occult. Contemporary critics such as Terry Eagleton have linked Stoker's Gothic sensibilities with the 'political unconscious of Anglo-Irish society, the place where its fears and fantasies most definitively emerge',[131] while Alison Milbank emphasises Stoker's sense of 'doubleness' 'as being both part of a quasi-imperial order and yet a victim of outside systems'.[132] One of his lesser-known stories, 'The Burial of the Rats' (1914), confronts this social and psychic displacement, depicting a young Englishman in Paris, strangely in exile from his fiancée, who finds himself constantly drawn to the dust heaps on the outskirts of the city. Although he originally professes his journeys to be a sociological experiment, exploring the life of a *chiffonier* (a ragpicker), his desire transforms into an obsessive personal quest 'to penetrate further', to 'trace dust to its ultimate location'.[133] In line with a quintessential Freudian case study, he stays and strays too long on his final visit, becomes trapped in a plot by an old woman to ensnare him and manages to barely escape after a filthy yet baptismal flight through a sea of stinking rubbish and excrement.

> My feet had given way in a mass of slimy rubbish, and I had fallen headlong into a reeking, stagnant pool. The water and mud in which my arms sank up to the elbows was filthy and nauseous beyond description, and in the suddenness of my fall I had actually swallowed some of the filthy stuff, which nearly choked me, and made me gasp for breath. Never shall I forget the moments during which I stood trying to recover myself almost fainting from the foetid odour of the filthy pool, whose white mist rose ghostlike around.[134]

Again, the slimy ooze evokes the Kristevan feminine devouring the Englishman before he is rebirthed into the symbolic order. In his rejection of filth, he eschews the womb and, in part, his genealogy (and sexuality), although he cannot completely remove the fetid odour that lingers like a 'ghost'. Like a rat, the traveller becomes a part of the sewage, a transgressor of boundaries and a transmitter of disease, a popular metaphor for the Irish at the time, alluding to Stoker's own crisis of identity. Elizabeth Tilley also suggests that Stoker's dust heaps evoke Ireland's 'Bog of Allen' and argues that the story portrays 'an unconscious desire for assimilation, disgust at that desire and ultimately separation of the self from the source of anxiety, the bog in all of its manifestations and historical guises'.[135] In withdrawing himself from the filth, he attempts to remove the stain of his own attraction to this underworld, and in the end, the *gendarmes* arrive at the scene in a reinforcement of social, national and bodily order. However, the nightmare of the experience haunts him, as he retells the tale in a constant resurrection of the past, alluding to the enduring presence of this tainted vision in his dual consciousness.

The attraction and repulsion to the 'other' is also given significant treatment in Stoker's *Dracula* (1897), but the representation of waste is extended beyond the borders of self-identification to a larger, fearful web of foreign invasion. Many critics have dwelled on Dracula's foreignness, reading his body as a potential pollutant from the East, as he accumulates his army of infected slaves to descend upon the city of London, the height of Western civilisation. Maud Ellmann, in particular, juxtaposes these geographical oppositions in a hierarchical map of high and low, progress and degeneration.

> The West is associated with the middle class, the East with the feudal aristocracy; West means love, where East means lust; West normality, and East perversity. In the Eastern figure of Count Dracula, Stoker seems to summon up the whole gamut of perversions – sadism, masochism, rape, necrophilia, paedophilia, incest, oral sex, group sex, and voyeurism – and then to repress them violently through the retribution enacted by the Western heroes.[136]

Thus, Dracula is a residuum, a waste product of Eastern decadence that threatens to contaminate London with his excessive thirst and perverse desires. The boxes or coffins of soil from his native land that he disperses throughout London so that he can be reinvigorated from lying in them become the subterranean infiltration from beyond that need to be sterilised and sanitised by Van Helsing and other vampire hunters in order to protect the city.

Like the eyes of slum-investigating Mayhew or the colonial apprehension of Marlowe, Jonathan Harker enters Dracula's territory with a voyeuristic penchant for alterity in 'one of the wildest and least known portions of Europe'. In Dracula's castle, he descends through a sewer-like passage and encounters Dracula in his dormant state, lying like 'a filthy leech, exhausted with his repletion':

> I shuddered as I bent over to touch him, and every sense in me revolted at the contact . . . This was the being I was helping to transfer to London, where for centuries to come, he might, amongst its teeming millions, satiate his lust for blood, and create a new and ever widening circle of semi-demons to batten on the helpless. The very thought drove me mad. A terrible desire came upon me to rid the world of such a monster.[137]

A formidable sanitary engineer, Harker then sets out to embank the city from the threat of this contagion, as he organises a sewage system of his own invention in the form of blood transfusions. Like the underground pipelines, fluids are emptied into a receptacle, in this case the body of Lucy Westenra, and the waste flowing through her veins is treated and purified of its toxicity. Although the figure of Lucy as a sewage treatment plant may not be palatable, Stoker also uses the female body in *The Lair of the White Worm* (1911) as a locus of filth, disease and death. In a Kafkaesque revelation, the beautiful Lady Arabella turns out to be a worm that lives beneath the house, 'a round fissure seemingly leading down into the very bowels of the earth' that reeks of 'the draining of war hospitals, of slaughter-houses, the refuse of dissecting rooms . . . the sourness of chemical waste and the poisonous effluvium of a bilge of a water-logged ship whereon a multitude of rats had been drowned'.[138] In this overflowing, infested image, all the repressive elements threaten to erupt onto the surface of the city. In order to contain these psychic anxieties, the Western heroes in *Dracula* resort to Western techniques of measuring, calculating and anticipating in order to flush the vampire out of the heart of the city.

Mina surmises in her final journal entry that Dracula could have used many networks to escape, from roads to railroads, but finally deduces that it must have been through the sea that he found his way back to his homeland. Like the conduits of a sewer, water has the only purifying potential to drive out foreign matter and the agents of contamination. However, there is a lingering fear still left in London, as traces of Dracula and the conundrum surrounding his identity continue to plague the urban consciousness. Critics have read the strong physical resemblance of Dracula to the Jew, and thus reinscribe his character as a victim rather than a persecutor, aligning him with those who faced double prejudices in pograms in Russia as well as persecution in the East End. Freud's analysis of the 'Rat Man' is appropriate here in comparison to Dracula's identity as the demonised 'other'.

> The notion of a rat is inseparably bound up with the fact that it has sharp teeth with which it gnaws and bites. But rats cannot be sharp-toothed, greedy and dirty with impunity: they are cruelly persecuted and mercilessly put to death by man, as the patient had often observed with horror.[139]

In all of his beastly manifestations, Dracula's ambivalent character allows for a reflective meditation on the actual source of filth: is it the foreign body that attempts to settle into the city, or the city that uses violence and hatred to drive out its alien presence? As Mina realises at the end of her final entry, 'It is as if some haunting presence were removed from me. Perhaps ... My surmise was not finished, could not be; for I caught sight in the mirror of the red mark upon my forehead; and I knew that I was still unclean.'[140] The dirt continues to defile long after Dracula's presence is removed, gesturing towards an impurity perhaps of another sort, of Western civilisation's strident rationalisation of their xenophobia and colonial ideology in their treatment of, and interaction with, other races and cultures.

The attempts to embank the city against the polluting effects of foreigners take on a different guise as a narrative of detection in the tales of Sherlock Holmes. Written over four decades, the first half of the stories were written and published before the passage of the first Aliens Act in 1905, which attempted to regulate the flow of immigrants into England. Within this historical context, Arthur Conan Doyle's introduction of detective Holmes sheds sanitary light once again into the foreign underworld, exposing possibilities of contamination in an effort to preserve the body of quintessential Englishness. The narrator of the tales, Dr Watson, proves to be an eminent filter for exposing and diagnosing foreign ills of a corrupted city. As a wounded veteran of the Afghan wars, he has already been contaminated by 'savages' and wanders back to London, 'that great cesspool into which all the idlers and loungers of the Empire are irresistibly drained'.[141] Extending this circulatory metaphor, Joseph Childers comments on the blockages in the imperial sewage system:

> The London to which he returns is indeed the heart of the empire, but that organ no longer functions efficiently. Rather than the pump that keeps men and materials moving along the arteries feeding the farthest-flung extremities of empire, it has become a backwash of imperial detritus, susceptible to infection from without and sepsis from the pool of filth that has accumulated within.[142]

In this congested, infested city, imperial detritus takes on multiple forms, from foreigners who have flowed into the city as well as the English themselves, who return after having been tainted by the colonising impulse and ensuing idleness. Which one poses a greater threat to the Empire and civilisation remains questionable at best.

In *A Study in Scarlet* (1887), Doyle constructs a narrative of a revenge murder of an American in London that ignites a wave of paranoia within the city. Although the aetiology of the crime points closer to home, newspapers in the story circulate warnings of contamination, recommending 'a closer watch over foreigners in England' and an admonition to 'all foreigners' to 'settle their feuds at home'.[143] In the construction of an exterior criminal entity, England overlooks its own stained hand in the production of imperial filth and the reabsorption of it into the city. As Holmes and Watson revisit the original transgression, the real crime is actually committed by Englishmen while performing a service to the Empire. Ronald Thomas argues that in the heated foreign rhetoric at the turn of the century, the Holmes mysteries brought England 'face to face with its own criminal guilt and impending colonial revenge, and the means with which to defend itself against both'.[144] Criminal filth from within and colonial filth without then merge in the liminal spaces of the city to produce a retributive underworld where it becomes harder to distinguish the proper English gentleman from the ostensibly foreign perpetrator.

The contaminating imperial touch becomes more pronounced in *The Sign of Four*, where Holmes and Watson trace the path of the stolen treasure Agra, which passes through multiple English and foreign hands. Originally stolen by an English soldier, Jonathan Small, with the help of Sikh cohorts, the treasure belonged to a murdered rajah during the Mutiny in India. This stained jewel then becomes the haunting object of imperial violence, both an object of power and of filth that pollutes everyone in its path. When Holmes and Watson finally overtake the English culprit along the bank of the polluted Thames, his physical deformity, a peg leg, drags him into the quagmire of his own guilty muck.

> He yelled in impotent rage and kicked frantically into the mud with his other foot, but his struggles only bored his wooden pin the deeper into the sticky mud. When we brought our launch alongside, he was so firmly anchored that it was only by throwing the end of the rope over his shoulders that we were able to haul him out and drag him, like some evil fish, over our side.[145]

Again, the Thames becomes the sewer through which polluted identities and histories are brought to light. Merging with the filth of the river, the captured criminal complicates the notion of English purity until he is physically dragged over to 'our side' or the 'proper side' that reflects the ordered and meticulous world of Holmes and Watson. Although

The Sign of Four has been read as a 'scathing indictment' of the 'grasping nature of imperialism and the economic impetus of the ideology of "great expectations"', the narrative also reveals the erosion of the English character when the Empire returns 'home' to the metropolis, endangering its constituents and contaminating its history with the taint of its imperial aggression abroad.[146] By recycling foreign filth as one of England's own, the tale destabilises what it means to be British and interrogates the eugenic virtue of racial purity at a time when the fate of the Empire paradoxically depended on embanking its shores, while allowing the flow of human and material capital in and out of its borders.

Beyond Cleanliness

> . . . when written, shit does not smell.
> Roland Barthes, *Sade, Fourier, Loyola* (1971)

The discourse of underground sewers always contained within it the elusive goal of sanitising the city of impure matter in all its deviant forms. Social investigators, sanitary inspectors, detectives and soap all attempted to monitor, trace and remove the sources of disease and depravity. The construction of the sewers coincided with the need and desire for an ordered space, creating new vertical topographies in the city; however, in an effort to promote circulation and protect the urban body, more contradictions surfaced to create a dialectical relationship with some of the key social, cultural and political issues of modernity. As one critic notes, 'Repression, nevertheless, does not mean elimination. The sewers do not rid the society of what it wants to suppress. Like an archaeological formation, they simply hide the traces of history from sight at the same time they preserve them.'[147] The moments of their eruption onto the surface then become crucial markers of modernity, as the efforts to contain material and psychological messes become central to the formation of a modern consciousness.

In the Parisian identification of sewers and filth, there was a greater affiliation towards the abject matter, as writers and artists used the subterranean space for a bolder confrontation with the social and political residuum of the modern metropolis. Victor Hugo firmly elevated the sewer to a mythic and psychic level, while Félix Nadar opened up the space to the naked eye when he became the first photographer to use artificial light in photographing the underground system in 1861, which before had only existed in the imagination (Fig. 1.7). In this particular image, the sewer boat glides around the curve towards an overwhelm-

Figure 1.7   Félix Nadar, *Égouts de Paris* (1860). © Médiathèque du Patrimoine, Dist. RMN-Grand Palais / Imaginechina.

ingly bright light at the end of the tunnel, creating an atmospheric depiction of an underworld journey that is completely removed from its association with waste and its perfunctory removal. As Walter Benjamin comments, his photographs marked 'the first time that the lens is given the task of making discoveries'.[148] Such haunting reproductions of the

underground then contributed to the continuous discursive and subversive potential of the subterranean space in a city that embraced its
shadows below. Although Hugo lamented after the sewers were cleaned
up that 'nothing is left of the cloaca's primitive ferocity', filth continued
to erupt in other forms, lingering like Marx's spectre, in the formation
of social, spatial, and aesthetic sensibilities.[149]

In London, the sewers were also a marker of civilisation, but conceded
to a more shadowy presence in the Victorian imagination. As Ruskin
once declared, 'a good sewer . . . is far more nobler and a far holier
thing . . . than the most admired Madonna ever painted'.[150] However,
in its aesthetic and literary representation, the materiality of the sewers
was supplanted by a more haunting substitution and supplementation
in the River Thames that both polluted and purified the city, associating filth with the poor, prostitutes and foreigners. In its spectrality, the
discourse of the sewers was inevitably intertwined with the discourses
of sanitation, evolution and imperialism, as England attempted to
define itself against dirt, pollution and the 'other' in all its haunting
manifestations. Thus, the devaluation and revaluation of high and
low cultural products of society in reference to refuse underscores the
enduring significance of the underground metaphor. Rosalind Williams
argues that '[t]he subterranean environment is a technological one – but
also a mental landscape, a social terrain, and an ideological map'.[151]
The cartography of waste provides a powerful counter-narrative to
the rhetoric of social, sexual and racial purity, while opening up new
theoretical underpinnings of the way cities are built, ordered and defined
today.

Notes

1. Alain Corbin, 'L'Hygiène publique et les "excreta" de la ville préhauss-
   mannienne', cited in Reid, *Paris Sewers and Sewermen*, p. 1.
2. Marcus, 'Reading the Illegible', p. 266.
3. Mayhew, *London Labour and the London Poor* [1851], vol. 2,
   pp. 394–5.
4. See for example, 'Father Thames Introducing His Offspring to the Fair
   City of London', *Punch* (3 July 1858).
5. For a detailed account of the diseases that swept through London, see
   'Fever! Fever!', in Wohl, *Endangered Lives*, pp. 117–41. See also Pelling,
   Cholera, Fever, and English Medicine.
6. The miasmatic theory was later disproved by John Snow who published a
   pamphlet in 1849, *On the Mode and Communication of Cholera*, which
   identified contaminated water as a source of the outbreaks. However, he
   was not taken seriously until the 1880s, when German scientist Robert

Koch isolated the *Vibrio cholerae* bacteria, which confirmed Snow's earlier findings. See Koch, 'The Etiology of Cholera', pp. 327–69.

7. Greenhow, *Second Report of the Medical Officer*, p. 27.
8. *The Lancet* (15 November 1856), cited in Budd, *Typhoid Fever*, p. 181.
9. O'Connor, *Raw Material*, pp. 11, 40.
10. Chadwick, *Parliamentary Papers*, p. 651. Italics are my own.
11. Cited in Melosi, *The Sanitary City*, p. 53. See also Halliday, *The Great Stink of London*.
12. *The Builder*, 30 April 1859, p. 292.
13. Doxat, *The Living Thames*, p. 41. For more on Bazalgette's contributions, see also Halliday, *The Great Stink of London*.
14. Klingender, *Art and the Industrial Revolution*, p. 178. See also Barringer, *Men at Work*.
15. See Keating, *The Working Classes*, p. 10.
16. John Leech, 'Capital and Labour', *Punch*, 5 (29 July 1843), p. 48.
17. Marx, *Capital*, pp. 279–80.
18. See Himmelfarb, *The Idea of Poverty* and Flint, *The Victorian Novelist*.
19. Stallybrass and White, 'The City: The Sewer, the Gaze and the Contaminating Touch', in *The Politics and Poetics of Transgression*, p. 125.
20. Engels, *The Condition of the Working Class in England*, pp. 75, 58.
21. Chadwick, *Report on the Sanitary Conditions*, p. 274.
22. Mayhew, *London Labour*, vol. 1, p. 2.
23. Himmelfarb, *The Idea of Poverty*, p. 53.
24. Anthony S. Wohl, Introduction to Hollingshead, *Ragged in London in 1861*, p. xix.
25. Wilson, *The Sphinx in the City*, p. 37.
26. Originally a phrase coined by Lord Chesterton, but associated more with Douglas, *Purity and Danger*. See p. 44.
27. Corbin, *The Foul and the Fragrant*, p. 5.
28. Ibid. p. 143. Italics are my own. Also as a 'fingerprint' of identity, body odours allowed people to locate the status of an individual in a crowd. Corbin dwells on the scents of linseed, gum, spinning mill, tobacco and other industrial processes in identifying labourers.
29. Freud, *Civilization and Its Discontents*, p. 100.
30. Ward, *Circulation or Stagnation*. Cited in Read, *Theatre and Everyday Life*, p. 219.
31. Read, *Theatre and Everyday Life*, p. 217.
32. Winter, *London's Teeming Streets 1830–1914*, p. 8.
33. Cited in Read, *Theatre and Everyday Life*, p. 218.
34. Clark, *The Painting of Modern Life*, p. 45.
35. Reid, *Paris Sewers and Sewermen*, pp. 35–6.
36. Pike, 'Sewage Treatments: Vertical Space and Waste in Nineteenth-Centry Paris and London', in Cohen and Johnson (eds), *Filth*, p. 68.
37. The most notable connection between sewers and politics revolved around the journalist and 'friend of the people' Jean-Paul Marat, who hid in the sewers and gained mythic status in the French cultural imagination. For more, see Hibbert, *The French Revolution*, p. 142.
38. Christiansen, *Tales of the New Babylon*, p. 96.

39. Hugo, *Les Misérables*, p. 1064.
40. Maxwell, *The Mysteries of Paris and London*, pp. 191–2.
41. Maxime du Camp, in *Paris: Its Organs, Functions, and Life until 1870*, cited in Reid, *Paris Sewers and Sewermen*, p. 48.
42. See Dobraszczyk, *Into the Belly of the Beast*.
43. Keating, *The Working Classes in Victorian Fiction*, p. 130.
44. Dickens, *Little Dorrit*, p. 29.
45. Dickens, *Bleak House*, p. 13. For more on Dickens's passion for sanitary reform, see Sutherland, 'Dickens's War on Filth'.
46. Forster, *The Life of Charles Dickens*, p. 11.
47. Dickens, *Nicholas Nickleby*, p. 409.
48. Steig, 'Dickens's Excremental Vision', p. 348. For more on Freud's discussion of anality and repression, see Freud, *The Complete Letters*, pp. 279, 280.
49. Cited in Brown, *Life against Death*, p. 293. The relevant texts by Freud are 'Character and Anal Eroticism', pp. 167–75, and 'On Transformations of Instinct as Exemplified by Anal Eroticism', pp. 127–33.
50. Ellen Handy, 'Dust Piles and Damp Pavements', p. 120.
51. Ibid. p. 2.
52. Ibid. pp. 841, 849.
53. For more on the criminal underworld, see Thomas, *Victorian Underworld*.
54. See Benjamin, *Charles Baudelaire*.
55. Keating, *The Working Classes in Victorian Fiction*, p. 223.
56. Engels, *The Condition of the Working Class in England*, p. 298.
57. Gaskell, *North and South*, p. 175.
58. Zola, *Germinal*, p. 353.
59. Gissing, *The Nether World*, p. 58. This form of resignation is also expressed in Orwell, *Down and Out in Paris and London*. Published in 1933, Orwell's novel depicts the underworld of the two cities and canvasses the lives of waiters, tramps, beggars, prostitutes and homosexuals through the eyes of an educated, middle-class narrator who ends up in the slums.
60. Stephen Gill, Introduction to Gissing, *The Nether World*, p. xiv.
61. Bulwer-Lytton, *Vril*, p. 32.
62. Letter dated June 1871, cited in Williams, *Notes on the Underground*, p. 128.
63. Wells, *The Time Machine*, p. 48.
64. Ibid. p. 79. Wells's later novel, *The Sleeper Awakes* (1899) also deals with similar themes and has been linked to Fritz Lang's film *Metropolis* (1927) in its representation of technology and social sublimity.
65. Williams, *Notes on the Underground*, p. 155.
66. Wells, *The Time Machine*, p. 48.
67. Cited in Thomas Aquinas, *Summa Theologiae*. See *On Faith, Summa Theologiae*, p. 207.
68. Cited in Nead, *Victorian Babylon*, p. 71.
69. Parent-Duchâtelet, *On Prostitution*, p. 72.
70. Acton, *Prostitution Considered*, p. 49. For more discussion on prostitutes and their association with the river, see Nead, *Myths of Sexuality*.
71. Wilson, *The Sphinx in the City*, p. 9.

72. Cited in Corbin, *The Foul and the Fragrant*, p. 177.
73. Baudelaire, 'Hygiene Projects', p. 70. For more on *Mon coeur mis à nu*, see <http://www.bmlisieux.com/archives/coeuranu.htm> (accessed 22 June 2009).
74. Léonard, *Les Médecins de l'Ouest au XIX Siècle*, cited in Corbin, *The Foul and the Fragrant*, p. 148.
75. Vigarello, *Concepts of Cleanliness*, p. 230.
76. Corbin, *Women for Hire*, pp. 210–11.
77. For more on the link between prostitutes and venereal diseases, see Spongberg, *Feminizing Venereal Disease*.
78. C. Wouters, 'Negotiating with de Swaan', unpublished manuscript (Amsterdam, 1970), cited in Stallybrass and White, *The Politics and Poetics of Transgression*, p. 136.
79. Cited in Bell, *Reading*, p. 58.
80. Pittard, *Purity and Contamination*, p. 4.
81. Ibid. p. 67.
82. Women were given advice on how to avoid the stares of men in such publications as *The Girl's Own Paper*, while maps organised specific walks around the West End to avoid such confrontations. For more on the development of the culture of walking women, see Walkowitz, *City of Dreadful Delight*.
83. Walkowitz, *City of Dreadful Delight*, p. 1.
84. Wilson, 'The Invisible Flâneur', p. 109). For more discussions on the sexuality of the *flâneur*, see Wolff, 'The Invisible Flâneuse', pp. 37–46, and Turner, *Backward Glances*.
85. Foucault, *The History of Sexuality*, pp. 105–6. Italics are my own.
86. Walkowitz, *Prostitution and Victorian Society*, p. 3.
87. Cited in Dyos and Wolff, *The Victorian City*, p. 698.
88. Menninghaus, *Disgust*, p. 86.
89. Zola, 'Courrier de Paris', *Illustration*, p. 66.
90. Zola, *Nana*, pp. 204–5.
91. Ibid. pp. 44–5.
92. Sartre, *Being and Nothingness*, p. 782. Kristeva, *Powers of Horror*, p. 70.
93. Zola, *Nana*, p. 389.
94. See, for example, Sartre's vision of jelly and slime in *Being and Nothingness*, p. 772.
95. Zola, *Nana*, p. 480.
96. Mayhew, cited in Ditmore, *Encyclopedia of Prostitutes*, p. 564.
97. Hood, 'The Bridge of Sighs', p. 760, ll. 91, 66.
98. See Hartley, *Charles Dickens and the House of Fallen Women*.
99. Dickens, *Oliver Twist*, p. 62.
100. Ibid. p. 354.
101. Dickens, *David Copperfield*, p. 768.
102. Ibid. p. 582.
103. Bowlby, *Just Looking*, p. 77.
104. Parsons, *Streetwalking the Metropolis*, p. 226.
105. Ledger, *The New Woman*, p. 166.
106. James, *The Princess Casamassima*, pp. 92–3.
107. Gissing, *The Odd Women*, p. 164.

108. Schreiner, *Women and Labour*, pp. 132–3.
109. Richardson, *Love and Eugenics*, p. 57.
110. Barthes, *Mythologies*, p. 59.
111. Prendergast, *Paris and the Nineteenth Century*, p. 79.
112. Wilkins, *The Alien Invasion*, p. 95.
113. Davies, *Discovery of the True Causes*, pp. 162–3.
114. Engels, *The Condition of the Working Class*, p. 106.
115. In 1848, British authorities uncovered a plot to plant explosives in the London sewers to blow up parliament and government offices. See Lewis, *Edwin Chadwick*, p. 90.
116. Cited in Wright, *Clean and Decent*, p. 155. The rat imagery was not exclusive to the Irish and the lower classes. The term 'sewer rats', for example, was slang for City businessmen who regularly commuted to work by subway in the 1880s. See Lesser, *The Life Below Ground*, p. 98.
117. Letter to his wife, 4 July 1860, in *Charles Kingsley*, p. 107. Curtis, *Anglo-Saxons and Celts*.
118. See Cheyette, *Constructions of the Jew*.
119. Briggs, *Victorian Cities*, p. 330.
120. Said, *Orientalism*, p. 3.
121. John Snow's *Report on London* [1853], cited in Winslow, *The Conquest of Epidemic Disease*, pp. 256–7.
122. Prashad, 'Native Dirt/Imperial Ordure', p. 243.
123. Lévi-Strauss, *Tristes Tropiques*, p. 134.
124. Kristeva, *Powers of Horror*, p. 69.
125. Greenblatt, 'Filthy Rites', p. 2.
126. McClintock, *Imperial Leather*, pp. 208, 209.
127. Haraway, *Primate Visions*, p. 10.
128. Morris, *News from Nowhere*, p. 186. McClintock, *Imperial Leather*, p. 219.
129. See Morris, 'Advertising', pp. 195–200.
130. Laporte, *History of Shit*, p. 3.
131. Eagleton, *Heathcliff and the Great Hunger*, p. 187.
132. Milbank, 'Powers Old and New', p. 14.
133. Stoker, 'The Burial of the Rats', p. 104.
134. Ibid. p. 117.
135. Tilley, 'Stoker, Paris, and the Crisis of Identity,' p. 39.
136. Maud Ellmann, Introduction to Stoker, *Dracula*, p. xxiii.
137. Stoker, *Dracula*, p. 51.
138. Stoker, *The Lair of the White Worm*, pp. 97, 158.
139. Freud, 'Notes upon a case of obsessional neurosis (the "Rat Man")'.
140. Stoker, *Dracula*, p. 321.
141. Doyle, *A Study in Scarlet*, p. 4.
142. Joseph Childers, 'Foreign Matter: Imperial Filth', in Cohen and Johnson (eds), *Filth*, p. 202.
143. Doyle, *A Study in Scarlet*, p. 106.
144. Thomas, *Detective Fiction*, p. 220.
145. Doyle, *A Study in Scarlet*, p. 178.
146. Kestner, *Sherlock's Men*, p. 67.
147. De la Carrera, 'History's Unconscious', p. 841. For more on unconscious

messes as meaningful interventions in modernity, see Trotter, *Cooking with Mud*.
148. Benjamin, 'Paris', p. 150.
149. Hugo, cited in Reid, *Paris Sewers and Sewermen*, p. 143.
150. Cited in Wohl, *Endangered Lives*, p. 101.
151. Williams, *Notes on the Underground*, p. 21.

Chapter 2

Tubing It:
Speeding through Modernity
in the London Underground

... the coming of the railways to London from the mid-1830s onwards dealt the metropolis a bigger, and certainly more lasting, blow than anything since the Great Fire. Like the Great Fire, the railways shattered both the living and working arrangements of hundreds of thousands of Londoners. Like the Fire, they ate up vast quantities of labour, material, and capital, and destroyed acres of the metropolis in the process. Most importantly of all, like the Fire, they spun the population of London further away from the core, spreading the decay of the central districts, yet at the same time enabling Londoners to enjoy higher standard of space and cleanliness in their housing than in any other city in the world.

Simon Jenkins, Landlords to London (1975)

The contradictory forces of progress and destruction remained a powerful spectre in the Victorian underground, but the construction of the underground railway also created social and psychological fissures in the urban psyche, while irrevocably changing London's landscape. In many ways, its dual nature is captured in the Janus-edged façade of 23 and 24 Leinster Gardens in Paddington (Fig. 2.1). At first glance, the Georgian exterior, complete with plant trimmings and iron railings, is undifferentiated from the row of terrace houses that line the elegant street. However, just beyond the veneer of gentrification, a network of railway tracks disappearing into a dark tunnel reveals one of the few visible remnants of the original Metropolitan Line, where steam-engine trains emerged for ventilation purposes. This portal into the past represents the threshold between many of the inherent contradictions that underscored the inception, conception and representation of the first underground railway system in the 1860s. Like the sewers, the underground railway was considered an engineering triumph, the ultimate symbol of technological achievement, and a 'mythical event', yet it simultaneously represented chaos, disaster and a complete reconfiguration of London's streets and boundaries.[1] In the ensuing paradoxes, the underground railway propelled the urban traveller to an ambivalent form of modernity, one that

Figure 2.1   Hywel Williams, '23/24 Leinster Gardens' and 'The Scene Taken from Craven Hill Gardens'. Photographs. 22 January 2005. www.underground-history.co.uk

embraced convergence yet fragmentation, compression yet expansion, in a psycho-spatial and temporal re-evaluation of the metropolis.

In the first chapter, the sewers haunted the Victorian imaginary, most notably through its evocation of the poor, prostitutes and foreigners. Although the construction of the underground railway also stratifies the urban populace, it paradoxically unifies the city by creating a communal journey that is accessible to all travellers. Wolfgang Schivelbusch's seminal work *The Railway Journey* (1977) reveals how the railway destroyed the space between places, thereby radically destabilising the notion of distance. This new proximity, combined with the movement of people in and out of the city centre, created a Lefebvrian dialectic of clandestine encounters in the carriages below and underground identities in the neighbourhoods and suburbs above. As 'speed' became the dominant vision of the Underground in the latter part of the century, this chapter suggests that new temporalities created by underground travel contributed to the new aesthetic of Modernism and Futurism. In its final metamorphosis, the impact of such spatial and temporal disruptions produced a new psychology of the underground that mapped a territory of violence while privileging the subjective experience of travelling in a crowd. The struggle to maintain one's identity in the reification of the commuting experience then becomes the final battleground in the modernist space of anonymity and fragmentation.

Despite the tremendous impact of the underground railway on London's urban formation and expansion, there has been some speculation as to why this space escaped central treatment in mid-nineteenth-century novels and other literary representations. Although its progress is recorded meticulously and satirised in equal parts in the popular press, the underground railway is everywhere yet nowhere in literary endeavours, appearing as both fragments of fleeting encounters or as an invisible backdrop of social interconnections. Jack Simmons in *The Victorian Railway* (1991) argues that the railways were not subjects of literature in England, as they 'seem to make life more superficial', while France's more imaginative response to the power of the locomotive was 'a matter of temperament'.[2] Although David Pike has surveyed the treatment of the London Underground in Victorian theatre, from melodramas to pantomime, they are often a reflection and a critique of the railway disasters that accompanied its material history, rather than a more conceptual and psychological framework espoused in such works as Émile Zola's *La Bête Humaine* (1889) or Claude Monet's *Gare St Lazare* series (1877).[3] However, I argue that London's subtle treatment of the underground railway is equally powerful in the way its absence reveals the ambivalence felt towards the new technology and the subsequent fragmentation of the urban psyche. The invisibility of the Underground does not denote a *disappearance*, but a *prevalence* of ghostly traces that haunt the city in some of the crucial discourses of modernity. The underground railway's pervasiveness as a backdrop and a persistent shadow underscores its significance in the (sub)consciousness of the city and gestures at the structuring 'absence' it plays in aesthetic representations.

Derrida argues against the 'metaphysics of presence' and cites that one of the goals of deconstruction is 'to render enigmatic what one thinks one understands by the word "presence" and to see how "absence" is made strange'.[4] His irruption of binaries is useful here in conceptualising the underground railway as a 'ghostly presence' in nineteenth-century novels that challenges the way the city was imagined. For example, the character of various London neighbourhoods and the expansion of the middle classes to the suburbs cannot be read without the spectre of the Underground that haunts these transformations. Walter Benjamin has commented on the absence of physical crowds in Baudelaire's work that 'the crowd, of whose existence Baudelaire is always aware, has not served as the model for any of his works, but it is imprinted on his creativity as a hidden figure'.[5] In a similar vein, the underground railway does not become a tangible subject of conjecture until its deeper significance emerges latently on the surface of London's urban consciousness after the electrification of trains in 1890s. As the underground railway becomes an indispensable mode of travel, the transport system begins to receive more direct treatment, especially in art and literature, as a way of representing a new reality of psychological fragmentation. Furthermore,

the Underground's embodiment of speed becomes the basis for modernist aesthetics, while its function transforms into a lived space as bomb
shelters during both world wars. Throughout these social, technological
and political changes, the underground continues to maintain a form of
resistance to aboveground practices as it transitions from a private site
of hidden impulses and psychological repression to a more public and
publicly controlled space of anomie and alienation.

Spatial Annihilation, Production and Representation

. . . on one hand, the railroad opened up new spaces that were not as easily
accessible before; on the other, it did so by destroying space, namely the space
between the two points.
　　　　　　　Wolfgang Schivelbusch, *The Railway Journey* (1977)

In the development of the underground railway, the production and
destruction of space engaged in the spatial dialectic of the city, creating
new flows of movement of urban travellers. The history of the underground railway and the sewers suggests a similar rationale for their
immediate and necessary construction. Just as the drainage system was
being built to subdue cholera in the 1850s and 1860s, the underground
railway was constructed to counter another debilitating disease: the
overcrowding and congestion that inhibited the flow of movement on
the city streets. As historian Hugh Douglas remarks:

. . . towards the middle of the [nineteenth] century, London was dying –
slowly, painfully and with a great deal of protest. No physician had to be
called in to diagnose the trouble; it was all too apparent to those who lived
there, for, wherever they went, they encountered the great thrombosis of
traffic which clogged the highway, that were the veins and arteries carrying
the city's blood.[6]

In another incorporation of the corporeal metaphor, urban pathways
had to be cleared of the pathogenic crisis of stagnation in order for the
body of the city to run more efficiently. Gustave Doré's engraving of
Ludgate Hill depicting an overcrowded street, bustling with carriages,
horses and pedestrians against the backdrop of St Paul's Cathedral is
a testament to the claustrophobia and density encountered on a daily
basis, as the city population doubled in forty years and a quarter of a
million people commuted to London each day to work. Once again, the
only prescription for this arterial blockage was improved 'circulation',
as the solicitor to the City of London, Charles Pearson, advanced the
idea of 'trains in drains' in an effort to reduce the amount of traffic on

the city streets. Inspired by the initial engineering success of Brunel's Thames Tunnel in 1843, Pearson envisaged an underground network that would attract and connect all social classes in a fluid movement across the city's subterranean tunnels. Although many proposals were considered, from Joseph Paxton's 'arcade railway' to elevated pneumatic tubes, it was Pearson's vision of an underground system of steam-engine trains linking to all main-line railway termini in London that ultimately became a reality. Although Pearson died just six months before the opening celebrations of the first Metropolitan Line from Paddington to Farringdon on 9 January 1863, he was compared mythically to 'Cloacina the purifier', whose nobler aims were articulated in Henry Mayhew's *Shops and Companies of London* (1865):

> to gird London round with an iron belt of rails – the metal ring that is to wed the wealthy and fashionable West to the poor and squalid East, and to unite the healthy North to the pestiferous South.[7]

Implicit in this railway metaphor was the unifying prospect of underground transport, one that encircled the city, bridging classes and neighbourhoods, while democratising travel for all strata of society. This blueprint then became a site of competing visions, from nightmarish descents in Charles Dickens to the utopian and dystopian possibilities in H. G. Wells. As the circular and circulating metaphor appeared pervasively in the representation of the Underground, the ostensible 'centre' of the city shifted fluidly, in a reinscription and recircumscription of the city that followed the material development and extension of each Underground line. From delineating the Inner Circle in 1884, the iron girdle succeeded in unifying yet dispersing, centring yet decentring the social, cultural and psychic spaces and practices of the city.

However, the spatial significance of the underground railway cannot be fully comprehended without taking into consideration the representation of railways aboveground that initiated the transformation of the modern city. In J. M. W. Turner's painting *Rain, Steam and Speed – The Great Western Railway* (1844), a train speeding through the countryside blurs the distinction between foreground and background, sublimating the pastoral to the steam of industrial progress. As the underground railway became, in many ways, an extension and intensification of surface railway representation, it embraced a similar aesthetic and social conceptualisation as an all-consuming force that tore up streets and homes in a complete reconfiguration of the metropolis. The fragmentation and psychic ruptures to the city are critically observed by Charles Dickens in a familiar passage on the demolition of Staggs's Gardens in *Dombey and Son* (1848):

The first shock of a great earthquake, had just at that period, rent the whole neighbourhood to its centre. Traces of its course were visible on every side. Houses were knocked down; streets broken through and stopped; deep pits and trenches dug in the ground . . . There were a hundred thousand shapes and substances of incompleteness, wildly mingled out of their places, upside down, burrowing in the earth, mouldering in the water, and unintelligible as any dream.[8]

The nightmarish quality of this underground space is lent a further apocalyptic atmosphere in Dickens's reference to the train as 'monster Death' that subsequently kills Carker under the wheels of its inexorable progress. H. J. Dyos remarks that the railways left the city an incoherent mass of shapes, while 'entire neighbourhoods were relocated to already overcrowded adjoining areas which created filthy, dangerous slums'.[9] *The Illustrated London News, The Builder* and *The Illustrated Times* detailed the spate of demolitions occurring all over London during the early phases of the Underground construction, which depicted sublime landscapes of chaos and disorder. The contrast of Victorian buildings and monuments alongside the mangled confusion of excavations and demolished homes lent an aura similar to the recently unearthed ruins of Pompeii in the intertwining of the surreal present and an ancient past, or what Lynda Nead terms 'the archaeology of modernity'.[10] Thus, spatial and temporal interpenetration was a significant aspect of apprehending the Underground in both literary and visual representation.

In the mess of urban excavations, however, there was some intelligibility in the recircumscription of the city's social map. The demographic shifts were astutely predicted in an 1861 pamphlet by Reverend William Denton who observed:

the special lure to the capitalist is that the line will pass only through inferior property, that is through a densely peopled district, and will destroy the abode of the powerless and the poor, whilst it will avoid the properties of those whose opposition is to be dreaded – the great employers of labour.[11]

Indeed, it is little coincidence that the first Metropolitan and District Lines formed an Inner Circle that avoided financial, government and wealthy districts in the centre of town. In the spatial girdling of the city, the underground railway took on a similar role as the sewer in pushing the slums outward and embanking the heart of the city. However, despite its efforts to encircle, enclose and encapsulate, the construction of the first Inner Circle had more metaphorical associations with Dantean circles of the mythological inferno in the images of heat, steam and asphyxiation. One of the earlier apocalyptic images of the Underground appeared in 1862, when the sewer passages of the River Fleet flooded the railway tunnels of Clerkenwell in a devastating accident that seized the Victorian imagination. According to *The Illustrated London News*, 'the black hole of the Fleet Sewer, like a broken artery, pour[ed] out a thick rapid stream which found its way out fiercely . . . into the railway cutting', while the 'fallen roadway with the bent lamp-post and pavement, looks as if it had been sucked down by a whirlpool' (Fig. 2.2).[12] The vivid and dramatic depiction of the devastation underneath the city and its subsequent impact on the surface suggested the tension between the power of nature and technology as well as the oscillation between progress and destruction. An article in *The Times* recapitulates this sense of the sublime and the unknown in its denouncement of Pearson's plans:

> A subterranean railway under London was awfully suggestive of dark, noisome tunnels, buried many fathoms deep beyond the reach of light or life; passages inhabited by rats, soaked with sewer drippings, and poisoned by the escape of gas mains. It seemed an insult to common sense to suppose that people who could travel as cheaply to the city on the outside of a Paddington bus would ever prefer, as a merely quicker medium, to be driven amid palpable darkness through the foul subsoil of London.[13]

The infernal overtones of the Underground, with its proximity to noxious emanations and darkness, strengthened the association of underground travel with a descent into hell. When the Metropolitan Line was completed, the first trains, with steam engines and poor ventilation in the compartments, continued to plague the subterranean space with deathly associations. There were many reported cases of gas inhalation, and in 1867, three people died in separate incidents due to 'choke damp', leading to the mandatory use of ventilation shafts. In 1887, an American journalist, R. D. Blumenfeld, recorded in his diary:

> I had my first experience of Hades to-day, and if the real thing is to be like that I shall never again do anything wrong . . . The atmosphere was a mixture of sulphur, coal dust and foul fumes from the oil lamp above, so that by the time we reached Moorgate Street I was near dead of asphyxiation and heat.[14]

Yet despite the persistence of this infernal mythical overtone, nearly ten million travellers in the first year of the railway chose the 'quicker medium', as speed became the ultimate driver of underground and aboveground expansion and movement in the city. However, the fears and anxieties of travelling underground continued to plague the Victorian imagination in haunting ways.

The inevitability of technological modernity is portrayed as a more secularised form of hell in literary representations of the mid-to-late Victorian period. While sensational melodramas of train murders and

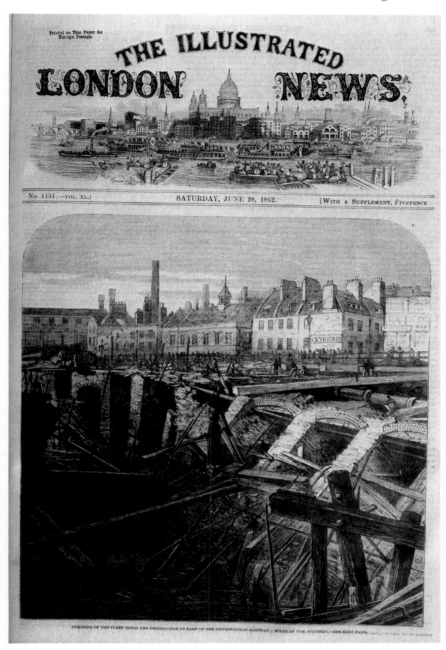

Figure 2.2 'The Bursting of the Fleet Sewer', *The Illustrated London News*, 28 June 1862. Courtesy of the University of Reading Library.

robberies entertained West End audiences, a subtler and a more disturbing social and cultural representation of the Underground haunts George Gissing's novels. In *The Nether World* (1889), the impact of the Metropolitan Line, especially the construction of Farringdon Station, is peripherally mentioned in the dug-up landscapes of Clerkenwell, but it functions as a Derridean absence in the relegation of the neighbourhood into the abyss of the slums. As a metaphorical underground space, the Inner Circle becomes the suffocating enclosure of the social depths represented largely on the surface of the city. The Underground experience here is also elided, but is echoed in a destructive journey on an aboveground railway into the countryside that begins in revelry but ends in a drunken fight and subsequent disintegration of relationships. The railway journey, like the Inner Circle, becomes a cyclical representation of unfulfilled promises and the inability of the lower classes to escape their fate despite their attempts to better themselves. Futility and resignation become critical themes in the representation of the railway, which Gissing later takes to the actual physical locus of the Underground as his characters are forced to participate in the urban movement dictated by new forms of transport.

In a centrifugal dispersion of the metropolis, the completion of the Inner Circle enlarges the centre of the city to the western suburbs such as Kensington, Bayswater and Westbourne while connecting the centre to the residential north-western suburbs of West Hampstead and St John's Wood. As the Underground becomes the dominant mode of travel amongst the middle classes, especially in the transition from steam to electrical traction in the powering of the locomotives in the 1890s, Gissing turns his attention to the lower-middle classes who face another type of urban hell, living and commuting from the periphery of the city. In *The Whirlpool* (1894), many families choose to relocate to suburbs, but in the new metropolis, there is only one choice for those who wish to negotiate a family and a job in the city. As the main character, Harvey Rolfe, observes with some scepticism, 'I feel as if we were all being swept into a ghastly whirlpool which roars over a bottomless pit.'[15] The Underground is only mentioned episodically, in fleeting transfers at Baker Street, for example, but its spectre haunts all of the characters' movements, rendering them powerless in the living and commuting arrangements created by the new social map. As the urban population continued to extend outward, London's day population increased significantly, from 170,000 people in 1866 to 360,000 at the beginning of the twentieth century.[16] A precursor to the development of suburban Metroland in 1915 and to the more contemporary 'doughnut effect' that empties out the urban core after working hours, the city centre became uninhabited or uninhabitable for the lower-middle classes, while new neighbourhoods at the outer edges become undifferentiated areas of itinerant commuters. As Gissing writes, 'Thousands of men, who sleep on the circumference of London, and go each day to business, are practically strangers to the district nominally their home.'[17] Unable to resist the flow of this rapid transformation, Gissing's characters become trapped in the perpetual vortex of urban development and expansion as the city's core expands concentrically into impersonal zones of faceless residential districts.

The underground railway also sweeps up urban dwellers in *In the Year of Jubilee* (1894), albeit in the power of consumerism and advertising. In this conceptual representation of the Underground as a commercial, capitalist space, Gissing compares the circulation of products and advertisements in the carriages with the superficial paraphernalia surrounding Queen Victoria's fiftieth jubilee:

> High and low, on every available yard of wall, advertisements clamoured to the eye; theatres, journals, soaps, medicines, concerts, furniture, wines, prayer – meetings – all the produce and refuse of civilization announced in staring letters, in daubed effigies, base, paltry, grotesque. A battleground of advertisements, fitly chosen amid subterranean din and reek.[18]

Although Gissing resents the vulgarity of the new corporatism exhibited underground, the commercial machine is unstoppable, as exemplified in the production of 'Jubilee Perfume', a 'Jubilee Drink' and the 'Jubilee Fashion Club'. William Morris sharply criticised the Underground corporate barons for the monopoly they had on urban transport, and in his utopian novel, *News from Nowhere* (1890), he portended the death of capitalism as he envisaged 'the whole society gradually falling into lower depths, till it at last reached a condition of barbarism'.[19] In a descent towards this vision, hoardings and advertisements multiplied on subway platforms and in the carriages, while bookstalls by James Willing and W. H. Smith began to proliferate, offering short, condensed novels for quick Underground consumption. In the ubiquity and claustrophobia of advertising culture, the Underground reflected a compressed version of the commercial streets above, which Gissing nightmarishly portrayed as his final circle of hell.

The underground railway, with its connections to surface railways, also haunted the outskirts of the city with its corrosive and corruptive presence, suggestive of Lefebvre's concept of 'representational space' in the transformation of the outer edges of the city. In *The Production of Space* (1974), Lefebvre argues for a redefinition of space, not as a fixed, geometric place, but of a socially produced phenomenon where spaces 'interpenetrate one another and/or superimpose themselves upon one another'.[20] This is helpful in conceptualising the Underground, as it constantly reshapes the meaning of the neighbourhoods above in a dialectical relationship. Thus, the outskirts begin to reflect underground tendencies, while the suburban becomes an extension and a reworking of the subterranean metaphor. In the scathing social satire *The Suburbans* (1905), the narrator degrades the landscape and comments that the 'suburban' is a 'sort of label which may be properly applied to pretty well everything on the earth that is ill-conditioned, undesirable, and unholy'.[21] Meanwhile, in E. M. Forster's *Howards End* (1910), 'the creeping red rust' of the suburbs intrudes on the countryside retreat, infecting all the characters in what Andrew Thacker argues is a 'novelistic meditation upon the spaces of national identity' in a tenuous interpenetration of social hierarchies that ultimately questions what it means to be English before the onset of World War I.[22] Anxieties of identity and transgression of social boundaries appear more humorously in Oscar Wilde's *The Importance of Being Earnest* (1899), where a double life in the city and country is made possible by the railway. The secret lives of the characters are exemplified in one protagonist's penchant for 'bunburying', a playful word with multiple underground connotations.[23] In the constant interchange of names and relationships, a resolution is only achieved when the identity of a railway orphan left in a handbag at Victoria Station is brought to light. Under the surface of pastoral calm, the outer regions, like the city centre, become a duplicitous space, where illicit transactions and social transgressions re-emerge through the connective social fibre of the Underground network.

Recuperating Meaning in the Underground

> I have known a man, dying a long way from London, sigh queerly for a sight of the gush of smoke that, on a platform of the Underground, one may see, escaping in great woolly clots up a circular opening, by a grimy, rusty iron shield, into the dim upper light. He wanted to see it again as others have wished to see once more the Bay of Naples, the olive groves of Catania.
> Ford Madox Ford, *The Soul of London* (1907)

Although the underground space and the streets above experienced an assault that overturned the physical, social and cultural landscape of the city, the completed technological product also offered Victorians more freedom of movement, especially for the working class and women in a new social reconfiguration of urban space. Visually, there were also contradictions that accompanied the construction and completion

Figure 2.3 *King's Cross Station, Metropolitan Line* (1863). Lithograph. London Transport Museum.

of the underground railway. Although earlier images portrayed the Underground as a terrifying, sublime landscape, later depictions relied on the popular use of cross-section diagrams that buttressed the notion of a rationalised subterranean space that mirrored the sanitised streets above.[24] A lithograph of King's Cross Station in 1868 epitomises the conquest over the unknown as modern materials of glass and steel created a safe haven for middle-class passage, contesting prior images of demolition and disaster (Fig. 2.3). The admission of natural light, and later gas and then electric light, was crucial in the representation of the Underground as a visible and visually comprehensible space. In this utopian vision, the underground railway offered the potential to eradicate some of the injustices above by allowing for the circulation and movement of all people across a wide geographic and social divide.

First and foremost, the Underground attempted to be a social leveller by catering to all classes of travel, bridging the stratifications created by its own inception. When Charles Pearson envisaged the railway service, he had hoped for a standard low fare for the working classes but died before this goal was achieved. At the opening of the Underground, the fares ranged from 6d. to 3d. one way, and from 9d. to 5d. for the return, depending on the class of travel. However, as so many poor districts were demolished in service of the railway, the return rate for workers was lowered to 3d., paving the way for the 1883 Cheap Trains Act obliging all railway companies to price fares specifically for workers.[25] In 1865, approximately 1,800 to 2,000 workmen were using the Underground every day, a steadily increasing number captured in Gustave Doré's and Blanchard Jerrold's 1872 etching of a bustling third-class platform in *London: A Pilgrimage*. Commenting on the ease of commute, one worker remarked, 'If a man gets home tired after his day's labour he is inclined to be quarrelsome with his missus and children . . . while if he gets a ride home . . . he is as pleasant a fellow again over his supper.'[26] The same technological force that tore up working-class neighbourhoods and cut up the city into areas of the rich and the poor also paradoxically offered better lifestyle choices for the displaced workers. In this democratisation and liberation of the underground space, the working classes were able to roam more freely in the city, take advantage of cheaper housing outside the urban centre, and participate more fully in the pleasures that the city had to offer.

In allowing for more freedom of movement in the city, the Underground also challenged the notion of social distance in the city, as carriages and platforms became a heterogeneous space of class interactions. As the private Underground enterprise also aimed to attract middle-class passengers, the commingling of classes was inevitable despite first-, second- and third-class carriages and separate waiting areas. The intrusion of the working class in first-class carriages, despite the surveillance of ticketing officers, became a recurring theme on the Underground. Mikhail Bakhtin's critique of carnival culture is useful here as the space of carriages also provided what Bakhtin described in his study as a 'temporary suspension of all hierarchic distinctions and barriers among men . . . and of the prohibitions of usual life'.[27] As one *Punch* cartoon in 1886 reveals, the first-class carriage was often 'invaded' by the working class, making for an 'unpleasantly lively' train ride, in a *carnivalesque* reconfiguration of social and spatial boundaries.[28] It is precisely this 'topsy-turvy' mêlée and the mixing of high and low culture that overturned the more rigid social topographies of surface practices. Eventually, class distinctions were removed, thereby democratising travel for all commuters, as the Central Line took the lead in introducing the one-fare system, otherwise known as the 'tuppenny tube'. The initial reaction to this historical event is captured in Eric Banton's impressions of the city in 'Underground Travelling London' in George Sims's four-volume compendium *Living London* (1901): 'The office boy, finding that these trains have no third-class carriages, has sat down in great content beside the City magnate, and still the heavens do not fall!'[29] This egalitarian vision of the city is echoed in the work of Marxist theorist Constantin Pecqueur who also believed in the humanising force of the communal journey:

> By causing all classes of society to travel together and thus juxtaposing them in a kind of living mosaic of all the fortunes, positions, characters, manners, customs, and modes of dress that each and every nation has to offer, the railroads quite prodigiously advance the reign of truly fraternal social relations and do more for the sentiments of equality than the most exalted sermons of the tribunes of democracy. To thus foreshorten for everyone the distances that separate localities from each other, is to equally diminish the distances that separate men from one another.[30]

Thus, physical and social distances were bridged in the collapsing of hierarchical boundaries in the Underground journey. In the shifting mosaic of the subterranean city, the intermingling of different people from all walks of life opened up the space to new experiences and encounters heretofore unimagined in the city. As a democratising force, the underground railway paved the way for more recuperative visions of the subterranean space and a conduit for more metaphorical journeys in literary representation.

The potential for underground transport to challenge and reconfigure hierarchies extended beyond class conventions. As an article in *The Quarterly Review* observed, the railways also brought about 'the emancipation of the fair sex, and particularly of the middle and higher classes, from the prohibition from travelling in public carriages, which with the majority was a prohibition from travelling at all'.[31] In recent scholarship, works by Judith Walkowitz and Deborah Epstein Nord have complicated the role of women in public spaces, questioning the notion that 'to be a woman on the street . . . was to be exposed to the illicit gaze of men'.[32] Furthermore, in *Shopping for Pleasure* (2000), Erika Rappaport highlights the significance of public transport in the 1880s in offering women the freedom of movement without being accosted in a city, where unattended females were previously associated with unwanted sexual invitation. Although magazines often pointed to the dangers and discomforts of railway travel for ladies, they also

> spent quite a bit of effort convincing women that they should ride London's trains, omnibuses and Underground . . . persuading readers that riding such conveyances was safe and respectable, that it was comfortable and easy, and that it would be a pleasurable and even poetic experience.[33]

It is this very 'poetic experience' that Ana Vadillo explores in her study, *Women Poets and Urban Aestheticism* (2005). Vadillo rightly questions the 'epistemology of the *flâneur*' as 'fewer people went out walking' and argues that there was a variety of women who travelled on public transport other than those 'invariably link[ed] to shopping'.[34] Although the role of the *flâneur* was inevitably transformed with the advent of public transport, the commuter was, in many ways, an extension of the lone walker in the modern metropolis. Public transport allowed women to see and to be seen in public spaces such as parks, shops, and the theatre on the surface of the city, and in the Underground, the female commuter/ *flâneuse* tried to remain more invisible, as her anonymity allowed her to step outside of middle-class propriety. The Underground stations and conduits provided an alternative city where the female commuter was able to explore other aspects of her selfhood outside of the world of commodities above. Thus, her 'non-presence' afforded her freedom of exploration in more psychological conjectures and mental flânerie, submerged in the roar of the speeding Underground train.

The presence of women in the Underground appears subtly and episodically throughout late nineteenth-century novels, but its significance is underscored by the intensity of their encounters and the subversive nature of their wanderings. The Underground carriage in particular appears pervasively as a site of contestation that resembles Foucault's 'heterotopia' in the way it 'invert[s] the set of relations that they happen to designate, mirror, or reflect'.[35] For example, the carriage is represented simultaneously as a public and a private space, allowing for random encounters that are often intensely personal in nature, while offering women both the freedom of movement and the potential dangers of such opportunities. Gissing's female characters often travel independently, from Alma Rolfe in *The Whirlpool*, who decides to spend the night in the city alone after missing the last train to the suburbs, to Monica in *The Odd Women* (1893), who experiences an intimate moment with Everard Barfoot in a first-class carriage: 'I don't know why he took me into this confidence. It happened first of all when we were going by train – the same train, by chance.'[36] Even Monica's more conservative sister Virginia turns to the Underground to satisfy her secret habit at a refreshment room: 'In front of Charing Cross Station she stopped, looked vaguely about her . . . [and] said to the barmaid in a voice just above a whisper, – "Kindly give me a little brandy".'[37] The pursuit of personal pleasures finds more destructive implications in Henry James's *The Wings of the Dove* (1902), when sexual undercurrents in a carriage between Kate Croy and Edward Densher propel them on a *derailed* pathway of buried passions and hidden ambitions. Furthermore, in Anthony Trollope's *The Way We Live Now* (1875), another illicit affair is discovered through an initiation to the Underground: 'That afternoon Hetta trusted herself all alone to the mysteries of the Marylebone underground railway, and emerged with accuracy at King's Cross . . . '[38] Robert Altick notes that many of Trollope's novels, from *The Claverings* (1867) to *The Eustace Diamonds* (1873), suggest the ways in which the railways became an acceptable form of middle-class transport as it became the preferred mode of travel in the expanding capital.[39] However, the sanitisation of the underground space to conform to Victorian ideals of middle-class propriety had the contradictory effect of producing more in-between spaces of moral transgressions. In opening the carriages to middle-class women, the Underground also became a hidden network of social interactions, offering women independence from the domestic sphere, but not without a frisson of unwanted attention and unavoidable temptations of the city. Although the Underground is never a central feature of any of these works, passing glimpses into a carriage or a descent into a Tube station suggest a hidden side of women's lives and the *détournements* that a subterranean journey can take.

Thus far, the recuperative aspects of the underground railway have been tinged with an undercurrent of danger, both physical and moral. The contradictions continued in turn-of-the-century representations of the Underground, even as electrification and lighting made the journey safer and the extension of the Underground to the outskirts of the city promised more fresh air and verdant pastures. As Schivelbusch argues, railways led to an 'annihilation of space and time' as greater distances were bridged more quickly, creating a 'new reduced geography'.[40] In the convergence of technological innovations such as electricity, telegraphy and telephony in the late nineteenth century, the new compact geography reflected greater and faster communication and mobility, to and from the suburbs, reconfiguring London's urban and social boundaries. While early nineteenth-century images of underground often depicted the tension between nature and technology, later utopian visions subverted this notion by recreating a dreamscape of an accessible countryside in the form of the garden suburbs in the 1880s and the introduction of 'Metro-land' in 1915. No longer was technology in conflict with nature; rather, the power of the locomotive could be harnessed for a reconnection with the pastoral in a symbiotic co-existence between the city and the countryside. Underground posters for this campaign played a key role in the surge of property developments in the suburbs in such areas as Golders Green, Sudbury Hill and Chiswick. The new links, especially to the north-west of the city,

> opened up new and delightful countryside to the advantage of picturesque seekers; ancient houses and old world ways. Within 50 minutes from Baker Street and for the cost of less than a florin [two shillings], if the visitor can be

economically disposed, he can enjoy a feast of good things, fresh air, noble parks, stately houses, magnificent trees, and sylvan streams.[41]

Despite the idyllic visual and commercial displays of the suburbs, these unspoiled outer areas of the city did not remain untouched by the darker side of the underworld in the literary imagination. With the underground railway as a backdrop, many authors chose the socio-spatial connection to the city to articulate a form of transgression that can only occur outside the social centre of Victorian propriety. In response to the new advertising campaign, art critic Roger Fry expressed his cynicism about the ability of the underground railway to deliver on its promises:

> [The Underground] build[s] up in the public imagination an image of something almost personal – as such they begin to claim almost the loyalty and allegiance of the public they exploit. They produce in the public a non critical state of romantic enthusiasm for the line. More and more the whole thing takes on an air of romance and unreality.[42]

Despite the simulacrum of the suburban experience and the glaring capitalistic exploitations on the part of railway developers, the Underground still maintained a crucial role in re-imagining the city, while situating itself as a proponent of, and a precursor to, the advent of modernist sensibilities.

In a reinvention of the metropolis, the underground railway not only expanded the core horizontally, but also stretched the city vertically in an obliteration of surface and subterranean distinctions. The Underground literally became the extension of the surface world, as technology allowed for more permeable movement between the layers and the city's surface. Although Wells paints a bleak picture of what the Underground portends in *The Time Machine* (1895), he gestures towards a technological future in his vision of a multi-tiered city connected by high-speed Tube trains in *The Sleeper Awakes* (1899). In this 'quasi subterranean labyrinth', the protagonist, Graham, observes the 'strange traffic of narrow, rubber-shod vehicles, great single wheels, two and four wheeled vehicles sweeping along at velocities from one to six miles a minute'.[43] The highly mechanised environment reveals the elimination of the line demarcating surface and depth, as speed of movement bridges this vertical topography in a new vision of urban transport. Although Wells remained critical of the institutional powers that capitalised on people's dependence on the state, he still saw the Underground and technology as a positive harbinger of social change and human progress. Challenging conventional notions of space, the Futurists later embraced this new vertical topography that reiterated

Wells's vision of a network of traffic that allowed for a fluid movement above and below the surface of the city:

> ... the futurist house must be like an enormous machine. The lifts must not hide like lonely worms in the stairwells; the stairs, become useless, must be done away with and the lifts must climb like serpents of iron and glass up the house fronts ... the street, which will no longer stretch like a footpath level with porters' lodges but will descend into the earth on several levels, will receive the metropolitan traffic and will be linked, for the necessary passage from one to the other, by metal walkways and immensely fast escalators.[44]

The new Underground was no longer underground. In its new verticality, the railway tracks merged with the pathways connecting streets and buildings in a sleek new interpretation of the cityscape that became the basis for modernist reinterpretations, captured in such futuristic films as Fritz Lang's *Metropolis* (1927) and William Menzies's adaptation of H. G. Wells's novel *Things to Come* (1936).

In its final trajectory to modernism, the underground railway underwent a dramatic reinvention when Harry Beck produced his iconic Underground Tube map in 1931, refashioning the streets above and propelling the traveller to a new perception of underground space. Tracing the transformations of the Underground map throughout history reveals how the patterns of train lines were originally subordinate to the streets above, following the paths and curves of an unruly city landscape (Fig. 2.4). However, it was the colour-coded, abstract space of Harry Beck's map that created a completely alternative subterranean space with straight lines and forty-five-degree angles, defying surface pathways and even straightening the Thames (Fig. 2.5). Resembling an electric circuit board, the new cartography had little to do with geographic verisimilitude and more to do with a new minimalist visual aesthetic. As David Pike argues:

> By simplifying the complex network of urban railway lines into a visually pleasing and easily legible map bearing little or no relation to either the experiential or the physical metropolis of London, Beck codified a particular modernist conception of space.[45]

In the new subterranean network, Beck's Underground map compressed and expanded the distance between points, distorting the urban traveller's spatial sense of the surface of the city. In its ability to recreate and recuperate meaning in the abstract, inorganic space of the Underground, Beck's map can ultimately be interpreted as an ironic artistic representation that continues to guide, as much as it misguides, the viewer's conceptualisation of the metropolis.

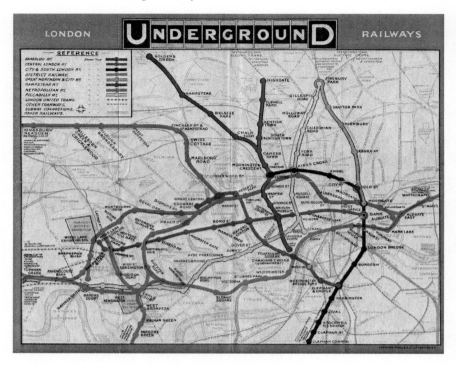

Figure 2.4   Pocket Underground Map (1908). London Transport Museum.

One of the persistent anxieties in the construction of the underground railway was the promise of a new technology that would profoundly change the way one inhabited the city and what forms these changes would take. Although earlier representations relied on a more destructive path towards progress, later images embraced modernity and modernism, casting a more redemptive light in the potential of the Underground to reimagine new possibilities for the future. By connecting the grandeur and aesthetic visions of the past and present, Michael Saler suggests that the Underground ushered in a form of 'medieval modernism' in which the transport system stood as a medieval cathedral of congregation and dispersal, an architectural feat that combined functionalism and formalism in creating a new form of social cohesion in the city.[46] From Pearson's initial vision of the system as a social democratiser to the modernist appeal of the Underground as a liberator of the imagination, the subterranean networks continued to be defined and redefined by the passengers in a socio-spatial dialectic that constantly questioned surface hierarchies and ideologies. As a contained place, a travelled space and a space that redefined the notion of 'space', the Underground embraced

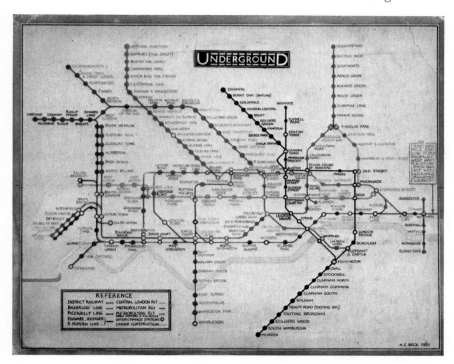

Figure 2.5   Harry Beck, first presentation drawing of the London Underground
Map (1933). London Transport Museum.

the perspectives of a modernist heterotopia that constantly played with
the contradictions within the city, resisting any totalising attempts to
be represented in any fixed terms. In the shadow of literary encounters
or as an invisible presence aligning characters' urban wanderings, the
Underground in its elusiveness maintained its ghostlike presence that
allowed for a fluidity of movement and identity in the city.

Temporal Dislocations

> What, then, is time? . . . If no one asks me, I know what it is. If I wish to
> explain it to him who asks me, I do not know.
>
> Saint Augustine, *Confessions* (397 AD)

> . . . all travelling becomes dull in exact proportion to its rapidity.
>
> John Ruskin, *Precious Thoughts: Moral and Religious* (1866)

Travels underground not only dramatically changed spatial relationships in the city, but they also transformed people's perception of

time, history and memory. From the intertwining of intimate lifelines to sudden irruptions of violent memories, the Underground contributed to a disorientating apprehension of time that recalibrated urban rhythms, while creating new artistic and literary representations of intertemporality. Although Schivelbusch argues that the railway 'annihilated' the sense of time, it also created a more diverse conceptualisation of time, and indeed, exploded the notion of time, as linearity was eschewed for a more polyvalent temporality in gauging the new rhythms of urban movement. In his critical study of time and space, Stephen Kern argues that in the nineteenth century, there was, on one hand, the idea of fixed time that established the Greenwich Meridian as Railway Time in the 1840s and the International Standard Time in 1884, dividing the world into twenty-four discrete time zones exactly one hour apart. On the other hand, technological changes in transport and communications shattered the concept of a single 'historical time' as movement and information flowed continuously at all hours, resulting in what Kern describes as the age of 'simultaneity'. Time was no longer absolute, universal and continuous; rather, new technologies raised questions about whether time was 'homogeneous or heterogeneous, atomistic or a flux, reversible or irreversible'.[47] In this fragmented landscape, the Underground also embraced a new sense of contingency, especially as the electrification of train lines in the 1890s expedited the journey to new metaphoric representations of the Underground that combined the past, present and future in an interpenetration of temporalities. In marking time yet disrupting it, the Underground ruptured time, which disorientated the traveller to a new aesthetic awareness of the urban environment.

Once again, the French apprehension of the railways and the Métro revealed more of an affinity towards the fragmentation of the present and the disassociation from the past. In particular, the fugacity of life inspired the Impressionists, who attempted to represent the passage of time and the perception of movement in many of their works. In particular, Claude Monet's series on Gare St Lazare in the 1870s attests to the fascination with motion, as the train arriving at the station is consumed in a billowing cloud of smoke, both revealing and occluding the power of the machine. Describing his method of capturing movement across time, Monet explains, 'One does not paint a landscape, a seascape, a figure. One paints an impression of an hour of the day.'[48] In this suspension of time, there is an obscuring of the present and a disruption of linear progression, where motion is captured in the broad brushstrokes of time passing yet standing still. Expressing his admiration for Monet's distinctive style, Émile Zola comments:

One can hear the roaring of the trains which are swallowed up in the overflowing smoke, rolling under vast hangars . . . Our artists ought to find poetry
in the stations as their fathers found it in the forests and fields.[49]

Zola also found poetry in trains and stations in his railway novel *La Bête
Humaine* (1890), while Maxime Du Camp celebrated technology as an
inevitable part of modernity: 'You, modern poet, you detest the modern
life. You go against your gods, you do not accept frankly your age. Why
do you find a gare ugly? It is very beautiful, a *gare*.'[50] Embracing the
temporal and the contingent, writers and artists articulated a new aesthetics of railway stations that extended itself to Underground stations,
evidenced by the Art Nouveau architecture of Métro entrances designed
by Hector Guimard in 1900, which combined the Gothic sensibility of
an entrance into the underworld with modern and distinct lettering and
ornamentation. Like Walter Benjamin's intermediary 'threshold spaces',
the urban train station became a critical point of contact between the
world above and below, the past and present, where meaning was continuously being articulated and negotiated.[51] Evoking Benjamin's glass-
covered arcades, the station remained an in-between space, a precipice
that joined different realities, temporalities and verticalities across the
urban landscape.

Against the backdrop of Paris, London's aesthetic response to the
new temporal rhythms of the city was more ambivalent, especially in the
earlier days of steam, when a descent into the underground resembled
that of a descent into hell. Although artists like James MacNeill Whistler
later attempted to blur temporal distinctions in such works as *Nocturnes*
(1871–7), which evoked neither dusk nor twilight, but a threshold or
a transition of time, literary representations in London often relied on
Dantean and destructive impressions of time speeding out of control in
their visions of underground travel.[52] The reification of the traveller or
the worker was a common theme in the adherence to new timetables
of the daily commute. Asserting the significance of collective time,
sociologist Émile Durkheim, in *The Elementary Forms of Religious Life*
(1915), argues that 'the foundation of the category of time is the rhythm
of social life . . . The divisions into days, weeks, months, years, etc.,
correspond to the periodical recurrence of rites, feasts, and public ceremonies.'[53] However, such natural rhythms were eschewed for a more
rigid temporality in the Underground, especially for the working class,
as the introduction of 'cheap trains' in 1865 enabled workers to travel
third class only at specific times. A daily train was provided between
4.55 a.m. and 6.00 a.m., while a return train departed at 6.15 p.m.,
creating a cyclical rhythm in which class, time and space interconnected

in a new flow of movement in the subterranean space. In synchronising the schedule of travellers, Foucault explains the historical significance of such temporal allocations as a powerful method of control:

> The *time-table* is an old inheritance. The strict model was no doubt suggested by the monastic communities. It soon spread. Its three great methods – establish rhythms, impose particular occupations, regulate the cycles of repetition – were soon to be found in schools, workshops, and hospitals . . . but in the nineteenth century, when the rural populations were needed in industry, they were sometimes formed into 'congregations' in an attempt to lure them to work in the workshops; the framework of the 'factory-monastery' was imposed upon the workers.[54]

The convergence of religion, prayer and work then instituted a new temporality that paved the way for a more industrialised pace in the capitalist rhythms of modernity. In his essay, Marxist historian E. P. Thompson elaborates that 'time discipline' was the result of the industrial revolution and that the modern capitalist state could not have existed without it, although it was a form of labour exploitation.[55] As time ultimately became equated with production and money in the nineteenth century, the Underground's ability to deliver the people, and thus the goods, 'on time' became a critical form of the mechanising progress in a new exterior or 'objective' time.

However, the underground railway also breaks up 'subjective' time, as the new pace of underground travels disorientates the commuter in a new perception of speed and place. Dickens laments the new pace of activity within the city in his article 'An Unsettled Neighbourhood' (1855), decrying the proliferation of senseless urban movement:

> Everybody wants to be off somewhere. Everybody does everything in a hurry. Everybody has the strangest ideas of his or her business to go 'down the line.' If any Fast-train could take it, I believe the whole neighbourhood of which I write: bricks, stones, timber, ironwork, and everything else: would set off down the line.[56]

This sense of expediency then gave rise to the form of restlessness so familiarly associated with urban travel: 'railroad fatigue'. In ascertaining the aetiology of this new phenomenon, *The Journal of Public Health and Sanitary Review* notes:

> The causes of evil are not to be found in the noise, vibration, and speed of the railway carriage . . . but in the excitement, anxiety, and the nervous shock consequent of the frequent efforts to catch the *last* express; to be in time for the fearfully punctual train.[57]

Thus, the stresses of travel that enslaved the individual to the exterior pace of a regimented schedule also contributed to the psychological restlessness in the urban traveller. In 1883, Edmondo de Amicis, a visitor to London, is sucked into the vortex of the Underground and reiterates the mayhem and confusion of his first descent:

> At one time, finding myself near a station, I thought I would make a trip in the Underground railway. I go down two or three stairs and find myself suddenly thrown from daylight into obscurity, amid feeble lights, people and noise, trains arriving and departing in the dark . . . The trains do not succeed, but pursue each other. The other train comes, I jump in and away we go like an arrow . . . I jump down; the train disappears, I am shoved through a door, half carried up a stairway, and find myself in daylight. But where? What city is this?[58]

In his underground journey, de Amicis experiences the spatial and temporal fragmentation that juxtaposes each successive moment next to each other in a montage of sensorial experiences. Although he is retrospectively describing his experience of the journey, he breaks into the present tense at the moment he crosses the threshold into the Underground, lending immediacy to the confusion of his underground wanderings. This sense of asynchrony in space and time, the past and the present, is articulated in Mikhail Bakhtin's description of the 'chronotope', where:

> . . . everything must be perceived as being within *a single time*, that is, in the synchrony of a single moment; one must see this entire world as simultaneous. Only under conditions of pure simultaneity can there be revealed the true meaning of 'that which was, and which is and which shall be' . . . To 'synchronize diachrony', to replace all temporal and historical divisions and linkages with purely interpretative, extratemporal and hierarchicized ones – such was Dante's form-generating impulse, which is defined by an image of the world structured according to a pure verticality.[59]

Again, simultaneity is what renders an experience incomprehensible yet reveals the new conditions of subjectivity that modernity poses on the Underground commuter. Like Dante's layers, temporal distinctions collapse in the vertical representation of the underworld where the past, present, and the future are indistinguishable and concurrent. To find meaning in such a disjointed journey forms the new basis of subterranean literary explorations, but like time itself, such images flicker in and out of images and subjective musings, adding more phenomenological layers to the complex experience of time speeding past.

Despite the fragmentation of time and space often associated with the Underground journey, there was a more fluid representation of temporality that sought to depict the tracks of the railway as the path of life in a metaphysical reappropriation of the Underground. Speed was no longer exterior or technological; rather, it expressed the fugacity of modern life. This intimate connection was most likely inspired by the number of fatalities that occurred on the railways as well as by the more obvious function of stations as a point of departure and arrival, but the metaphor of the railway journey as a passage through life was a popular embarkation point for many writers in the mid to late nineteenth century. The narrator in Dickens's 'Mugby Junction' (1866) encapsulates the fleeting nature of life in an Underground journey:

> . . . a shadowy train went by him the gloom of which was no other than the *train of life*. From whatsoever intangible deep cutting or dark tunnel it emerged, here it came, unsummoned and unannounced, stealing upon him, and passing away into obscurity.[60]

In the humanising metaphor of the railways, David Seed also observes in Dickens's fiction that the railway journey becomes a significant metaphor for psychological incursions, even in an off-handed remark by Mr Toodle in *Dombey and Son*: 'What a Junction a man's thoughts is . . . to be sure!'[61] Once again, the network of the Underground appears as a persistent shadow that connects people and ideas to the city, a palimpsest above which lives are written and erased. Ethnologist Marc Augé sheds light on this space of interconnectedness and reinvigorates the language of the Underground in his philosophical meditation, *In the Metro* (1986). In his dreamlike interpretation of the Underground journey, Augé attempts to counter the discourse of alienation in the subterranean passages by articulating a new poetics of the quotidian train ride and infusing it with more personal significance: 'It is obvious that every day in the metro there are individuals who are taking their first trip and others their last.'[62] Indeed, in literary representations of the Underground, tales of the novelty of a traveller's first descent are countered by narratives of death at the end of the journey, such as Anthony Trollope's Ferdinand Lopez in *The Prime Minister* (1876), who wanders around the Metropolitan Line to Euston Station, only to jump off the platform and be 'knocked into bloody atoms' at Tenway Junction.[63] Furthermore, Augé accurately perceives, 'Near hospitals one always finds a florist, an undertaker, and a subway station.'[64] Reflecting the path of life and death, the Inner Circle of the Underground also comes to symbolise the cyclicality of nature and the junctures of life, or what Augé terms *les correspondences*, the lines that intimately connect travellers and their itineraries in the symbolic subterranean space. In compressing, expanding, shattering and encircling time, the Underground plays with a multiplicity of temporal meanings that redefine the urban pace and space of life in the metropolis.

The shifting nature of time is also articulated in the Underground's disruption of the past, as history and memory intermingle with the present in a new interpenetration and overlapping of temporalities. In the earlier days of the steam engine, a sense of anxiety permeated the language of time spent underground, as overlapping schedules and competing time-tables created what Mark Turner describes as 'temporal *asymmetry*' and a crisis in the interpretations of time.[65] Thomas Trollope exemplifies this and eulogises the past in his memoir *What I Remember* (1887):

> But perhaps the underground railways have most of all revolutionised the London habits of the present day. Why, even to me, who knew cabless London, they seem to have become indispensable. I loathe them! . . . and yet the necessities of time and place in the huge overgrown monster of a town seem to compel me to pass a large portion of my hours among the sewers, when I find myself a dazed and puzzled stranger in the town I once knew so well.[66]

In the new technological environment, Trollope nostalgically looks back to reconstruct an image of a city he believes to have known, recalling Freud's observation in *Civilization and Its Discontents* that there is the 'amazing' tendency of men to idealise the past in which 'the inroads of agriculture, traffic, or industry threaten to change . . . the earth rapidly into something unrecognizable'.[67] Here, the intrusion of the underground railway into the city threatens to cut the connection with the past and disrupts the older rhythms of the city, replacing them with a faster pace that dislocates the self and destabilises subjectivity. Thus, the ability to recall and retrieve the past becomes of primary importance in the Victorian city, exemplified by the fascination to document history and to refer back to ancient and classical texts to comprehend its own meteoric rise to, and potential fall from, the height of civilisation.

In a final temporal reassertion, the underground railway does more to propel the urban dweller to the sense of the future, as technological improvements in the 1890s propel the subterranean networks to new utopian and dystopian reappropriations. Rather than nostalgia for the past that steam engines evoked, the new Underground system, with the introduction of electric traction, evoked a smoother, more effortless journey, placing speed at the forefront of modernity. *Punch* cartoons regularly regarded the transition from steam to electricity as one of the great triumphs of modern invention and mythologised the advent of a new powerful locomotive in sketches, such as the cartoon in 1900 of Electra banishing the Steam Locomotive Underground Demon, declaring, 'Now they've seen *me*, I fancy your days are numbered'.[68] No longer was the underground space demonised in the choking sensation of the Underground journey; rather, the cleaner air and efficiency of service sanitised and uplifted the experience as a voyage to a technologically advanced society.

In this reinvention, the underground railway begins to take a more central role in the depiction of the futuristic city, but not without its attending fears of urban collapse and degeneration. H. G. Wells had already taken this new landscape to the realm of science fiction, but E. M. Forster's short story 'The Machine Stops' (1909) was more vehement in its articulation of an underground society whose technological advancement has made the inhabitants subservient to the whims of a mechanised system. Following a narrative of a son's quest to reconnect with his mother, the story develops along Freudian lines, not only to reconnect with the womb, but to discover the power of 'direct experience' that was destroyed by the civilising agent of modern technology. In the journey, the mother realises that she must plunge into a terrifying tunnel in a re-enactment of the past in order to see her son face to face: 'By a vestibule, by a lift, by a tubular railway, by a platform, by a sliding door – by reversing all the steps of her departure did Vashti arrive at her son's room, which exactly resembled her own.'[69] Here, Forster gestures at the significance of the Underground journey in recovering memory, history and genuine experience while alluding to the paradoxical idea that the retracing of steps is an equally potent form of progression and human advancement. Forster revives the organic image of urban circulation, but he subverts the concept by dehumanising people as mere objects in service of the Machine and casting the subterranean networks as a means of sustaining this power structure in a Marxist division of capital and labour. The new lines of technological advancement no longer resemble Augé's *correspondences* that recover meaning in the fluid movement of people and ideas in the subterranean passageways. Forster's warning of an age of inhumanity echoed many of the anxieties at the turn of century about the dangers of uncontrolled technology and the potential of such power to destroy civilisation, a prescient view in the face of the looming international tensions that would lead to the outbreak of war. Time was speeding towards its own destruction.

Despite conflicting visions of the future in a mechanised era, aesthetic apprehension of machinery, speed and technological progress reached its apotheosis in celebrating 'the noise, the tumult, the ugliness, the inhumanity', as London found itself at the forefront of the Futurist movement. On his visit to London in 1912, the founder of Italian Futurists, Filippo Marinetti, told *The Evening News* that travelling on the Underground had given him 'what I wanted – not enjoyment, but a totally new idea of motion, of speed' and triumphantly declared, 'London itself is a futurist city!'[70] The Futurist movement, in effect, demanded a desensitisation and a defamiliarisation with humanity in a reification of the passenger as an object to be conveyed through the cogs of the city. In the atomisation of time and space, the movement severed the underground space with the past and reimagined it as a mechanised utopia in a temporal propulsion towards modernism. Focusing on electricity as the primary driver of Futurism, Marinetti continued to delineate a radical departure from the past:

> Why should we look back, when what we want is to break down the mysterious doors of the Impossible? Time and Space died yesterday. We already live in the absolute, because we have created eternal, omnipresent speed.[71]

In the exhilaration of the new technology, the Futurists attempted to capture the speed of man's progress in a new aesthetic vision of the city, and the Underground was one of the key substructures that would sustain the life and vigour of this revolutionary movement. The outpouring of aesthetic interest in the Underground is what David Welsh terms 'Tubism' as it reconfigured how transport functioned in the iconography of the city.[72] In this new architectural vision, man is subservient to space; indeed, there is no evidence of humanity in the iron and glass constructions that overshadow all traces of organic forms in the new outline of the city. The speed of, and towards, the future is privileged in the atomised works of Cubism, while harsh, interrupted lines sever the concept of time into a smattering of perspectives. Futurist painter Umberto Boccioni painted a series entitled *States of Mind* (1911) that depicts farewells at train stations, but in the emotional upheaval, human faces disassociate into inanimate patterns and geometric shapes. In this dark vortex, a departing train cuts up the vague figures in a cloud of smoke, ultimately suggesting the split between human emotions and the automatism of the machine. It is a brutal celebration of destruction and locomotive power, a far cry from the dreamy plumes of Monet's *Gare St. Lazare* that shrouded the machine in mystery and ambiance. The new technology was harsher, edgier and steelier in its resolve to overtake human subjectivity in a powerful new interpretation of the locomotive.

However, in London's artistic and literary representation, there is an absence of such revelation and more unrelieved pessimism in the prospect of speed to deliver anything other than the ghost of death and destruction. The only English artist who inherited the Futurist vision, Christopher Nevinson, painted a single canvas of the Underground called *The Non-Stop* (1914), celebrating the speed and dynamism of the London Tube system (Fig. 2.6). However, echoing the structuring absence of the Underground in so many narratives of the city, this canvas has since been lost with no surviving studies or copies. The only

Figure 2.6   Christopher Nevinson, *The Non-Stop* (1918). Oil on canvas. Missing

description that remains is one review that described *The Non-Stop* as 'a circular picture of the interior of a compartment in a "Tube", in which the vibration of seated figures and strap-hangers was kaleido-scopically expressed in vivid bright colours'.[73] In this 'kaleidoscopic' interpretation of subterranean space, time is suspended and shattered into a montage of disparate perspectives. Wyndham Lewis, who based the Vorticist avant-garde movement as a response to Futurism, described his vision as 'an absolute revolution in the principles that govern the visual arts in response to a fundamentally altered world'. [74] In its severance with the past and Victorian ideals of aesthetic realism, the Underground presented itself at the forefront of a brave new city of utilitarian and utopian ideals. However, such ideals were short-lived with the onset of World War I, when the Underground turned into a temporary bomb shelter and storage space in an abeyance of time, as the city waited restlessly for the siege to end and for time to start anew.

In a final *détournement*, time comes to a grinding halt in the underground, as World War I suspends and subsumes the past, present and future in an eternal purgatory of 'trench time'. Although painter Christopher Nevinson initially embraced Futurism in his (now absent) canvas of the Underground Tube, his later realisation of subterranean space reveals a return to sobering realism in the wake of life in the barracks. In *The Underground War* (1918), anonymous soldiers pass through a protective structure that eerily resembles an Underground carriage, while aboveground, a barbed-wired fence cuts them off from the rest of the world, painted in dark, menacing tones (Fig. 2.7). Psychiatrist Eugène Minkowski describes the loss of time and the boredom of life in the trenches of war:

> The monotonous life in the trenches sometimes made us forget the date of the day of the week . . . We substituted another 'calendar' for them, more appropriate to the situation: we simply counted the days that had passed since we came to the front and those which separated us from our return to the rest camp . . . We succumbed to the tedium and the monotony of the succession of days, and we fought off the boredom – obviously an essentially temporal phenomenon which penetrated our being like a viscous mass, threatening to reduce it to nothing.[75]

In the existential abeyance of temporal movement, the trenches adopted a new measurement of time, a new calibration of days to counter the tranquilising effects of waiting in a stagnant underground space. This new form of hell that threatened to atrophy all sensations of life and living was echoed in the urban underground space, as creativity and productivity stalled in the face of imminent attacks.

In the suspension of time, the Underground became a shelter in both world wars to escape the warring present on the surface of the city, and many stations were used to store artefacts and artwork in a desperate return to, and preservation of, the past and its symbolic associations[76]

Figure 2.7   Christopher Nevinson, *The Underground War* (1918). Oil on canvas. © Bonhams, London, UK / The Bridgeman Art Library.

The link between the trenches and the Underground is also made explicit in Ford Madox Ford's poem 'Antwerp' (1917), where Charing Cross serves as both a historical Tube shelter and also as a mythological space of Hades where women and children await the dead. The poem begins with an image of the station at midnight, with a crowd of women and children '[a]ll with dead faces, waiting in all the waiting-places', but the image traverses spatially and psychologically to the war front, as they transform into 'the women of Flanders' who 'await the lost that shall never again come by the train'.[77] There is a sense of time passing slowly, but ultimately the poem renders time and people stagnant in the repetition of images that function more as a necropolis for the departed soldiers as well as for their spiritually dead family members who wander like ghosts in the Tube station. As Stephen Kern concludes, 'The war shut off direct access to the immediate future and opened an abyss between the present and the distant future for everyone, even the Futurists.'[78] In the temporal and spatial void, many of the Futurists met their deaths in the trenches, rendering their ideology of a technocracy obsolete. In a subversion of surface and underground images, the streets now presented the potential for hell in the air raids of a new warring era, while the underground represented the purgatory of those who had to endure the wait of a history that raged on without them. As the Wellsian hero in *The Sleeper Awakes* astutely reflects, 'We were making the future ... and hardly any of us troubled to think what future we were making'.[79] In this retrospective analysis, there is a call for a return to subjective time, or the need for individual conscious-ness to mediate the acceleration of mechanised time, in a prophetic warning about the dangers of technology's ability to accelerate the world to its own self-destruction. Here, history and the past reassert their significance as ideas about the nature of time come full circle in re-establishing the lines between different temporalities in a desperate attempt to make the world cohere in an incoherent war of competing ideologies.

Signal Failure and Psychological Disjunctions

Under the surface of flux and fear there is an underground movement,
Under the crush of bureaucracy, quiet behind the posters,
Unconscious but palpably there – the Kingdom of individuals.
        Louis MacNeice, 'The Kingdom' in *Collected Poems* (c. 1943)

In the spatial and temporal flux of the Underground, physical and psychological effects on the traveller become a critical hermeneutic through which writers, sociologists and medical practitioners attempted to understand a new form of subterranean consciousness. From its inception, the Underground journey was already equated with disaster. Conditions in dark tunnels, heightened visual and auditory stimuli as well as close proximity to other bodies all contributed to a range of discourses about altered mental states, which in many ways anticipated the Freudian model of the unconscious. In the cultural imagination, the surface railways were associated with the destruction of the pastoral idyll, while the Underground Tubes dealt more with the psychic disrup-tions of the internal landscape. Of particular interest was the impact of accidents underground, the experience of which reverberated in the narratives of its victims and in nineteenth-century sensationalist drama and murder mysteries. Although the underground railway often served as a backdrop for plays, one popular drama, *After Dark* (1868) by Dion Boucicault, used it as a centrepiece for its finale, in which a man is killed under a train at King's Cross.[80] Such visual and cultural fears became embedded in the Victorian imagination and inculcated a sense of the unknown and the unexpected in the subterranean journey. In her study of earlier train disasters, Jill L. Matus argues that 'the railway accident was to Victorian psychology what World War I and shell shock were to Freudian' and sees 'the awareness of trauma as part of modernity itself'.[81] As embedded anxieties and unconscious fears begin to play a crucial role in the understanding of the mind, the Inner Circle here becomes an apt metaphor again for the thought processes that traversed inner and outer consciousness, a liminal line that, once crossed, created disruptions in the psychic and urban landscape. The use of the railway metaphor in representing the traffic across these mental states appears as early as 1866 in *The Gay Science*, a study of psychology and aesthetics, which reported:

> Between the outer and inner ring, between our unconscious and conscious existence, there is a free and a constant but unobserved traffic forever carried on. Trains of thought are continually passing to and fro, from the light into the dark, and back from the dark into the light.[82]

Already implicit in the scientific language is the accessibility to an unknown self and the journey that is required to bring the unconscious to light. The awareness of such invisible 'trains' of thought then becomes a crucial mode of understanding the past, repressed memories and unbidden fears on subterranean journeys, alluding to the Freudian layers of consciousness.

In the anonymity and darkness of underground space, there was a heightened form of desensitisation and an inward turning of consciousness that marked the subterranean journey. By 1864, the phenomenon of 'accident shock' became a critical issue as railway companies became legally liable for their passengers' safety and health, leading to numerous medical diagnoses of this 'invisible' problem. Due to the impact on the nervous system that surfaced in such outward manifestations as hysterical fits, spasms and anxiety, the condition was often referred to as 'railway spine' in medical assessments.[83] In addition to symptoms arising from accidents, there were other shocks that were psychically absorbed by the overstimulation wrought by the speed of the trains. In his significant study, 'The Metropolis and Mental Life' (1903), sociologist Georg Simmel describes the necessity of a protective 'organ' to shield oneself from the threatening nature of urban life, resulting in the kind of detachment and apathy attributable to a 'new metropolitan type individual'.[84] Applying his critical ideas to the train ride, Simmel also notes that increased velocity on trains led to 'intensification of nervous stimulation which results from the swift and uninterrupted change of outer and inner stimuli'.[85] Reports of fatigue and muscle strain from the jolts suffered on the train were widely reported in *The Lancet* and led to the use of upholstery to absorb the shock that still cushions the carriages today. One of the earlier models of trains called the 'padded cell' also attempted to create a more comfortable journey, enclosing the passengers in a protective membrane in an attempt to obliterate the sense of movement and discomfort in the carriage. Although the model was discontinued, the compartment reveals Simmelian links to the psychology of the Underground journey, especially in the detachment the traveller must maintain in a space that inhibits visual or verbal exchange. This sense of isolation is echoed in Walter Benjamin's observation of the lack of communication in new forms of urban transport:

> Before the development of buses, trains and streetcars in the nineteenth century, people were quite unable to look at each other for minutes or hours at a time, or to be forced to do so, without talking to each other. Modern traffic increasingly reduces the majority of sensory relations between human beings to mere sight, and this must create entirely new premises for their general sociological feelings.[86]

The reduced personal contact and a sense of anonymity meant one had to reject or repress outer stimuli, thereby submitting entirely to an inner realm of the subconscious. In interiorising the Underground journey, the traveller's visual focus turned to imaginary dreamscapes in books, advertisements and the ubiquitous Underground map as the gap between inner and outer worlds widened.

In recent years, many critics have historicised trauma in the context of railway accidents and have suggested the spectre of violence was often a part of the narrative of the city.[87] Charles Dickens's short story 'The Signalman' (1866) is a haunting example of such psychological upheaval created when the line between the conscious and the unconscious is transgressed. Dickens himself was involved in a major railway accident from which he never fully recovered, and although this story evokes the horror of this memory, it also exemplifies the cathartic impact of the narrative process.[88] In this ghost story, an anonymous narrator descends into a signalman's box and becomes unwittingly involved in a repetitive dream cycle of a terrifying train wreck. The descent into this alternate threshold transports the narrator to a darker, more foreboding realm:

> His post was in as solitary and dismal a place as ever I saw. On either side, a dripping-wet wall of jagged stone, excluding all view but a strip of sky . . . the shorter perspective in the other direction terminating in a gloomy red light,

and the gloomier entrance to a black tunnel, in whose massive architecture there was a barbarous, depressing, and forbidding air. So little sunlight ever found its way to this spot, that it had an earthy, deadly smell; and so much cold wind rushed through it, that it struck chill to me, as if I had left the natural world.[89]

Evoking the terror and the sublimity of the Underground, Dickens depicts the railway tunnel as a dangerous, unconscious space, alluding to metaphors of enclosure and death. When the narrator first meets the signalman, he is mistaken for an 'apparition', an uncanny Lacanian encounter in which the signalman suggests, 'I was doubtful . . . whether I had seen you before.'[90] This refracted image of the narrator then becomes linked with a spectre that the signalman continues to see in the tunnel, which ultimately portends the signalman's own death in a train crash. The projection of the narrator's unconscious memory through the ghost of the signalman reveals the psychological distance between inner and outer consciousness, as the Underground serves as a structural framework for unearthing these psychic layers of memory. The ability to narrate then becomes the only effective means of connecting the events in a release from the horrors that attend such violence.

In digging through the layers of urban consciousness, the Underground is also represented as a site of violence and libidinal impulses that mirrors Freud's model of repression and aggression. Although the anxieties of the potential disaster of train crashes subsided by the late nineteenth century, the sense of violence in the Underground still lingered as a tangible threat to the metropolis. As Schivelbusch notes:

If the normal functioning of the railroad was thus experienced as a natural and safe process, any sudden interruption of that functioning (which had become second nature) immediately reawakened the memory of the forgotten danger and potential violence: the repressed material returned with a vengeance.[91]

Such interruptions to the quotidian train ride were expressed in narratives and actual accounts of robberies and murders that depicted the Underground as a dangerous, transgressive space. In the 1880s, Fenian attempts to bomb the Circle Line lent an aura of terror during the political upheaval, the impact of which will be discussed more in detail in Chapter 4 on underground revolutions. Furthermore, by the 1890s, when electrification took hold of the underground railways, the underground space became less haunted and became more central to the imagination in tales that terrorised the commuters in a new underground map of violence.[92]

One short story that reignited fear in the Underground was John

Oxenham's 'A Mystery of the Underground' (1897), published serially under a pseudonym in the popular weekly, *To-Day*. Mimicking the reportage of sensational journalism, the series followed the hunt for an 'underground murderer' who killed unsuspecting City businessmen in a random spate of violence, which actually led to a drop in Underground commuters each Tuesday evening that it was published.[93] Alarms were raised all along the southern part of the Circle Line from Blackfriars to Sloane Square in a new psychogeography of middle-class crime. Another tale that adds a palimpsestic layer to the terror of underground space is Baroness Emmuska Orczy's 'The Mysterious Death on the Underground Railway' (1901), in which a wealthy woman's body is discovered at Aldgate station. Like many popular tales, illicit themes of adultery, betrayal and false identity converge in the underground networks, as the murder is eventually traced back to her own husband.[94] In retracing the events, the police conclude that the victim encounters the murderer on Gower Street and is found murdered at Aldgate, the terminus in real and metaphorical terms. Furthermore, Arthur Conan Doyle's 'The Bruce-Partington Plans' (1917) also locates Aldgate station as a junction of more violence, as the body of a civil servant is carried on top of the train along the Circle Line until it falls off at the station in the East End. The murder victim, who is found with a stolen plan of a government submarine, connects the station to a wider web of international spies and underground espionage in a breach of national security. As Jeffrey Richards remarks on the duality of the Underground, 'The station became at one and the same time one of the principal forces in society for order, regulation, and discipline, and a new focus for violence, crime, and immorality.'[95] In this bifurcation, the Underground reasserts itself as a space of conscious control and a subconscious locus of violence that harbours the mysteries of the city and underground identities, particularly through the genre of crime and detective stories.

Amidst the violence underground and aboveground, a final psychological theme surfaces at the turn of the century as the city prepared itself for war: the meditation on the solitude and the collectivity of the Tube ride. In the growing anonymity of the newly mechanised underworld, artists and writers responded to the uncertainty and the dangers of war in restless and melancholic images of urban transport. Augé comments that 'the prosaic definition of the metro' is 'collectivity without festival and solitude without isolation'.[96] Such psychological contradictions of the Underground experience were expressed in striking visual responses to the weariness of urban life and the disjuncture from humanity in the world above. Maxwell Armfield's painting *Oxford Circus Underground Station* (1905) expresses a form of solitude and self-estrangement as an

Edwardian woman blends into the shadow on a platform while a train is on the threshold of piercing through a dark tunnel. In the repetitive semicircles that frame the painting, the woman's dark figure is echoed in the tunnel of the Tube, the exit in the background and the overarching shape of the entire platform. She is subsumed into the technological design of the station as her identity is overwhelmed by the force of the architecture and the power of the oncoming train. In another defeatist image, Roger Fry's Omega mural (1916) depicts a weary woman climbing up the stairs of a Tube station against the backdrop of the corporate logo 'UndergrounD' that is cut off at an angle, undercutting the power of the ubiquitous sign. Henri Lefebvre regarded the hours spent in transit as a dehumanising period where bodies were reduced to commodities passing through production in a wasted interval of 'constrained time', echoing Ruskin's criticism that travellers were mere 'human parcels who dispatched themselves to their destination by means of the railway, arriving as they left, untouched by the space traversed'.[97] These two images are also striking in their representation of solitary female commuters in the early twentieth century. Rather than exhibiting the novelty of Underground journeys, the paintings illustrate futility combined with an inward turning that demonstrates a new awareness of her environment. As Parsons argues, lone *flâneuses* found 'an external anonymity in the crowd that then allows them the freedom to conduct a female pilgrimage, both the "voyage out" and the "voyage in"'.[98] I suggest that this invisibility and anonymity gave her another form of agency in the city in the form of interiority and introspection that Virginia Woolf later inherits in her vision of the Underground journey.[99] Although the commodification of time and the reification of commuters appeared as pervasive motifs in underground representation, the quotidian element of the journey also allowed for new forms of individual 'trains' of thought to lead the commuter into the more private, psychological realm of his or her consciousness.

Poetry also conveyed a sense of anomie, as well as collective identity in the Underground in the image of passive travellers who lose themselves in the moving carriage or on a crowded platform. In his modernist poetry, Ezra Pound combines subjectivity and detached objectivity in the communal *lack* of identity in the Underground experience. In his pared-down poem 'In a Station of the Metro' (1913), Pound reinvents Poe's attraction to the crowd, but without the visual exchange of the *flâneur*.

> The apparition of these faces in the crowd;
> Petals on a wet, black bough.[100]

In merging the organic image of petals with the faces trapped in a technological subterranean space, Pound infuses the indistinguishable crowd

with a subjective, albeit dark, beauty. Although there is no individualism, the 'apparition' attempts to temper the mechanical with the poetic,
the objective with the subjective experience in an 'in-between' spectral
guise that interrupts the usual binaries of underground representation.
Commenting on the nuances of collectivity in the Underground, Augé
observes:

> Transgressed or not, the law of the metro inscribes the individual itinerary
> into the comfort of collective morality, and in that way it is exemplary of
> what might be called the ritual paradox: it is always lived individually and
> subjectively; only individual itineraries give it a reality, and yet it is eminently
> social, the same for everyone, conferring on each person this minimum of
> collective identity through which a community is defined.[101]

The identity of this 'minimum community' is the most pronounced
in the use of Underground stations as shelters that fought against the
dehumanising effects of war. Although most of the historical focus is
on World War II shelters, the succession of raids during World War I
also prompted approximately 12,000 people to seek shelter at Finsbury
Park and 9,000 people at King's Cross in 1915. The sense of purgatory
in World War I was captured in works such as Walter Bayes's painting
The Underworld (1918), where figures are slouched listlessly at different angles in the stillness of subterranean time, and a Tube exit only
leads to another grim tunnel of haunting figures lingering in the distance
(Fig. 2.8). They no longer wait for trains on the platform, but merely
wait for time and the war to pass. In this collective space and time, the
Underground Tube station serves as a womb and a tomb, paving the
way for a more extensive subterranean network that will ultimately
become a lived space and a new underground city during World
War II.

Disembarkation

> These cathedrals of the new humanity are the meeting points of nations, the
> centre where all converges, the nucleus of the huge stars whose iron rays
> stretch out to the ends of the earth.
>   Théophile Gautier, quoted in Jean Dethier (ed.), *All Stations* (1981)

The construction of the underground railway, in its sheer monumen-
tality and enduring influence, reveals a complex intersection of social,
geographical and aesthetic lines and patterns that remapped the city.
Considered one of the most dramatic symbols of modernism, the
Underground ushered in a new sense of the ephemeral and the contin-

Figure 2.8   Walter Bayes, *The Underworld* (1918). Oil on canvas. © Imperial War Museums (Art. IWM ART 935).

gent as speed determined the flow of movement and expansion. As a structuring device, the Inner Circle remained a liminal space that unified yet dispersed the core of the metropolis while maintaining a ghostlike presence in literary representation, flitting in and out of narratives like a passing glimpse in a moving carriage. While creating new neighbour-hoods and extending urban boundaries on the surface of the metropolis, the Underground also became its own lived, travelled and imaginary city of real and metaphoric journeys. As David Pike observes:

> While the nineteenth century was dominated by the representation of above-ground space as if it were subterranean, and the increasingly predominant experience of the underground space in the everyday life of the lower classes, the twentieth century was characterized by the representation of subterranean space as aboveground, and the increasing predominance of underground space in the everyday life of the middle classes.[102]

While the underground and aboveground constantly mirrored and con-tradicted each other in artistic and literary representations, many urban practices on the surface were eschewed in inventing the new heterogene-ous, subterranean city. Class and gender distinctions became blurred as access was widened, and separate classes and carriages were eliminated in favour of a more democratic journey. However, the benefits of the Underground were always in a delicate equipoise with the destructive ele-ments that lent an aura of violence and terror to the subterranean space.

Jack Simmons, in his overview of railway history, remarks that in nineteenth-century England, railways were not subjects of literature, as they did not 'touch the soul'; rather, they became a 'mere commer-cial instrument . . . [p]art of textile mills, ironworks, and shipyards as instruments of a powerful commercial economy'.[103] On the contrary, it touched the soul too greatly, so much so that it had to be repressed in the form of a shadow, an invisible but omniscient presence that supported the aesthetic and novelistic ambitions in the nineteenth century, only to emerge as a central subject of treatment in the modernist and avant-garde sensibilities of the twentieth century. Its dramatic reinventions of time, space and urban subjectivity attest to the prevalence of, and preoccupation with, the Underground throughout the years, and the 7/7 Tube attacks in London are a reminder of the fragility of this deeply symbolic and resilient subterranean space.

Notes

1. Dickens, *The Railway through Dickens's World*, p. 8. See also Schivelbusch, *The Railway Journey*.
2. Simmons, *The Victorian Railway*, p. 216.
3. Some of the main theatrical productions that use the Metropolitan Line as a backdrop include Boucicault's *After Dark*, J. B. Buckstone, *Little Miss Muffet and Little Boy Blue or, Harlequin and Old Daddy Longlegs* (1861) and M. du Terreaux's *Waiting for the Underground* (1866). For more details, see Pike, 'Underground Theater', pp. 102–38.
4. Derrida, *Of Grammatology*, p. 70. It is also interesting to note in the context of absences that the Inner Circle, which eventually became the 'Circle Line', does not actually exist. Referred to as a 'virtual line', the Circle Line does not have any tracks or stations of its own, but shares the same tracks of the Metropolitan and District Line, with only two sections of its own between High Street Kensington and Gloucester Road and between Tower Hill and Aldgate. For more, see Croome, *The Circle Line*.
5. Benjamin, 'On Some Motifs on Baudelaire', p. 165.
6. Douglas, *The Underground Story*, p. 13.
7. Mayhew, *Shops and Companies of London*, p. 143.
8. Dickens, *Dombey and Son*, pp. 120–1.
9. Dyos, *Exploring the Urban Past*, pp. 25–6. Although laws required 'demolition statements' to list the number of residents displaced, the accuracy of such numbers were in doubt, as the official figure of the people displaced in the construction of the Paddington to Farringdon line was 307 people. Recent research suggests the number was closer to 1,000 houses and 12,000 inhabitants. For more details, see Simmons, *The Railway in Town and Country*.
10. See Nead, *Victorian Babylon*, p. 32. Although excavations in Pompeii began in 1711, systematic digging did not begin until the mid-nineteenth century, as Victorians became fascinated with antiquity, and Pompeii became a popular destination for the middle classes.
11. Cited in Douglas, *The Underground Story*, p. 106. In the case of Temple Station, trains were not originally allowed to blow whistles so as not to disturb the barristers. For more details in the social stratification in the

construction of the underground network, see Kellett, *The Impact of Railways*.

12. 'Bursting of the Fleet Ditch' in *The Illustrated London News*, 28 June 1862, p. 139.
13. *The Times*, 30 November 1861, cited in Wolmar, *The Subterranean Railway*, p. 41.
14. Blumenthal, *R. D. B.'s Diary*, pp. 6–7.
15. Gissing, *The Whirlpool*, p. 14. H. G. Wells applauded Gissing's work, claiming that the novel 'was the very figure for the nineteenth-century Great City, attractive, tumultuous, and spinning down to death'. See Wells, *Anticipations*, p. 44.
16. Barker and Robbins, *A History of London Transport*, p. 208.
17. Ibid. p. 381.
18. Gissing, *In the Year of Jubilee*, p. 309.
19. Morris, *New from Nowhere*, pp. 316–17.
20. Lefebvre, *The Production of Space*, p. 87.
21. Crosland, *The Suburbans*, p. 8.
22. Thacker, *Moving through Modernity*, p. 47.
23. Wilde, *The Importance of Being Earnest*, p. 19.
24. Many engravings were also commissioned directly by railway companies to gain support for the construction process. See Richards and MacKenzie, *The Railway Station*.
25. For more details on the fare system, see Freeman and Aldcroft, *Transport in Victorian Britain*, p. 149.
26. Cited in Trench and Hillman, *London under London*, p. 139.
27. Bakhtin, *Rabelais and His World*, p. 10.
28. 'First-Class Underground Study' in *Punch*, 11 September 1886.
29. Banton, 'Underground Travelling London', p. 150.
30. Constantin Pecqueur, *Economie sociale*, 1, pp. 335–6, cited in Schivelbusch, *The Railway Journey*, pp. 74–5.
31. *Quarterly Review*, 74 (1844), 250. The Underground was also one of the first organisations to employ women in the nineteenth century, first as 'fluffers' who dusted off the rails at night, and then as ticket staff during World War I. For more on the social history of women and transport, see Rotandaro, *Women at Work*.
32. Nord, 'The Urban Perpipateti', p. 352. See also Nord, *Walking the Victorian Streets*.
33. Cited in Rappaport, *Shopping for Pleasure*, p. 122.
34. Vadillo, *Women Poets and Urban Aestheticism*, pp. 23, 13.
35. Foucault, 'Of Other Spaces', p. 24. Foucault specifically denotes the train as a heterogeneous space, because 'it is something through which one goes, it is also something by means of which one can go from one point to another, and then it is also something that goes by'.
36. Gissing, *The Odd Women*, p. 359.
37. Ibid. p. 20.
38. Trollope, *The Way We Live Now*, p. 385. Trollope's *The Claverings* (1867) and *The Eustace Diamonds* (1873) also attest to the presence of the underground in the middle-class imagination.
39. Altick, *The Presence of the Present*, pp. 442–4.

40. Schivelbusch, 'Railroad Space and Railroad Time', p. 32.
41. Cited in Edwards and Pigram, *The Romance of Metroland*, p. 18.
42. Cited in Green, *Underground Art*, p. 74.
43. Wells, *The Sleeper Awakes*, p. 112.
44. Sant'Elia and Marinetti, 'The Futurist Manifesto of Architecture', pp. 36–7.
45. Pike, 'Modernist Space', p. 101. This playful rendering of the Underground is also reflected in a contemporary painting *The Great Bear* (1992) by Simon Patterson. Mimicking Beck's iconic map, he replaces the names of stations with names of philosophers, actors and celebrities, forcing the viewer to look at the map more closely and to interrogate the purpose and accuracy of such maps.
46. See Saler, *The Avant-Garde in Interwar England*. In keeping with medieval aestheticism, the architecture of Underground stations like Charles Holden's Balham Station and Uxbridge Station were modelled after English cathedrals, while Travertine marble from Italy was used in the renovation of Piccadilly Circus in 1925.
47. Kern, *The Culture of Time and Space*, pp. 9, 11.
48. Ibid. p. 21.
49. Cited in Robinson, 'Zola and Manet', p. 55.
50. Ibid. p. 66.
51. Guy Debord's 'plaque tournant' indicated a space where a 'turning' was possible from an anticipated direction of movement, giving the urban traveller a sense of agency in the city. See Sadler, *The Situationist City*. Walter Benjamin defined 'threshold spaces' as the spaces of transit, such as trains, stations, bridges, squares, buses and streets. See Menninghaus, 'Walter Benjamin's Theory of Myth', pp. 292–325.
52. See also Whistler's 'The Ten O'Clock Lecture' (1885) that discussed the 'exquisite tune' of 'Nature' at nightfall in which the industrial landscape of the city was transformed into Italian bell-towers and palaces.
53. Durkheim, *The Elementary Forms of the Religious Life*, pp. 10–11.
54. Foucault, *Discipline and Punish*, pp. 149–50.
55. Thompson, 'Time', pp. 56–92.
56. Dickens, 'An Unsettled Neighbourhood'.
57. *The Journal of Public Health and Sanitary Review* (1855), 1, p. 425. Also, Sir James Crichton-Browne in 1892 found heart disease and deaths from cancer and kidney disease increased 'due to the tension, excitement, and incessant mobility of modern life'. Beard, in *American Nervousness* (1881), argued that the telegraph, railroads and steam power have enabled businessmen to make 'a hundred times' more transactions in a given period than had been possible in the eighteenth century, causing a host of physical ailments, such as neurasthenia, neuralgia, nervous dyspepsia, early tooth decay and even premature baldness. Nordau, in *Degeneration* (1895), also argued that the onset of modernity came too fast. 'No time was left to our fathers. Between one day and the next, with murderous suddenness, they were obliged to change the comfortable creeping gait of their former existence for the stormy stride of modern life, and their heart and lungs could not bear it.'
58. De Amicis, *Jottings about London*, pp. 24–5.

59. Bakhtin, 'Forms of Time', p. 157.
60. Dickens, 'Mugby Junction', p. 477. Italics are my own.
61. Seed, 'Mystery in Everyday Things', p. 49.
62. Augé, *In the Metro*, p. 59.
63. Trollope, *The Prime Minister*, p. 520. Tenway Junction is now Willesden Green. As early as 1877, medical reports noted, 'Recently, suicide by falling before a railway train has exercised an extraordinary fascination for disordered minds.' For more, see Cox, *The Principles of Punishment*, p. 57.
64. Augé, *In the Metro*, p. 9.
65. Turner, 'Periodical Time in the Nineteenth Century', p. 187.
66. Trollope, *What I Remember*, p. 22.
67. Freud, *Civilization and Its Discontents*, p. 325.
68. 'Notice to Quit' in *Punch* (27 June 1900).
69. Forster, 'The Machine Stops', pp. 98–9.
70. Cited in Paolozzi, *Eduardo Paolozzi Underground*, p. 28.
71. Marinetti, 'The Founding and Manifesto of Futurism', p. 22.
72. Welsh, *Underground Writing*, p. 8.
73. Cited in Paolozzi, *Eduardo Paolozzi Underground*, p. 28. The painting was first exhibited at the London Group, but since then has been lost. Another Futurist artist, Gino Severini, attempted to capture the 'complex of dynamic elements' of trains in his work *The Nord-Sud* (1912). Literary styles also reflected this intense focus on dislocations of identity, space and time in such urban texts as Andrei Bely's *Petersburg* (1913) and John Dos Passos's *Manhattan Transfer* (1925).
74. Wyndham Lewis, *Blast*, 1 (July 1914), p. 24. His later Cubist painting, *One of the Stations of the Dead* (1933), also treats the theme of death in the Underground that mimics the wait at a Tube station.
75. Minkowski, *Lived Time*, p. 14.
76. Of significance was the use of Aldwych station to house the Elgin Marbles as well as many of the paintings from the National Gallery.
77. Ford, 'Antwerp', pp. 81–2.
78. Kern, *The Culture of Time and Space*, p. 298.
79. Wells, *The Sleeper Awakes*, pp. 96–7.
80. Boucicault, *After Dark*.
81. Matus, 'Trauma, Memory, and Railway Disaster', pp. 414, 417. Also see *Studies on Hysteria*, p. 213, on the connections Freud makes between railways and the history of trauma.
82. Dallas, *The Gay Science*, 1, p. 207. Carpenter also comments in *Principles of Mental Physiology*: 'And as our ideas are thus linked in "trains" or "series" which further inosculate with each other like the branch lines of a railway or the ramifications of an artery, so, it is considered, an idea which has been "hidden in the obscure recesses of the mind" for years – perhaps for a lifetime, – and which seems to have completely faded out of the *conscious* Memory . . . may be reproduced as by the touching of a spring, through a nexus of suggestion, which we can sometimes trace-out continuously, but of which it does not seem necessary that all the intermediate steps should fall within our cognizance' (pp. 429–30).

83. For more, see Drinka, *The Birth of Neurosis*, pp. 108–22, and Harrington, 'The Neuroses of the Railway', pp. 15–21. The term 'railway spine' was first used by Erichsen in *On Railway* and is often seen as a precursor to later symptoms of hysteria and post-traumatic stress disorder.

84. Simmel, 'The Metropolis and Mental Life', p. 411.

85. Ibid. p. 410.

86. Benjamin, 'On Some Motifs in Baudelaire', p. 191.

87. See Matus, 'Trauma, Memory, and Railway Disaster', Seed, 'Mystery in Everyday Things', and Nicholas Daly, 'Blood on the Tracks', pp. 47–76.

88. Dickens nearly died in a railway accident in 1865 when he was travelling from Folkestone to London. For more biographical details, see Ackroyd, *Dickens*, and Dickens's own critical article, 'Need Railway Travellers Be Smashed', *Household Words*, 29 November 1851, pp. 217–21.

89. Dickens, 'The Signalman', p. 2.

90. Ibid. p. 3.

91. Schivelbusch, *The Railway Journey*, p. 130. A contemporary example of violence and terror is Murakami, *Underground*, which interviews the victims and perpetrators of the 1995 Tokyo sarin gas attack in the Underground.

92. In a new terrorist map of the Underground, it is interesting to note that nineteenth-century narratives of crime and violence also centred around the Tube stations that were bombed in the more recent 7/7 attacks in London. Aldgate, King's Cross and Edgware stations are all haunted by spectres of disaster, from Fenian bombings to *fin-de-siècle* crime narratives, creating more disturbing *correspondences* in the subterranean space.

93. Oxenham, 'A Mystery of the Underground', pp. 270–7.

94. Baroness Orczy, 'The Mysterious Death on the Underground Railway', in Glen and Karen Bledsoe (eds), *Classic Mysteries II* (Los Angeles: Lowell House, 1999), pp. 8–18.

95. Richards and MacKenzie, *The Railway Station*, p. 94.

96. Augé, *In the Metro*, p. 26.

97. Cited in Schivelbusch, *The Railway Journey*, p. 39.

98. Parsons, *Streetwalking the Metropolis*, p. 227.

99. More specifically, Woolf's texts 'The Mark on the Wall' (1917), *To the Lighthouse* (1927), and *The Waves* (1933) liken a woman's 'stream of consciousness' to an Underground journey.

100. Pound, 'In a Station of the Metro', p. 33. Eliot in *The Wasteland* (1922) and *Four Quartets* (1943) also evokes the perpetual solitude of Underground travel.

101. Augé, *In the Metro*, p. 30.

102. Pike, *Subterranean Cities*, p. 2.

103. Simmons, *The Railway in Town and Country*, pp. 216, 218.

Chapter 3

The (Un)Buried Life:
Death in the Modern Necropolis

From one year to the next, they say, the Eusapia of the dead becomes unrecognizable. And the living, to keep up with them, also want to do everything
that the hooded brothers tell them about the novelties of the dead. So the
Eusapia of the living has taken to copying its underground copy. They say
that this has not just now begun to happen: actually it was the dead who built
the upper Eusapia, in the image of their city. They say that in the twin cities
there is no longer any way of knowing who is alive and who is dead.

Italo Calvino, *Invisible Cities* (1972)

The haunting image of 'twin cities' in all its destabilising connotations, from the Gothic sense of doubling to the image of the World
Trade Center, reveals how death permeates the urban landscape with
the sense of the unknown, the unexpected and the unseen. In antiquity,
the underground as a burial space for the dead, from Egyptian tombs
to the Roman Catacombs, was predicated on the sacred belief that the
afterlife below was just as important, if not more crucial, than the lived
experience above. Indeed, the elaborate architecture of underground
altars and temples in these civilisations attests to the power of the belief
that the house of the living is but a 'temporary abode'.[1] Although this
symmetry between the living and the dead persisted in Western escha-
tology throughout the centuries, grounded in the significance of the
Christian burial and the vertical representation of heaven and hell, it
was in the beginning of the nineteenth century that the meaning of death
and, consequently, the metaphysical space of the underground was violently uprooted by the movement of cemeteries away from churches and
away from the centre of the city. Michel Foucault connects the spiritual
break with the spatial dislocation in his designation of the cemetery as
another 'heterotopia', a space of 'otherness' or a counter-site that con-
tests previous social and cultural practices:

[I]t is only from that start of the nineteenth century that cemeteries began
to be located at the outside border of cities. In correlation with the indi-

vidualization of death and the bourgeois appropriation of the cemetery, there arises an obsession with death as an 'illness.' The dead, it is supposed, bring illnesses to the living, and it is the presence and proximity of the dead right beside the houses, next to the church, almost in the middle of the street, it is this proximity that propagates death itself . . . The cemeteries then came to constitute, no longer the sacred and immortal heart of the city, but the other city . . .[2]

The correlation of death and illness then aligned the corpse with diseases and pestilence, placing cemeteries in the same medical discourse as the sewers in the secularisation of burial practices. This correlation inevitably took the subject of death from the religious realm to a political one in the eradication of graveyards and cemeteries from the city centre. Various historians have commented on this loss of faith in the afterlife or the 'end of death', so to speak, most notably James Stevens Curl, who contemplates what altered society's perceptions to 'drive death underground'.[3] By teasing out the discourses involved in this radical shift in perceptions of death from the sanitary debates in the 1830s and 1840s to the introduction of cremation in the 1880s, I argue that although death and commemoration were removed from the Church's domain to a more secular and commercial realm, the underground space continued to maintain its connection to the sacred and the spiritual, despite the ideals of urban rationalisation and a departure from religion that defined modernity.

Thus far, the underground has been inextricable with the engineering feat that accompanied its representation as an inorganic, artificial space that both reflected and disrupted the urban contours of modern life. Although the cemetery, to some extent, was a product of technological interventions, the underground space of death, for the most part, maintained an organic image as a place of rest from the confusion and turbulence of life above. If the subterranean space of the sewers and the underground railways raised conceptual questions regarding the vertical hierarchy of capital and labour, the empowered and the disenfranchised, the cemetery interrupted the binaries demarcating life and death, science and spiritualism. In her sociological study of death, Elizabeth Hallam investigates various metaphors of death that complicate traditional notions of the living and the dead. She considers a 'matrix of the body' that can be divided as:

socially and biologically alive: socially and biologically dead
socially dead/biologically alive: socially alive/biologically dead.[4]

In this new space of identity, the underground no longer contained the biologically dead individual, as the body mapped itself onto a nexus of social relationships in which the body's resonance outlasted its corporeal essence. As multiple forms of death erupted onto the cityscape, literature and art responded to the Victorian fascination with death in ways that resuscitated the dead body in material and spiritual ways. The Gothic tradition and the rise of the supernatural then accompany this emphasis on the afterlife to become the underlying metaphor for psychoanalytic and deconstructive theories from the 'spectres of Marx' to the 'ghosts of modernity', which become the prevalent mode of apprehending the city of the dead.[5] As Nicola Bown observes in her study of the Victorian supernatural:

> What is uncovered, once the veil is lifted, is often something missing, something that should be there and maybe once (at least in fantasy) was . . . But these losses are often incomplete and leave a remainder. It is here the supernatural comes into play; the remainder is imagined as a haunting.[6]

In many ways, this haunting closely parallels the psychological projection of loss that Freud articulated in his essay 'Mourning and Melancholia' (1917). The inability to relinquish or replace the lost object becomes a psychic wound that embeds itself in the unconscious only to surface in violent repetitions of that unconscious memory.[7] Although bodies and burial grounds were moved beyond the city walls, the concept of death and the afterlife was not destroyed, but merely deferred, as the underworld of the dead circled back to the heart of the metropolis in Derridean hauntings, a recourse to the *revenant* and the spectre of the dead and the undead in a collapsing of the liminal boundaries between the two worlds. This chapter begins by charting the transformation of society's attitude towards the dead body and then examines the multitude of ways the city came to be haunted by the ghosts of the dead, the past and the unconscious in a spectralisation of the metropolis. In literary representations, what was underground was more important than ever as its traces were unearthed and resurrected literally and textually in the Gothic imagination.

The Disposal of the Dead: Shifting Attitudes towards the Corpse

Man is the animal who buries his dead.
L. V. Thomas, *Anthropologie de la mort* (1975)

In line with the sanitary debates and health reforms informing the development of the sewers in the mid-nineteenth century, urban burial grounds became another source of contagion as the dead body became a site of religious, medical and political contestation. Mary Douglas has pointed out that dirt and waste that transgress symbolic boundaries between the body and social structures are 'specially invested with power and danger'.[8] This threat was also embodied in the corpse as it crossed physical and psychic boundaries in the Victorian imagination. The prevalent image of overcrowded graveyards and rotten corpses piled on top of one another signified a cultural shift towards death from the eighteenth century, where 'graveyard poets' from Thomas Gray to Edward Young exalted death in the Arcadian, pristine spaces of elegiac reflection, meditation and melancholy.[9] In the early nineteenth century, Percy Bysshe Shelley echoed this effusive sentiment in his penchant for death: 'The cemetery is an open space among the ruins, covered in Winter with violets and daisies. It might make one in love with death, to think that one should be buried in so sweet a place.'[10] However, such romantic notions were soon displaced by doubt as Victorians began to question their dependence on the Christian burial for spiritual sustenance. Alfred Tennyson's epic poem *In Memoriam* (1850) grapples with this crisis of faith as the narrator attempts to mourn for the dead, but cannot articulate the hope for salvation in a constant monument and erasure of that monument to the departed. In this self-conscious elegy, the poet constructs the possibility of consolation, trusting that when God's plan is understood, all will see '[t]hat not one life shall be destroy'd / Or cast as rubbish to the void',[11] but he undercuts his hopes with the spectre of uncertainty:

> Are God and Nature then at strife,
> That Nature lends such evil dreams?
> So careful of the type she seems,
> So careless of the single life . . .
>
> I falter where I firmly trod,
> And falling with my weight of cares
> Upon the great world's altar-stairs
> That slope thro' darkness up to God[12]

In this vertical representation, Tennyson alludes to Charles Lyell's recent scientific discoveries that uncovered layers of buried time or geological time. Such views of nature clashed with the Christian view of eternal life and, more importantly, an afterlife, which the narrator interrogates through his fragmented consciousness. The absence of the departed and the potential absence of meaning in the burial and mourning process haunts the poem in fissures and gaps that represent what is ultimately unknowable and inarticulable. Isobel Armstrong associates the trauma of grief in the poem with Freud's process of mourning, citing the work of

Figure 3.1   Henry Alexander Bowler, *The Doubt: Can These Dry Bones Live?*
(1855). Oil on canvas. Tate Images/Digital Images. © Tate, London 2012.

psychiatry with 'the geological idea of concealed process, the energy at
work *underground*'.[13] Such layers of signification captured the spiritual
crisis of the time, which duly inspired other artists, most notably Henry
Alexander Bowler, whose painting *The Doubt: Can These Dry Bones
Live?* (1855) also raised the spectre of uncertainty in the juxtaposition
of secular and religious symbols (Fig. 3.1). In the painting, a woman in
mourning dress leans contemplatively over a tombstone, pondering the
possibilities of resurrection against the inscription on the tombstone,

'Resurgam' ('I shall rise again'). The butterfly, also representing rebirth, sits on the skull drying above the grave, further interrogating the potential of spiritual resurrection against the biological processes of birth and decomposition. The underground, which was traditionally seen as a conduit through which souls could pass, became a site of tension at a time when scientific discoveries uncovered layers of history beneath the earth's surface, and the ideas of evolution came to clash with the theological implications of a proper burial.

As discourses of death reflected the dissonance between religious and secular beliefs, social and sanitary changes in London also problematised the rituals of death observed by the Church and inculcated by the middle classes. Most notably, the spatial practice of having burial grounds near the church was regarded as a grave threat, as decomposing bodies were believed to release 'mephitic vapours' of cholera while poisoning the soil and the water supply in the environs. The corpse then became, in Kristevan terms, 'the utmost of abjection' in its 'unbounded' state, as its putrid body and porous surface threatened to contaminate the city with its matter and fluids.[14] As the decomposing body destabilised physical and psychic borders, the subterranean space of death merged with the rhetoric of disgust in the sewers, aligning them in a pestilential image of death and disease. To illustrate the dangers to the Victorian body politic, British physician Henry Thompson, an early advocate of cremation, gave notable examples of two gravediggers who perished in 1841 descending into a grave in St Botolph's churchyard in Aldgate and concluded that 'cholera was unusually prevalent in the immediate neighbourhood of London graveyards'.[15] Mirroring the miasmatic theory of the sewers, the pythogenic theory of the cemeteries also cited the proximity to infectious sources and the inhalation of the airs surrounding them to be a deathly combination. *A Report from the Select Committee* in 1842 exemplified this toxic phenomenon by citing a notorious discovery at Enon Street Chapel in Clement's Lane, revealing how closely the living consorted with the dead. The investigation found almost 12,000 bodies buried in the cellars, which were built over an underground sewer into which the corpses slid, releasing intolerable odours during services and ceremonies. The church eventually closed and became a congregation hall for tea-dances (its proximity to corpses being the main macabre attraction), but the image of the underground as a resting place for the dead, separate from the living world above, was supplanted by a more porous image of pestilence and pollution. The proximity to the church no longer afforded the living or the dead a safe passage in this life or the next. Of course, not all graveyards were attached to churches, as Charles Dickens notes in his survey of 'strange churchyards . . . entirely detached from churches' in *The Uncommercial Traveller* (1861) and in his sordid description of the unmarked pauper's grave in *Bleak House* (1853), where bodies rose to the level of first-floor windows of nearby houses. However, the secular break with the Church that was prescribed by sanitary reformers created the psychic schism between the world of the dead and the possibility of an afterlife. In the removal of burials from churches, Christian ideals of resurrection had to be replaced by another form of return, a Gothic form of haunting which will be revisited later in this chapter.

As with previous underground associations, the labouring classes bore the heavier blame and consequences of improper burial. Unable to afford timely funerals, the poor often kept the dead bodies in their single-room lodgings in a domestication of the dead that often met with morbid results. In his Condition-of-England novel, *Alton Locke* (1850), Charles Kingsley descends to the slums, 'the wildernesses of Bermondsey', where the underground serves as the spatial convergence of the poor, the sewers and the dead:

> Downes pushed past . . . unlocked a door at the end of the passage, thrust me in, locked it again, and then rushed across the room in chase of two or three rats, who vanished into cracks and holes. And what a room . . . through the broad chinks of the floor shone up as it were ugly glaring eyes, staring at us. – They were the reflections of the rushlight in the sewer below. The stench was frightful – the air heavy with pestilence. The first breath I drew made my heart sink, and my stomach turn. But I forgot everything in the object which lay before me, as Downes tore a half-finished coat off three corpses laid side by side on the bare floor.[16]

In this claustrophobic descent, there is no distinction between the pestilence of the body and the pestilence of the sewers, mediated by the prevalence of rats that transgress yet connect these filthy realms. Indeed, Kingsley's exploration of social injustices not only reflects the insalubrious conditions of the poor, but the toxic relationship between the living and the dead, which one critic has described as being forged not by 'affection' but by 'infection'.[17] The ritual of kissing corpses was also highlighted as a dangerous threat in a further isolation of the dead body as a carrier of disease and a threat to the living. Although inadequate measures for the burial of the poor made poverty the culprit of contagion, reformist George Alfred Walker, in his sensational exposé *Gatherings from Graveyards* (1839), which appeared the same year as Thomas Carlyle's *Chartism*, warned of the larger social implications of improper interment:

> Let those who at present supinely look on and disregard the dangers threatening their poorer neighbours from the vast sources of disease, remember that

pestiferous exhalations arising from the numerous infecting centres of the metropolis, are no respecters of persons.[18]

Known as 'Graveyard Walker', he published detailed accounts of desecrated graves, dismembered bodies and the dangers of putrefaction, which, combined with the cholera outbreaks of 1831 and 1837, created a sensational stir and precipitated new regulations on the closure of burial grounds in the city. What Walker prescribed emphatically was the 'ENTIRE REMOVAL OF THE DEAD FROM THE PROMIXITY OF THE LIVING'.[19] However, in campaigning against intramural interment, Walker not only separated the body from the city, but also relegated the corpse to an abject matter to be disposed of in the same manner as excrement in the tide of sanitary reforms sweeping across the city.

The argument for the closure of burial grounds and the construction of extramural cemeteries was not a new one. Christopher Wren had recommended it after discovering massive graves under St Paul's Church in 1673, while France had already paved the way in the construction of the grand Cimetière du Père Lachaise in 1804 that was to become a model for garden cemeteries in the UK. However, England's hostility towards the country that 'killed the King and denied their God' delayed their urbanisation scheme until Walker's reports compelled Edwin Chadwick to extend his section on the dangers of decomposing bodies in his 1842 *Report* to a more comprehensive argument against ghastly unsanitary burial practices, exploitation of the poor and the 'multiform monopoly' of funeral homes.[20] Informed by the vision of builder John Claudius Loudon, Chadwick recommended 'garden-cemeteries' in the suburbs, transferring the aegis of burial practices from the Church to the government in a complete secularisation and rationalisation of the spaces for the dead. James Curl contends that Chadwick's plans were 'hygienic and essentially utilitarian' and notes that the burial reforms were viewed as 'antipathetic to the whole complex of sensibility that had developed from the sentimental and the picturesque, and could even be construed as unChristian, almost irreligious'.[21] Although Chadwick received much criticism from the public, the removal of Dickensian graveyards and Walker's overflowing cesspits were well underway with the construction of Kensal Green in 1832 and the construction of more cemeteries following the railway boom of the 1830s and 1840s. In an innovative merging of the two expanding 'industries', the first London necropolis railway opened in 1854, carrying funeral traffic from Waterloo to Brookwood Cemetery in Woking, Surrey.[22] An advertisement for the 'The London Necropolis' reveals a train speeding towards sylvan fields, but its first-, second-, and third-class single tickets for coffins reveal a more morbid preoccupation with the economic return on its silent passengers (Fig. 3.2). In response to the free market enterprise that overtook the city, *The Builder* reported in indignation:

> What a merciless, remorseless pursuit is that of moneymaking! How loath-some is the hollow show of reason with which the unseemly actual motive is glossed recklessly over . . . Let us eat, drink, and be merry, whoever may die. *Sauve qui peut.*[23]

By the time the Metropolitan Burial Acts 1852 took effect, ending all intramural burials and creating a national system of public cemeteries run by joint-stock companies, decentralisation and dispersal in the metaphorical and metaphysical sense had already taken root. The underground ceased to be a resting place, but a contested and rational-ised space, where hopes for resurrection were only available in the visual landscape of broken urns, angels and funereal ephemera that adorned the graves. No longer attached to the family home, the Church or God, the dead body became a free-floating, circulating signifier for the displacement of Victorian anxieties concerning death and the afterlife. The unwholesome graveyard was banished and new sanitised models of Victorian cemeteries emerged to ostensibly replace it; however, I argue that rather than *substituting* the old burial grounds, they were a Derridean *supplement* to the messiness of the experience of death and mourning, which returned in symbolic traces and Gothic absences in the urban imagination.

In the relegation of the dead to a mere corpse, exhumations became a common occurrence and the clearance of dead bodies a necessary fact of urban life. Dante Gabriel Rossetti's exhumation of Elizabeth Siddal from Highgate Cemetery in 1869 to retrieve his book of unpublished poetry was an infamous case in point, while Jeremy Bentham's desire to donate his body for dissection and public viewing demonstrated a utilitarian approach to dealing with corporeal remains. Meanwhile, graveyards were often cleared to build railways and sewers, leading to novelist Captain Marryat's observation that 'The sleepers of the railway are laid over sleepers in death', while the popularity of the music-hall song 'They're Moving Grandpa's Grave to Build a Sewer' revealed the sardonic humour with which these changes were received.[24] However, the late nineteenth century witnessed a further secularisation of death when cremation emerged as a possibility and a solution to burial problems, a radical proposal that overturned the sensibilities of the people and the clergy. The leading advocate, Sir Henry Thompson, was a surgeon and Nonconformist who formed the Cremation Society of England in 1875 and argued for a treatment of the dead that would be best for survivors at a time when funeral customs were 'an extravagant imposition'[25] for the poor, while overcrowding and pollution of rivers still persisted despite burial reforms. For Thompson, the answer was to expedite nature's processes with a little scientific assistance:

> Given a dead body, to resolve it into carbonic acid, water, and ammonia, and the mineral elements, rapidly, safely, and not unpleasantly ... To treat our dead after this fashion would return millions of capital without delay to the bosom of mother earth, who would give us back large returns at compound interest for the deposit.[26]

Here, the same argument that was used in the construction of the sewers was being recycled in the argument for cremation. The dead were relegated to waste, as the circulatory metaphor reasserted itself in the sanitary, scientific and social climate of the mid-nineteenth century. Despite the initial uproar surrounding cremation, it became legalised in 1884, and the first official cremation took place in 1885, followed by the opening of Golders Green Crematorium in 1902. Although the number of cremations grew steadily throughout the end of the nineteenth century, it did not signal the disappearance of the underground in the funereal practices for the dead. Before ashes became commonly scattered, they were usually placed in urns or caskets that were then buried, attesting to the persistent need for a symbolic subterranean space through which the soul can pass. The frontispiece from William Tegg's *The Last Act* (1876) demonstrates this tension as the cremation rite is celebrated under the auspices of a clergyman in an odd combination of religious and secular traditions. Aboveground, mourners gather to watch a coffin being lowered, but underground, the furnace operator prepares to perfunctorily reduce it to cinders. As James Curl notes, the failure to see a coffin lowered was like a 'coitus interruptus' or an 'unlived climax'.[27] In the consummation of the act, there was still a greater emphasis placed on the idea of passage, the transition from the physical to the metaphysical, as well as the importance of ritual in honouring the dead.

Geographies of the Dead

'Mourir, à Londres, c'est être bien mort!'
  Henry James, *The Altar of the Dead* (1895)

The places and spaces of the dead always maintained a deep connection with time, from their basis in antiquity to their commemoration of the past and as a repository for memory. In this form of revival or

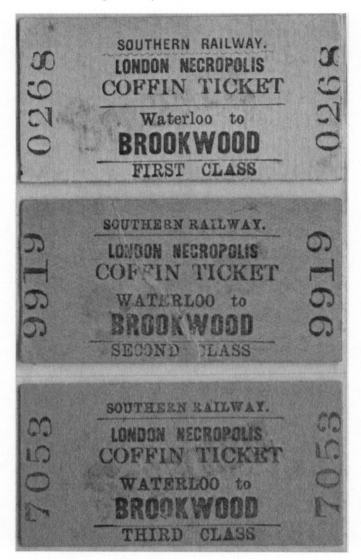

Figure 3.2   First, second, and third class one-way coffin tickets from Waterloo to Brookwood Cemetery (1855). Reproduced with the permission of Birmingham Libraries & Archives.

return, a new psychogeography of the dead begins to emerge against the backdrop of the centrifugal movement of graves from the urban centre to the outer periphery. As most of the cemeteries, from Highgate and Abney Park Cemeteries in the North to the Norwood and Nunhead Cemeteries in the South encircled the city and created new borders to the expanding metropolis, a new cartography of death emerged that depicted the outer limits of cemeteries as heaven and the inner city, a living hell. Furthermore, distinct subterranean spaces like wells, vaults and catacombs became new epicentres or 'auras' of the dead, as the city itself became a haunting and haunted labyrinth of streets teeming with spectres of the past, present and even future. As Dickens reflects in the 'City of Absent' in *The Uncommercial Traveller* (1860):

> . . . it was a solemn consideration what enormous hosts of the dead belong to one great city . . . if they were raised while the living slept, there would not be the space of a pin's point in all the streets and ways for the living to come into.[28]

In the overcrowded city, where death rates were commensurate with the explosive population growth, the subterranean world of the dead was evoked in ghostly terms as spirits that emerged from the underground to consort with the living. French sociologist Jean Fourastié has remarked that

> when the cemetery was to be found in the centre of the village, that is to say, in and around the church, death and its rituals were to be found at the centre of life. The expulsion of the dead beyond the boundary of the village preceded in fact the expulsion of the dead from our everyday life.[29]

However, I argue that the very separation from the church and the village did not lead to an 'expulsion', but an 'explosion' of the dead in the Victorian urban landscape. In the construction of new necropoli in the outskirts, even idyllic suburbs were not immune from spectral interference, while anxieties about death persisted in haunting visions and visitations in the Lefebvrian urban interstices produced by the living and the dead.

It is interesting to compare this haunting in contrast to Paris's appropriation of the dead, as it throws into relief the ways in which London's circumvention of death actually led to its own confrontation with Gothic revenants that came to haunt the city. Although Paris also built cemeteries outside the city walls, there were spaces of death within the city centre that allowed for a more direct confrontation with, and a closer affinity to, the ways of dying and being buried. Laman Blanchard observed in 1842 that the Parisian man of wealth possessed a town house, a country house, a box at the Opera and a tomb in Père Lachaise.[30] In the alignment of the tomb with private, domestic and social spheres, the cemetery came to be accepted as a part of everyday life. Moreover, in 1784, the government closed down one of the largest cemeteries in Paris, Cimetière des Innocents, in an effort to sweep away the overflowing graveyards and the surrounding *charniers* (charnel houses) that were seen as a source of contamination to the adjacent outdoor food and meat market, Les Halles. The bones of nearly six million Parisians were transferred to the Catacombes in the centre of the city, which ultimately came to symbolise the domestication of the dead and the incorporation of the underground space into city life. Like the sewer tours, walks through the subterranean corridors of skulls and bones gained popularity in the mid-nineteenth century, advertising to the bourgeois viewer that human ingenuity had cleared the air above and reordered the world below. Such direct experience with spaces of death emerged in literary representations as a locus of subversion, from Alexandre Dumas's *The Mohicans of Paris* (1864), where secret societies congregate in the labyrinthine passageways, to Elie Berthet's novel *Les Catacombes de Paris* (1854), which recreates the underground as a space of revolution.[31] The fact that the Catacombes were constructed within the city walls played a crucial role in posing a radical challenge to the state whose seat was also centralised within the capital. Furthermore, other spaces of death, in particular the morgue, also became a socially produced space of fascination and fear as corpses were revealed to the public in another exposure of the dead to the living. Even Charles Dickens admitted, 'Whenever I am in Paris, I am dragged by invisible forces to the Morgue.'[32] However, rather than a site of subversion, the morgue was reappropriated by institutional forces as a means of surveillance and a warning to those involved in underground criminal acts. In his analysis of the morgue as panoptican, Alan Mitchell suggests that while the morgue became a tourist attraction, it was also 'an essential agency for law enforcement and the detection of criminals' and 'the shrine of positivism . . . inseparable from the growing prestige of nineteenth-century science'.[33] Poised between the private and the public realms, the morgue begins to resemble another heterotopia, a 'simultaneously mythic and real contestation of the space', where crowds gather to witness the thrill and the horror of the spectacle.[34] Through such direct visual displays, death and its association with the underground came to be articulated in real and concrete terms, integrating the discourse of death into the very fabric of the Parisian urban landscape.

In contrast, London's incorporation, or rather ex-appropriation, of the dead was marked by ghostly resurrections that came to dominate the haunted city in a submersion of the city into the underworld. Dickens continuously evokes these otherworldly dimensions in such striking descriptions as this pestiferous burial ground for Nemo in *Bleak House*, which was written and published during the time of the burial debates:

With houses looking on, on every side, save where a reeking little tunnel of a court gives access to the iron gate . . . here they lower our dear brother down a foot or two, here sow him in corruption, to be raised in corruption: an avenging ghost at many a sick-bedside, a shameful testimony to future ages how civilization and barbarism walked this boastful island together.[35]

Here, homes and graves, villainy and virtue, the past and present all converge in the burial ground, emphasising the contradictions and dislocations inherent in the underground space. In a proselytising tone, Dickens raises the spectre of retribution against the inadequate burial measures for the poor, as the graveyard comes to symbolise the physical and moral deterioration of society. There was more psychic fragmentation in the urban landscape when buried bodies had to be moved to make way for competing underground technologies, such as the railway and the sewer. In 1865, an estimated 8,000 bodies at St Pancras Churchyard had to be moved to accommodate the construction of the Midland Railway. Unlike Paris's stylised removal of bones to the Catacombes, London's clearance was more haphazard and disjointed, leaving visual traces of death everywhere on the surface of the city. As historian Simon Bradley observes:

Trial diggings for the work had been mismanaged. The Vicar of St. Pancras noted skulls and thigh-bones scattered heedlessly about, and complained to the Bishop of London, who prevailed on the Home Secretary to stop it . . .[36]

Thomas Hardy, who supervised and witnessed the excavations at St Pancras, sardonically relays his experiences in his poems, most notably in 'In the Cemetery' (1911), which envisages mourners 'squabbling' over mistaken identities in an upturned graveyard:

But all their children were laid therein
At different times, like sprats in a tin.
'And then the main drain had to cross,
And we moved the lost some nights ago,
And packed them away in the general foss
With hundreds more. But their folks don't know,
And as well cry over a new-laid drain
As anything else, to ease your pain!'[37]

The general 'foss' of urban exhumations reveals the anonymity and the undifferentiated spaces of burial where the body no longer signified in the face of modern burial practices. Although the bones were moved to peaceful cemeteries in the suburbs, the return to nature did not offer complete consolation, as the decline of religion also contributed to a sense of emptiness in the underground space. Spatially, this crisis of faith takes form in the image of wells in literary representation that sought to substitute and supplement the experience of death in social and psychological terms. From the horror of the bottomless well that Nell peers into in *The Old Curiosity Shop* and the well that stores bodies and secrets in Mary Elizabeth Braddon's *Lady Audley's Secret* (1862) to the longing for spiritual and corporeal unity in Radclyffe Hall's *Well of Loneliness* (1928), the hollow and dry well becomes symbolic of the void and emptiness in death, constantly in tension with a vision of pristine burial grounds where nature can follow the cyclical pattern of birth, death and regeneration.

The tranquil suburban cemeteries were utopian by nature and design, but they also offered more than a resting place for the dead. John Claudius Loudon, the key advocate for garden landscaping, argued that 'botanical riches' would 'improve morals' and 'cultivate the intellect' as well as serve as 'historical records' in his influential work on the significance of architecture in national cemeteries.[38] Furthermore, *A Report on a General Scheme for Extramural Sepulture* (1880) elaborated that 'national sepulture is a part, and a most important part, of national religion', further emphasising the role of the cemetery's architecture in the institutional appropriation of the mourning process.[39] The cemetery became a moral imperative and the embodiment of peace afforded to the dead and the survivors during an incredibly disruptive age of industrialisation, urbanisation and social change. As G. K. Chesterton muses in *The Rolling English Road* (1914):

> . . . to see undrugged in evening light the decent inn of death;
> For there is good news yet to hear and fine things to be seen,
> Before we go to Paradise by way of Kensal Green.[40]

For the Victorians, the cemetery preserved a vision and a version of death that transferred their longing for an imagined afterlife to an organic landscape of history and memory. In many of the grand cemeteries, from Kensal Green to Highgate, weeping trees, hardy cedars and clinging ivy commingled with broken columns, towering obelisks and marble angels in a Greek and Egyptian revival that sought to produce an eternal resting ground, yet a space of otherness separate from this world. As Gothic or pseudo-Gothic architecture also became an important feature of new cemeteries, new fantastical images permeated the Victorian consciousness in a new geography of the living and the dead.

If the outlying cemeteries represented heaven, the centre of the city alternatively became a modern version of hell. Steeped in the Dantean tradition of the *Inferno* and Milton's *Paradise Lost*, death and damnation were initially perceived on a vertical axis as a descent into Hades or the lower depths. However, the image of hell also transformed into a horizontalised and secularised version of a 'hell on earth', haunted by the living dead in Victorian literary representations. Theologian Frederick Denison Maurice, a friend of Tennyson, remarked in his ontological study on the metaphysics of being, 'What is Perdition but a loss? . . . real Hell was the absence of God from the human soul.'[41] As science, technology and industry began to erode the fundamentals of Christian beliefs in God, the ability to locate hell underground was a tenuous effort at best. Rather, the language of the infernal underworld came to suffuse the metaphoric descriptions of the city, as rapid urbanisation cast its dark shadows into the lives of its inhabitants. Visually, John Martin's painting *The Last Judgment* (1853) gives a sense of the fusion between hell and industry as a railway train descends into a hell-like ravine, while God and the angels look on benevolently from on high. This example of the apocalyptic sublime continued to forge the long-held relations between the destructive power of technology and the forces of evil. A more horizontal representation of the city as hell is readily apparent in Gustave Doré's illustrations for Jerrold's *London* (1872), which portray alienated figures huddled in masses near docks, brothels and opium dens, exemplifying another geography of social, if not biological, death. In particular, Doré's 'The Bull's-Eye' (1872) illuminates, in this case with a police searchlight, how the poor and the destitute in a particular area of the East End represents hell in all of its poverty and moral turpitude (Fig. 3.3). Rather than casting its light on the importance of purity and self-improvement as other images of police lanterns have done, this depiction leaves little room for possible redress or escape from the underworld of poverty. Echoing the sentiments of social reformers, Condition-of-England writers such as Charles Kingsley, William Booth and Elizabeth Gaskell also applied the attributes of hell to the social conditions of the working classes. George Gissing was particularly prolific in his use of this metaphor, from *Workers in the Dawn* (1880) to *The Nether World* (1889). The latter recreates hell as an East End enclave where people are trapped in 'the city of the damned':

> Over the pest-stricken regions of East London, sweltering in sunshine which served only to reveal the intimacies of abomination; across miles of a city of the damned, such as thought never conceived before this age of ours; above streets swarming with a nameless populace, cruelly exposed by the unwonted light of heaven . . . the train made its way at length beyond the utmost limits of dread, and entered upon a land of level meadows.[42]

Again, the intimate connection between trains and death is reasserted, but what is more interesting is the parallel between the city and Dante's rings of hell. Rather than concentric circles funnelling downward to the lower depths of the inferno, Gissing's circles spiral outwards from the centre of the city in a horizontal ripple, connecting east London with the lowest depths of depravity. In this secularisation of hell, the underworld literally surfaces in the image of the social abyss, without any potential for salvation or grace.

The liminality of hell shifts from the social realm to a more potent psychological space as the urban streets and rivers overflow with the dead and the undead in a new ghostly appropriation of the city. Matthew Arnold has already suggested the division between surface and depth to represent the psychic layers of the urban consciousness in his well-known verse, 'The Buried Life' (1852), in which he expresses the duality of everyday existence in the harrowing life of the city:

> But often, in the world's most crowded streets,
> But often, in the din of strife,
> There rises an unspeakable desire
> After the knowledge of our buried life . . .[43]

The idea of a hidden side amidst the crowds of the metropolis immediately evokes the shadowy figure of the *flâneur*, who is also caught between the split notion of being a part of, yet detached from, the social life of the crowd. The figure of the *flâneur* then transposes himself as a melancholic wanderer in another poem, James Thomson's *The City of Dreadful Night* (1879), as a haunted figure and literally, the walking dead. In this transformation, the *flâneur* becomes a flattened figure, a dejected by-product of urban modernity who haunts the city in search of visual exchange; however, his gaze is never returned. The poem was first published in the secularist *National Reformer* and paints a barren landscape where a lone walker is adrift amongst the ruins of a city, accosted by the derelict, dehumanised faces of modernity. As a figure of an atheist, he finds no substitute for the spiritual emptiness within, and as critic Curtis Dahl comments, Thomson's poem 'expresses an unrelieved and hopeless pessimism deeper even than sometimes posed by the gloominess of Swinburne'.[44] The city becomes a labyrinth embedded in such underground imagery as 'gulfs' and 'abysses', where 'mansions [are] dark and still as tombs' and 'lanes are black as subterranean layers'.[45] In this spiritual wasteland, the individual is split from himself and unable to maintain a holistic vision of the world:

> As I came through the desert thus it was,
> As I came through the desert: I was twain,
> Two selves distinct that cannot join again.[46]

Figure 3.3   Gustave Doré *'The Bull's-Eye'* (1872). Wood engraving. © Museum of London.

Echoing the sense of doubling so manifest in Victorian urban landscapes, Thomson presents irreconcilable identities that haunt the deadened streets, embodying the ephemeral, contingent nature of the *flâneur*. In many ways, Thomson's morbid *flâneur* then comes to represent the purgatorial state of so many individuals trapped in the wasteland of modernity, reinforcing the recurring underground theme that hell is indeed a city on earth.

Resurrection, Resurrectionists and the Revenant

It is only the Darknesse that can give trew Forme to our Work and trew Perspective to our Fabrick, for there is no Light without Darknesse and no Substance without Shaddowe.

Peter Ackroyd, *Hawksmoor* (1985)

As the topography of the city transformed to resemble the underground space of the dead, literature also reflected different forms of resurrection that revealed the potential of the spirit, the psyche and the unconscious to spill onto the surface of the city. Despite the decline of religious rites attending burials and the elimination of burial grounds from the city centre, Victorians persisted in looking for ways to make the body signify, whether through material commemorations or Derridean hauntings, advancing what Thomas Laqueur defines as a 'pluralism of death'.[47] Perhaps no other author engaged with the anxieties of death and the history of Victorian funereal practices as prolifically as Charles Dickens. From Mr Mould in *Martin Chuzzlewit* (1844) to Mr Omer in *David Copperfield* (1850), undertakers were well represented to handle the body count in his novels. John Ruskin argued that the death rate in *Bleak House* was 'a representative average of the statistics of civilian mortality in the centre of London', while T. S. Eliot remarked that Dickens had 'a love for death'.[48] Many contemporary critics have engaged with this fixation, most notably Andrew Sanders in his comprehensive survey *Charles Dickens Resurrectionist* (1982), which meticulously charts the mortality rate in his works, emphasising the shifting depictions of death and the subsequent possibility for social resurrection and moral restitution. However, what I wish to focus on specifically are Dickensian landscapes that are haunted by the *spectral*, or what Derrida has described as 'neither dead nor alive, it is dead and alive at the same time'.[49] The moments where meaning slips between the ontological gaps between the living and the dead are crucial markers of modernity and reveal the inheritance Derrida terms 'hauntology'. As Julian Wolfreys notes in his study of the Victorian Gothic, 'spectrality resists conceptualization and one cannot form a coherent theory of the spectral without that which is spectral having always already exceeded any definition'.[50] As an uncontainable force in modernity, the text is haunted by the writer, the period in which it is written, as well as by the characters who exceed their characterisations and bleed across the text in a myriad of spectral guises. Thus, the *revenant*, or the one 'who only comes in coming back', is an intervention that appears to compensate for the declining significance of death in a resuscitation of forms of being that refuses to die.[51] In these haunted and haunting structures, ghosts, doubling and the Freudian 'uncanny' become a repetitive motif that deals with the trauma of death in a continuous 'recall to life' that substitutes and supplements the act of mourning. As the physical underground space no longer promises a passage to eternal salvation, 'undergroundness' in spectral and ghostlike manifestations of memory and the unconscious become the predominant mode of apprehending a form of a spiritual afterlife in the modern city.

One of Dickens's earlier works that reveals his preoccupation with death is *The Old Curiosity Shop* (1841), which, on the surface, narrates a tale of one girl's search for an eternal resting place, but subtextually dislocates itself from this linearity in its multiple points of spectral interference. In his introduction, Norman Page notes the spatio-temporal reversal in Nell's journey across the map of England against the passage of history running backwards:

> For the contemporary industrial world, with its nightmarish scenes of wretchedness and pollution and fires that burn fiercely and ceaselessly as hell fire, is left behind, and the end of the journey is a pre-industrial rural community.[52]

Despite this regressive interpretation of her journey from the fiendish industrial city to a pristine place of rest, her urban past constantly punctuates the peaceful countryside through ghostly interferences that haunt the narrative. In particular, the material memory of the old curiosity shop returns with its deathly paraphernalia of 'suits of mail standing like ghosts in armour here and there, fantastic carvings brought from monkish cloisters . . . strange furniture that might have been designed in dreams'.[53] In the countryside, Nell must confront these spectres again, in the form of glass-eyed waxworks resembling corpses in her room, to the graveyard with its crumbling ruins and ghostly carvings where she chooses to be buried. The underground as a repository for memory thus resurfaces in objects and things that become a projection of death and a form of material mourning. Nell's deep affection for the churchyard echoes the legacy of Romanticism, but this too is deflected by an uncanny encounter with a woman who comes to the graveyard to mourn for her deceased husband. Resembling Nell's own journey, the woman's visit to the cemetery also reverses time to a place that she associates with another life, as she remembers it with her deceased husband. Nell observes the woman whose mourning resurrects her younger self, along with a ghostly resuscitation of her imagined dead self:

> And now that five-and-fifty years were gone, she spoke of the dead man as if he had been her son or grandson with a kind of pity for his youth . . . and yet

she spoke about him as her husband too, and thinking of herself in connexion with him, as she used to be and not as she was now, talked of their meeting in another world as if he were dead but yesterday and she, *separated from her former self*, were thinking of the happiness of that comely girl who seemed to have died with him.[54]

Like this multivalent figure who is of this world and yet not, Nell's subjectivity is constantly split through multiple selfhoods, radically destabilising the world between the past and the present, living and the dead. In a further blurring of these subjective and temporal boundaries, the woman at the grave then ominously states, 'Death doesn't change us more than life, my dear.'[55] This constancy is visually reinforced in the almost identical illustrations by George Cattermole of Nell lying asleep at the beginning of the narrative and of her 'at rest' near the closing chapter, which arrests time in a way that makes life and death indistinguishable. The narrator's comment that 'death is sleep . . . Lay death and sleep down, side by side, and say who shall find the two akin?' questions the entire basis of the text and the ghostly quality of Nell's wanderings.[56] In this substitution and supplementation, or what Derrida terms repetition with *différance*, it can be argued that the entire text hinges between the two worlds of the living and the dead, and that it is impossible to separate the real from the unreal. Nell has been haunting the text all along.

The ambiguity between the living and the dead is no less pronounced in Dickens's *Christmas Books* (1844–8), which not only deal with the theme of revenance, but also follow a recurring temporal pattern of publication: a tale of return that returns each year. In his 1874 biography of Dickens, John Forster recalled that Dickens 'had something of a hankering' for ghosts, and while the *Christmas Books* forged the cultural association of ghosts and the holidays, they also expressed the Freudian unconscious landscape of grief and loss.[57] Although contemporary psychoanalysis has linked the experience of trauma with repetition and memory, the sense of loss is also a haunting that disrupts the sense of linear or progressive time. Although *A Christmas Carol* (1844) mirrors *The Old Curiosity Shop* in its treatment of a life frozen in time, 'The Haunted Man' (1848) presents a character that wishes to erase time in order to put an end to the repetition of painful memories. As a professor of chemistry, Redlaw already lives a buried life in his underground 'vault-like dwelling', where flickering gaslight casts shadows of memory against the hard instruments of scientific rationalism. However, it is the unquantifiable, the unspeakable stuff of his subterranean, psychological existence that paralyses his sensibilities. As the text opens with the laconic utterance, 'the dread word GHOST, recalls me', the apparition and the word that signifies it can only be articulated through a form of return or 'recall' that invariably haunts his psyche.[58] However, in this case, it is the *absence* of repetition that is at the centre of the tragedy, as Redlaw begs the ghost, who eerily resembles him, to eradicate the ghosts and memories of his past. What ensues is more trauma and cruelty, whereby action is disassociated from memory or moral imperative. Like a contagion, everyone with whom he comes in contact also loses the very humanising act of remembering, fulfilling his wish but not without the unintended consequences of unrelenting egoism and heartlessness. When Redlaw begs the ghost to ironically reverse the reversal of memory, what is reinstated is not the institution of Victorian norms, but social and psychological abnorms; indeed, he no longer desires to be 'disghosted', as repetition and memory allow for the phenomenological apprehension of reality and in a Dickensian world, a possibility of moral redress. Thus, science and spectrality stand side by side, if not dialectically, as the underworld of ghosts humanise the world of science and progress in the urban psyche.

The concept of revenance becomes further complicated in the context of medical discourse, especially in the furore and debate regarding 'bodysnatchers' or 'resurrection-men', who profited from violating graves at night and selling the corpses to researchers for the purposes of dissection. Historically, it was a phenomenon that began in the late eighteenth century, and the two different terms for these grave robbers reveal the dual-edged role they played in the creation of a new social and cultural attitude towards death and burials.[59] 'Bodysnatchers', connoting a transgression or stealing, becomes interchangeable with 'resurrectionists', a religious term of spiritual renewal and rebirth, which then becomes reappropriated for more scientific and economic purposes in a new commoditisation of the dead body. The ascendance of Victorian middle-class values that embraced the sanctity of the grave raised more anxieties about this nocturnal trade, especially as the desire for the body to remain intact and commemorated as part of the living was a sacred belief immortalised in such poems from William Wordsworth's 'We Are Seven' (1798) to Matthew Arnold's elegy 'Geist's Grave' (1881).[60] However, in a momentous intervention by the government, parliament passed an Act for Regulating Schools of Anatomy in 1832 which not only legalised the act of disinterment, but enlarged the supply of bodies for dissection by allowing medical schools to obtain bodies not only of criminals, but also those of the poor who had not prearranged for their own burials. According to Ruth Richardson, the act merely transferred the stigma of punishment and criminality to poverty:

The political strategy of the Anatomy Act forced the poor to provide for themselves or face the consequences. Dissection after death became one of the darker elements in the terrible stigma of the pauper's funeral, and one of the props with which the fear of the workhouse was supported. So potent was the fear of 'the House' that people were induced to starve, to emigrate, to turn to prostitution, even to commit suicide, rather than enter workhouse portals.[61]

To be denied a proper burial was feared, but to be chosen as a subject of dissection was an abominable, unspeakable indignity that the working classes were now forced to consider. This fear manifested itself in the proliferation of corrupt burial clubs, captured in works like George Gissing's *The Nether World* (1889), which took advantage of the meagre incomes set aside by the working classes to afford a proper burial. The necessity of a proper burial and ritual is articulated by Mr Mould in *Martin Chuzzlewit* (1844) who explains:

> Why do people spend more money ... upon a death ... than upon a birth? ... I'll tell you why it is. It's because the laying out of money with a well-conducted establishment, where the thing is performed upon the very best scale, binds the broken heart, and sheds balm upon the wounded spirit.[62]

Again, the powerful association between underground interment and a safe passage to the next life that distinguished a 'good' death from a 'bad' one was a fundamental belief that could not be compromised in the Victorian imagination.

The anxieties surrounding graves, burial, disinterment and dissection reflect the growing concerns of an era that was grappling with the potential emptiness of death and the need to hold onto some hope for spiritual sustenance. In the narratives emerging from the burial crisis, there is a splitting of consciousness, a new awareness of mortality and a heightened consciousness of terror. Dickens, again, engaged with these themes of mortality most directly in *A Tale of Two Cities* (1859), which was published some twenty years after the Anatomy Act. Dickens himself was exposed to the parliamentary process while working for his uncle, Charles Barrow, on *Mirror of the Parliament* and frequently uses the figure of the resurrectionist in his later works, from Gaffer Hexam and Rogue Riderhood in *Our Mutual Friend* (1865) to Durdles in *The Mystery of Edwin Drood* (1870). In *A Tale of Two Cities*, the overarching motif of bodies 'recalled to life' is anchored materially by Jerry Cruncher's underground trade, which is obliquely referred to as 'an unlawful occupation of an infamous description'.[63] His circumlocutions and references to 'fishing expeditions' add humour to a humourless trade, but also allude to the unspeakable nature of his covert operations, as if the very articulation of the act would destroy the delicate foundations of a collective consciousness already divided between two cities. As critic Albert Hutter suggests, while Cruncher's comical grave-robbing scenes highlight Dickens's nihilistic break with Christian doctrines of resurrection, the death of Sydney Carton represents the 'elevated type of Christ [who] both literally and figuratively, stands for the idealized and religious concept of "Resurrection"'.[64] As Carton ascends the guillotine, he reinforces his Christ-like role as he utters his final words: 'I am the Resurrection and the life, saith the Lord: he that believeth in me, though he were dead, yet shall he live: and whosoever liveth and believeth in me shall never die.'[65] However, I would argue that those are *not* his final words and that Carton's death cannot be simply reduced or contained in the religious imagery or an affirmation of a potential afterlife. Rather, his final words are transferred and uttered by his ghostly double who is about to face the same fate. The final words of the woman to whom Carton secretly confided before he died reveal a more secular nuance to his final heroic utterance:

> I see a beautiful city and a brilliant people rising from the abyss, and, in their struggles to be truly free, in their triumphs and defeats, through long long years to come, I see the evil of this time and of the previous time of which this is the natural birth, gradually making expiation for itself and wearing out . . . It is a far far better thing that I do, than I have ever done; it is a far, far better rest that I go to than I have ever known.[66]

In this revolutionary imagery of freedom and regeneration, a resurrected voice echoes the struggles of the 'abyss' and suggests that the afterlife of Carton will haunt generations to come, in a repetitive recall to life and recall to democracy. In Dickens, the mistaken 'Carton' who dies for his silent cause thus destabilises the meaning of death and renewal, religion and secularism, repression and liberty in a textual embedding of multiple signification. Like the language of death and the afterlife, Dickens blurs the spatial, temporal and linguistic divisions between the biblical utterance and the unspoken, unseen potential of a metaphorical and metaphysical resuscitation.

The limits of language in the discourse of death and resurrection is further complicated in the unconscious realm of Robert Louis Stevenson's Gothic short story 'The Body Snatcher' (1884), in which the nocturnal exhumation of dead bodies awakens 'terrors of the conscience'.[67] Touching upon the notorious Burke and Hare trial of 1828, where two resurrection-men turned to murder in order to supplement their supply of bodies to medical institutions, Stevenson's short story also relies on the cold-blooded murder of a man whose body is given to dissection.[68] Rather than for profit, however, the main grave robber, Fettes, kills out of malice in the ultimate transgression of religious, moral and psychological boundaries. Although the assassins try to forget their heinous deed, the crime returns to haunt them one night when the body, after it had been sold and dissected, subsequently returns in the body sack of a freshly disinterred body:

> A nameless dread was swathed, like a wet sheet, about the body, and tightened the white skip upon the face of Fettes; a fear that was meaningless, a horror of what could not be, kept mounting in his brain . . . The light fell very clear upon the dark, well-moulded features and smooth-shaven cheeks of a too familiar countenance, often beheld in dreams by both of these young men. A wild yell rang up into the night; each leaped from his own side into the roadway; the lamp fell, broke, and was extinguished . . .[69]

This 'nameless' horror reflects the Kristevan terror that cannot be uttered, a haunting that can only be defined by an absence or a break with the symbolic order. Like the preverbal realm of the Lacanian mirror stage, there is an encounter with oneself and the 'other' in a subconscious space *a priori* language that can only be expressed as haunting. In his evocation of the Gothic, James Kincaid further reinforces this ontological fissure:

> Consider the gothic, it's always got to reach towards what cannot be spoken; if all can be spoken, then there is no gothic . . . the gothic has to alert us of agencies we cannot explain. We cannot explain them because they lie outside the realm of the explicable, outside of language. It's not just that we don't know enough; knowledge is not the issue. If the gothic can be explained, it is no longer gothic.[70]

In the discourse of death, the Victorian corpse appears in a multiplicity of guises, reflecting the ambivalence towards the body in the burial practices of modernity. The Gothic tradition was driven by this very conflict between nature and science, visible and the invisible, sacred and the profane. In the unspeakable acts that defied some of the most sacrosanct human beliefs in God and the afterlife, the underground became symbolic of spiritual displacement and psychological upheaval. As Terry Castle remarks, 'By the end of the nineteenth century, ghosts had disappeared from everyday life, but . . . human experience had become more ghost-ridden than ever.'[71] In the separation of the corpse from the coffin, the churchyard, the city centre and other containers of its potential transition into the afterlife, the body's *absence* signalled not a religious resurrection, but a metaphorical, spectral return to the present in the Gothic haunting of the Victorian text and the imagination.

Feminine Resurrections and Spectral Dispossessions

> . . . the death of a beautiful woman is, unquestionably, the most poetical topic in the world.
>
> Edgar Allen Poe, *The Philosophy of Composition* (1846)

Although resurrections of men often grappled with the questions of science and spiritualism, religion and existentialism, the revivification of women resided primarily in sensational fiction that dealt with such underground topics as female sexuality, duplicity and even murder. One of the most pervasive motifs to emerge in Victorian Gothic literature is the female ghostly figure that transgressed physical, social and psychic boundaries in her ethereal revenance. Near a graveyard, over a tomb or in a reflection against a windowpane, the image of a haunted woman penetrated the domestic sphere in a literal and symbolic form of the *unheimlich*, or the unhomely. In his description of the feminine underworld, David Pike notes that the modern necropolis

> played on the attributes of an organic underground steeped in the feminine . . . the rest and quiet of death; escape from the superficies of earthly concerns; safety from the authorities and the persecutions of the world above; the physical shelter that caves have provided from time immemorial.[72]

Such poetical descriptions are echoed in Elisabeth Bronfen's study in which she argues that cultural constructions of women and beauty ultimately construed their death as a profoundly beautiful moment, captured in visual culture throughout the centuries. She specifically locates the roots of this aesthetic to Jurij Lotman's cultural myths of femininity and death in the interchangeability of the terms 'the grave', 'a house' and 'a woman' in the representation of enclosed spaces:

> The lack of boundaries between concepts such as womb, tomb, home, is traditionally linked to the analogy between earth and mother, and with it, that of death and birth, or death-conception and birth-resurrection. Death is here conceptualized as a return to a symbolic unity, to the peace before the difference and tension of life, to the protective enclosure before individuation and culturation.[73]

However, a woman who refuses to remain in the grave suggests rupture, ambivalence and a threat to the natural order of life and the permanence of death. As Victorian spaces of the dead were unable to maintain 'symbolic unity' in face of dramatic urbanisation, the image of a woman's death also conceded to a more sinister and uncontainable representation of otherness. Many of these resurrectionist tales take place within the home, as many authors, from Catherine Crowe and Mary Elizabeth

Braddon to Vernon Lee and Margaret Oliphant deployed the Gothic tradition to deflect female issues and concerns through this medium. Although this sections focuses primarily on Braddon, as her work links spectrality most tangibly with the underground space, many of these authors also used the supernatural to project all that was socially and psychologically repressed in the Victorian female psyche, from women's right to property to the expression of feminine sexuality. In ghostly repetitions and spectral guises, the dead female figure created new geographies of desire, beauty and madness in the haunting manifestations of her underground selves.

Key conceptual frameworks govern the representations of Victorian women's subterranean, often subversive, existence. In *Civilization and Its Discontents*, Freud configures the relationship between *eros* (love, life, unity) and *thanatos* (death, destruction, violence) as diametrically opposed yet irrevocably intertwined in the powerful combination of libidinal impulses.[74] Furthermore, Philippe Ariès observes that as death was removed from social life in European culture, it also became the source of fascination and fantasy.[75] The love for death prevalent in eighteenth-century eroticism and representations of necrophilia continued into the nineteenth century but with more emphasis on the uncontainability of women's sexuality. Although many of these ghostly encounters occur in the countryside or beyond London's city walls, they always remain linked to the city in the way they threaten to encroach upon urban spaces of rationalism and order. Women's deaths, their ghostly reincarnation and their attending madness are often depicted in the periphery of the city, but their empty graves often come back to haunt the city and the masculine order with a vengeance. Such morbid eroticism appears in its ghostly incarnation most vividly in *Wuthering Heights* (1847), in which Catherine Earnshaw-Linton is continuously resuscitated from her grave by her lover, Heathcliff, and her servant, Nelly Dean. Representing *thanatos* in its most destructive form, Heathcliff, who himself disappears into the city and is resurrected, returns to Wuthering Heights to reconnect with the deceased Catherine. Invoking her physically and spiritually, he refuses to let the dead remain underground, exhuming Catherine's coffin and proclaiming his desire to merge with her in the grave. Meanwhile, Nelly Dean constantly resurrects her textually through her narrativising of the past to Lockwood, a guest from London who inadvertently becomes entangled in the ghostly re-enactment of their love. In this double revival, Catherine can only appear as a liminal figure, an unburied ghost, whose traces linger like her signature scratched onto the window ledge or her diary that remains the sole evidence of her real voice. In a continuous doubling, her daughter Cathy also embodies her revenance as she too is trapped within the confines of Wuthering Heights, which Lockwood appropriately likens to 'being buried alive'.[76] If Heathcliff, in part, suffers from what Freud terms 'melancholia' in his inability to find a suitable substitute for his lost object, Catherine then prolongs this state in her tenuous refusal to accept death without Heathcliff.[77] At her deathbed, she recalls her childhood of playing 'among the graves', as she feverishly calls out to Heathcliff, 'I'll keep you . . . they may bury me twelve feet deep, and throw the church down over me; but I won't rest till you are with me.'[78] Thus, both Heathcliff and Catherine are both caught up in the macabre dance between desire and death, the former biologically alive but spiritually defunct, and the latter biologically dead but spiritually alive. Ultimately, Heathcliff accepts her death upon exhuming her coffin and seeing the sight of her dead (but not decomposed) body. However, before he reburies Catherine, he leaves the side of her coffin unhinged in a final act that leaves a loophole for her continual revenance. Although they are ultimately buried together, there is still a symbolic crack in the underground space that refuses to be hermetically sealed. In this geography of eroticism and necrophilia, the desire to be a part of another's dust in the womb/tomb of the earth connects the world of the living and the dead in a continuous haunting and resurrection of the female body.

When the theme of sexuality and death is taken to a dangerous extreme, female revenance takes a more threatening and violent turn, most notably in Sheridan LeFanu's Gothic short story, 'Carmilla' (1872). Although Bram Stoker's *Dracula*, which was inspired by LeFanu's work, also treats the theme of uncontrolled female sexuality, 'Carmilla' intensifies it through a lesbian lens, through which the young narrator, Laura, is sexually awakened by the seductive advances of the beautiful vampire, Carmilla. Unlike her spectral predecessors, Carmilla represents the world of the undead in a physical sense, as a body that is caught between two somatic states. The buried, dormant body re-emerges in the daytime, penetrating young female bodies and relying on their blood for their survival, a resuscitation which Bronfen notes is entirely antithetical to the notion of a religious resurrection:

> In a cultural sense the vampire's false death is a serious falsification of Christian notions of death as the sleep before Judgement Day. The empty grave of the vampire, with its permeable plate, suggests that these bodies are not waiting for any teleologically oriented resurrection but, based on a cyclic notion of return, reappear prematurely in the world of the living, with their bodies preserved whole.[79]

In the story, the underground in its permeable state allows for a vampiric reawakening of Carmilla, who is the embodiment of Countess

Mircalla (an anagram of her name), a vampire who has preyed on young girls for centuries. Her 'amphibious existence' passes seamlessly between night and day, the living and the dead, underground and aboveground, haunting Laura in her childhood and later in her early adulthood.[80] Echoing Catherine's unrelenting attachment to Heathcliff, Carmilla spends intimate moments with Laura with 'the ardour of a lover' and asserts her possession of her: 'You are mine, you shall be mine, you and I are one forever.'[81] However, in the physical, psychic and sexual unity the vampire seeks with the host body, the undead can only survive at the sacrifice of the living. When an avenging father, whose daughter also fell victim to Carmilla's advances, appears on the scene, he not only unveils her identity and uncovers her grave, he also disinters the coffin and decapitates her in a Freudian gesture of castration. Indeed, Carmilla must be masculinised or reduced to an asexual Medusa-like figure before the General finally kills her. When he first attempts to strike her with an axe, her 'slender hand . . . closed like a vice of steel' on his wrist.[82] After he violently kills her, the acts of vampirism do come to a temporary end in the village, but Carmilla's traces remain prone to revivification as Laura still imagines her touch and 'the light step of Carmilla at the drawing-room door'.[83] Like Catherine's coffin, Carmilla's death remains unsealed, signifying the inability of the underground space to completely enclose its dead or to entomb homoerotic tendencies.

Perhaps the most popular novel to fix the image of the ghostly female *flâneuse* in the Victorian imagination is Wilkie Collins's *The Woman in White* (1860). Death, here, comes in a multiplicity of disguises: first as a psychic death in the figure of Anne Catherick, the woman in white who is metaphorically buried alive in an insane asylum; the fictional death of her double, Laura Fairlie, who must stage her own death in order to uncover her true identity; and the near-death experience of her lover, Walter Hartwright, who buries himself in the African wilderness after realising that his social position would not confer him the hand of Laura. All three characters must be resurrected in some form to uncover the conspiracy hidden underneath layers of Victorian propriety that would reveal the secret behind the 'mercenary marriage plot'.[84] Death and madness are closely intertwined in the figure of Anne Catherick, whose elusive presence flickers in and out of moonlit pathways, the vision of the revenant in her ghostly white dress. When Walter first encounters her in London when she escapes the asylum, 'every drop of blood in [his] body was brought to a stop by the touch of a hand laid lightly and suddenly on [his] shoulder'.[85] He is at once aroused and terrified by her embodiment of death, yet he must repress this desire and displace it onto another love object, Laura, whose 'ominous likeness' aligns her with the 'deeper mystery in our souls'.[86] In an inverse relationship, as Anne is resurrected as a haunting figure in the text, Laura herself slowly dies as she becomes a prisoner of her fiancé Percival Glyde's evil machinations to steal her inheritance. When Laura stands face to face with her deathly double – amongst the graves, no less – she is horrified by the 'sight of her own face in the glass after a long illness'.[87] Like the Gothic doubling in *The Picture of Dorian Gray* (1890), youth and beauty must come at a steep cost in a dialectical relationship between the subject and its uncanny image. But who is the subject and who is the double? This slippery relationship is reinforced when Anne eventually dies but is buried as Laura, and Laura is reborn as an unidentified woman in an asylum, who is later freed by her lover, Hartwright. When Glyde's treachery and lies are brought to light, the buried secret that Laura and Anne are half-sisters through an illegitimate relationship is finally revealed, restoring order in a confirmation of social identity. In a symbolic act, Anne's name and date of death is reinscribed on her gravestone in the hope that the dead will indeed remain buried.

The need for the buried body to correlate with the inscription on the tombstone aboveground becomes more pressing in the subject of feminine sexuality in Mary Elizabeth Braddon's *Lady Audley's Secret* (1862). In her subversion of Wilkie Collins's novel, Braddon collapses the identity of the deathly woman and the beautiful double into one dangerous *femme fatale* whose duplicitous character was remarked by one critic as 'at once the heroine and the monstrosity in the novel'.[88] Braddon turned to the sensational genre of ghost stories during the years of the second Reform Bill of 1867, which led to Parliamentary acts protecting women's rights in the areas of property, education and marriage. Although her stories provoke the feminine spectre in domestic arenas, there are no ghosts in *Lady Audley's Secret,* merely the suggestion of one. This haunting image is captured in Lucy Graham, a beautiful child-like governess who captivates and marries an old baronet elevating her to the status of Lady Audley. On the surface, she epitomises Victorian femininity:

> Wherever she went she seemed to take joy and brightness with her. In the cottages of the poor her fair face shone like a sunbeam . . . [she] was blessed with that magic power of fascination by which a woman can charm with a word or intoxicate with a smile. Every one loved, admired, and praised her.[89]

However, beneath her alluring façade, Lady Audley is actually a married woman who abandoned her child, staged her own death and attempted to murder her husband in order to protect her new identity.

What the underground here represents is not just another possibility of resurrection, but a *reinvention* of feminine identity, the kind of refashioning that was afforded men by the work ethic popularised by Samuel Smiles's *Self-Help* (1859), but closed off to women except through marriage. Lucy merely takes this ethos to heart, but her real crime is in articulating it:

> I had learnt that which in some indefinite manner or other every schoolgirl learns sooner or later – I learned that my ultimate fate in life depended upon my marriage, and I concluded that if I was indeed prettier than my schoolfellows, I ought to marry better than any of them.[90]

In the unlawful act of bigamy, she disrupts the Victorian notion of femininity by manipulating men for her own gain. It is interesting to note that another sexual undercurrent, that of incest, is insinuated in the novel but is quickly extinguished as the male hero, Robert Audley, attempts to restore order in the household. A nephew of the baron and an old friend of Lucy's first husband, Robert utilises all the powers of detection to gather evidence against Lady Audley. However, throughout his investigation, it is clear that he is inevitably drawn to her sphinx-like vulnerability, an incestuous impulse he projects onto a nobler quest to protect his uncle's honour and help a friend in need. There are several underground metaphors used in his detection, from the subterranean passageway he uses to enter Lady Audley's bedchamber to the well in the garden where her first husband George was literally 'buried alive', but it is the grave of Helen Talboys, the original identity of Lady Audley, that contains the only evidence that the body does not match the inscription above. When Robert uncovers enough evidence to confront Lady Audley, she proclaims herself to be mad in order to avoid criminal punishment in a gesture that once again takes advantage of Victorian constructions of femininity to escape an unwanted fate. In a reversal of Wilkie Collins's novel, the woman does not need to be resurrected from an insane asylum to reveal the truth to the world, but she casts herself into self-imposed exile in order to contain the truth and keep it buried. In a diagnosis of her ills, the medical expert at the hospital informs Robert, 'The lady is not mad . . . She has the cunning of madness, with the prudence of intelligence. I will tell you what she is . . . She is dangerous!'[91] Like the decapitation of Carmilla, Lady Audley must be socially 'castrated' and buried in order to prevent her return and to control the contagion of her excessive femininity. The subterranean space for the dead becomes the space of anxieties as it allows for a fluidity of identity that was not possible before massive urbanisation allowed for greater social movement and anonymity of people from various stations in life. Lucy, who reinvents herself from her grave and gives herself a new identity in the city, is seen as a threat to the domestic social order that Victorians sought to protect, one that was dangerously on the brink of collapse as the guardians of the domestic sphere found new ways to express their intellect and their buried ambitions.

While Braddon's sensational novels often dealt with the plight of middle-class women whose invisibility in society returned in Gothic traces, her ghost stories from the 1860s also raised the spectre of the alienated woman but from a lower domestic sphere: that of the servant in the home. There has been a steady excavation of these marginalised voices in Victorian literature, including Pamela Horn's historical study *The Rise and Fall of Victorian Servant* and Bruce Robbins's *The Servant's Hand: English Fiction from Below*, which not only attest to their invisibility in literary representation, but their spectral omnipresence that often drives the plotline or functions as a crucial narrative device in connecting words and actions often unspoken or unseen. The role of female servants represents a nexus of many of the themes we have seen thus far. First, as a subaltern class not only in social terms but in physical terms, servants often inhabited the subterranean regions of the home, which rendered their presence in literature fleeting at best. Robbins argues that the randomness of literary servants is attributable to the fact that they are 'too minor, fragmentary, and marginal to any given text to be treated by work', echoing many of the salient features of subterranean spaces we have observed in previous chapters.[92] Secondly, servants also act as the subconscious of the home in the way they harbour the secrets of the family, if not the superego, as they take on the role of surveillance in monitoring the family's actions. In the psychological role they play in the rearing of children and the upkeep of the domestic sphere, Dickens writes in his 'Nurse's Stories' (1852), 'If we all knew our own minds . . . I suspect we should find our nurses responsible for most of the dark corners we are forced to go back to, against our wills.'[93] In this psycho-spatial representation, the nurse is both the object of and the force behind repressive instincts, the evocation of which would destabilise the home in the eruption of the *unheimlich*. The servant's uncanny presence then leads us to the final subterranean trope that associates her with ghosts and supernatural phenomena. As Eve Lynch explicates, the servant often expressed the liminality of the domestic sphere and the in-between world she inhabited:

> Like the ghost, the servant was *in* the home but not *of* it, occupying a position tied to the workings of the house itself. Like the spectral spirit, servants were outsiders in the home secretly looking in on the forbidden world of respectability.[94]

In her ghostly manifestation, the servant held a powerful gaze upon the household as a witness to, and the embodiment of, spectral revenance that uncovered long-held secrets that upturned the very foundations of Victorian domesticity. Whether she encountered ghosts in the attic or returned from the dead to haunt various rooms in the home, the servant's appearance in literature often signalled the return of repressed anxieties that literally would not die.

The physical, psychological and spectral convergence of these subterranean traces appears most potently in Elizabeth Braddon's short story, 'Ralph the Bailiff' (1861). In this sensational plot, a mistress of a haunted farm falls prey to servants who really control the social and economic dynamics of the household. Married to a farmer who killed his brother in order to inherit the farm, Jenny Trevor becomes haunted by hallucinations and nightmares that keep her a prisoner of her own home. Furthermore, her husband's sinister servant, Ralph, constantly shadows her and undercuts her authority, further dispossessing her of her social rank and psychological stability. When she discovers, while eavesdropping through a peephole, that her husband is not only a murderer but the father of a child borne by Ralph's sister and the former housekeeper, her entire world of marriage and domesticity crumbles before her. The 'unseen influence' that is 'sapping' Jenny's life gradually comes to light in the unexpected return of the old housekeeper, who is resurrected in a power reversal that recasts the servant as the real mistress of the home and her son the heir to the property.[95] Blurring the boundaries between 'upstairs' and 'downstairs', Braddon deftly incorporates the haunting metaphor to signify the threat from institutional and domestic forces, as Jenny physically and economically deteriorates, rendering her 'alien' and socially dead in her own home. Buried alive metaphorically, she becomes the servant and the ghost, whose spectrality represents the anxieties regarding women's right to property and inheritance in this exposé of social injustices that demonstrably inhibit women, as well as servants, from rising above their station in life. The social and political underground again appears in ghostly traces to resurrect buried discourses and haunt modernity with its insistence on shedding light on the invisible, the repressed and the marginalised voices of Victorian society.

Underground Mourning, Memory and Memorabilia

There is nothing . . . not nothing innocent or good that ever dies, and is forgotten. Let us hold to that faith or none . . . There is not an angel added to the host of Heaven but does its blessed work on earth in those that loved it here.
Charles Dickens, *The Old Curiosity Shop* (1841)

The final conceptualisation of the dead moves from social and spatial appropriations to the psychological and material realm of grief and mourning. How does the subconscious or the unconscious deal with buried emotions, and through what rituals did the Victorians incorporate the dead into the world of the living? How did the underground of the dead come to re-inhabit and reclaim the city? To this end, Freud's 'Mourning and Melancholia' is useful again in interpreting the spectrum of grief the individual experiences through the loss of one's love object. Freud described melancholia as a:

> profoundly painful dejection, cessation of interest in the outside world, loss of the capacity to love, inhibition of all activity, and a lowering of the self-regarding feelings to a degree that finds utterance in self-reproaches and self-revilings, and culminates in a delusional expectation of punishment.[96]

While in mourning 'it is the world that has become poor and empty; in melancholia it is the ego itself'.[97] Such external and internal manifestations of pain have been observed in the ghostliness and the haunting of the Victorian imagination, which often revealed the importance of expressing the past impinging on the present. Repetition or the 'return' of the dead signalled the process of mourning, which sometimes led to a re-entry to the real that distinguished itself from the interminable grief of melancholia. Although I do not wish to draw such distinct boundaries in the bereavement process, I contend that Victorian ideas of expressing grief often oscillated between these two extremes, leading to an inward turning as well as an outside projection of all that was inexpressible in death. The mourning process often aligned itself with the ghostly incorporation of the dead into the world of living that worked through the grief, while the stalemate of melancholy was projected onto the surface world of material objects and funereal ephemera that linked the mourner eternally with the underworld of the dead.

Such was the 'cult of memory' that pervaded Victorian funereal customs that sublimated the death of a loved one to literally a 'thing' of the past. The need to memorialise the dead was a pervasive feature of the Victorian psyche that alluded to the Freudian need to work through memory in order to find a substitution for the lost object. In *Specters of Marx*, Derrida also discusses the significance of hospitality in welcoming the pain that often accompanies grief, which is the 'inheritance' that one must accept to truly live:

> To exorcise not in order to chase away the ghosts, but this time to grant them the right, if it means making them come back alive, as *revenants* who would no longer be *revenants*, but as other *arrivants* to whom a hospitable memory or promise must offer welcome . . .[98]

In this subtle shift from the fear of a ghostly revenant to the anticipation of an *arrivant*, Derrida articulates the foundations of many poets who had to grapple with the unknown terrain of death and the imagined afterlife. Although Alfred Tennyson, Matthew Arnold and Robert Browning all invoked the spirit of the dead and offered them a hospitable place amongst the living, it is Thomas Hardy who most prolifically confronted death and revivified the lost object in a myriad of poetic resurrections. After the death of his wife Emma, Thomas Hardy dedicated a series of poems that portrayed the narrator as both the mourner and the mourned in an ambiguous world that constantly oscillates between the home and the churchyard, where an invisible presence constantly haunts both places, as well as the journey in between. In 'The Walk' (1912), the narrator returns from his usual walk only to notice the emptiness of his home expressed in the question:

> What difference then?
> Only that underlying sense
> Of the look of a room on returning thence.[99]

This 'underlying sense', which expresses both the absence of his wife and his buried grief, reveals the detached sense of mourning that transforms the home into a grave. In contrast, Hardy's poems about churchyards tend to be populated with people who have died, as the cemetery becomes the real 'home' for the departed. In 'Paying Calls' (1913), the narrator calls upon his 'oldest friends . . . [b]y mound and stone and tree', but while indulging in reminiscences, the narrator realises in the final line of the poem, 'But they spoke not to me'.[100] Despite the silence that greets him, it is the act of re-enacting his life for the narrator – and for Hardy, the writing of the poem itself – which resurrects the departed and works through the process of mourning. It is this performative act that Peggy Phelan alludes to when she states:

> Mimicry . . . is the fundamental performance of this cultural moment . . . In this mimicry, loss itself helps to transform the repetitive force of trauma and might bring about a way to overcome it.[101]

In this threshold between life and death, Hardy invokes ghosts, doubles and disembodied voices to memorialise them before their memories fade into oblivion, a 'second death' as he would term the passage in his poem 'The To-be-Forgotten' (1899).[102] In this repetition and mimicry, the grave, the home and the 'unhomely' all become part of the inheritance that Hardy welcomes in his poetry, which performs the work of mourning by uncovering the lives beneath the graves and giving them a potential afterlife.

If poetry offered an afterlife and perhaps an alternative space of mourning, material objects and funereal memorabilia represented a static, timeless projection of grief that can be seen as a refusal to work through grief in its unyielding melancholia. Implicit in Derrida's notion of resurrection is the need for the dead to penetrate the psyche of the individual, but as Pierre Macherey observes, Derrida's 'ghost of communism' also appears in the 'enigma of the commodity and in particular the fetishism of political economy that makes relations among men "return" fantastically in the form of relations among things'.[103] How do these 'things' interrelate and how do they connect the past and the present, the living and the dead, the object and the subject? Although much of the recent scholarship related to 'thing theory' in Victorian studies focuses on materiality and representation, Peter Schwenger's work, *The Tears of Things* (2006), uncovers another layer in the phenomenological apprehension of physical objects by linking them to the process of mourning. Schwenger sees the failure of the subject to grasp the object fully as the inchoate sentiment that is perceived as a lack. 'This perception, always falling short of full possession, gives rise to a melancholy that is felt by the subject and is ultimately *for* the subject.'[104] In this subjugation of the ego, there are traces of the narcissism found in Freud's melancholy, but it also suggests the inability of the object to bring about the full restitution of the subject. Thus, material 'things' not only point to an absence of another but also contribute to the absence in oneself.

The underground, subconscious longing for the departed expressed in funereal ephemera abounded in Victorian customs and rituals of death that reveal the roots of melancholia in its inability to let go of the lost object. Mourning clothes like the black crape and other accoutrements such as coffin-plates, mourning-cards, jewellery and mementos of hair all contributed to the projection of death onto the surface of everyday life. In *Mary Barton* (1848), the seamstress sewing black mourning clothes is referred to as being engaged in 'blackwork', while the manufacturing company, the Courtaulds, held a monopoly on crapes from the onset of funeral practices and can be seen essentially as an institution built on the dead. The commercialisation of death was a very visible aspect of Victorian society, one that did not elude Chadwick when he commented, 'Christian burial is made an article of traffic' and one in which shareholders would be reluctant when change 'does not promise an immediate return for the expense incurred'.[105] Similarly in Paris in 1887, writer Villiers de l'Isle-Adam responded to the flower-sellers and shops selling funereal accessories near Père Lachaise, 'Those are the people who invented death!'[106] Historically, Queen Victoria's bereavement over the death of Prince Albert offers one extreme example of grief steeped in material excess, from the Albert Memorial in Kensington Gardens to the mourning dress code she chose to adopt beyond the statutory two-year limit. Furthermore, she left his room untouched, signalling her inability to move beyond death, beyond time. Such immovability is also captured in Henry James's short story 'The Altar of the Dead' (1895), in which a woman builds her entire life around the memory of a man who wronged her and died. Revealing her private room to another man trapped in the world of the dead, he comments:

> The place had the flush of life – it was expressive; its dark red walls were articulate with memories and relics. These were simple things – photographs and water-colours, scraps of writing framed and ghosts of flowers embalmed; but a moment sufficed to show him they had a common meaning. It was here she had lived and worked, and she had already told him she would make no change of scene.[107]

The irony of death in life and life in death reveals again the pathological nature of grief, as the female protagonist fetishises her own life into the tomb. Memories are frozen as objects and memorabilia ultimately stop progression and prevent the passage of mourning to the possibility of recovery.

Of all objects, however, the Victorian photograph represented unconscious mourning and the desire to arrest time in a manner that visually confronted the world above with the spectre of the dead. The development of photography, which followed the daguerreotype, led to the so-called 'card portrait era' (1860–1900) in which portraits of individuals in different exposures created a haunting sense of doubling and spectrality. Although many critics, from Roland Barthes to Susan Sontag, have written on theories of photography, Eduardo Cadava's work directly links the photography with the cemetery:

> As its own grave, the photograph is what exceeds the photograph within the photograph. It is what remains of what passes into history. It turns on itself in order to survive, in order to withdraw into a space in which it might defer its decay, into an interior – the closed-off space of writing itself. In order for a photograph to be a photograph, it must become the tomb that writes, that harbours its own death.[108]

Every photograph then is a confrontation with death, a constant reminder of how one may be remembered in history, as history. As the 'deathliness' of photographs posed ruptures in time and the interpenetration of the past and the present, literary representations also relied on doubling and repetition that not only echoed the multiple projections of the self, but also the reproductive capabilities of an eerie new technology.[109] In particular, Thomas Hardy linked the photograph with death in haunting ways, often making the distinction between the person and the photograph ambiguous at best. In 'The Rival' (1917), a woman destroys an early picture of herself that her husband held dear because 'he loved not the me then living/ But that past woman still'.[110] Meanwhile, in poems such as 'The Faded Face'(1916) and 'Looking at a Picture on an Anniversary' (1913), the narrators attempt to find a likeness in their photographs, but they cannot bridge the gap between the subject and object. In a more direct link with the cemetery, Hardy's 'The Son's Portrait' (c. 1925) describes a father who loses his son in the trenches, but finds a photograph of his son in a junk shop, which he purchases '[a]nd *buried* it – as 'twere he'.[111] In this representation, the subject *becomes* the object, as the photograph becomes the only substitute for the love object in mourning. The photograph that is already a cemetery is buried in a grave, reflecting the layers of grief that immobilises the individual and prevents any chance of genuine closure. In the final surface manifestation of the underworld, death pervades the consciousness with visual confrontations of the tomb that awaits each individual in a melancholic deadening of the world around them.

Final Exhumation

. . . let it alone. It matters not how a man dies, but how he lives. The act of dying is of no importance, it lasts so short a time.
Samuel Johnson, James Boswell's *The Life of Johnson* (1791)

For the Victorians, it seemed that death lasted forever, either in eternal suffering or cyclical revenance that permeated the social, cultural and literary fabric of burial and funereal practices. The pervasiveness of death and the inordinate amount of time and money devoted to the deceased in preparation for burial revealed an era of fetishisation of tombs, crypts, altars, crapes, ornaments and all things otherworldly. Philipe Ariès notes that the erotics of death was sublimated into beauty in the 'cult of memory' and observes, 'The nineteenth century is the era of mourning which the psychologist of today calls *hysterical* mourning.'[112] However, as the significance of the body in burial practices came under pressure from sanitary reformers, the underground space no longer afforded a peaceful place of rest in the city. The movement of bodies to the suburbs and the creation of new garden cemeteries complicated the notion that the deceased should be buried near churchyards for the sake of their resurrection. The cremation debate ultimately secularised the subterranean space, as new forms of death allowed social and Gothic resurrections to surface in literary and aesthetic representations of mortality. There were the bodysnatchers, the ghosts who returned from the dead, the spectres who never died, the undead and the living dead who all consorted in the urban underworld that ultimately came to represent the city itself. As Catherine Arnold observes, 'London is one giant grave', and the myriad of haunting narratives that emerged from the underground is a testament to the critical importance it held in the Victorian imagination.[113]

The *fin de siècle* witnessed another shift in the darker appropriation of the deathly space, as the Gothic tradition fused with the anxiety of civilisation and the spectre of war in depicting urban landscapes of ruins. David Cannadine provides a fascinating insight into the changing faces of death resulting from World War I and contends that the era of 'hysterical mourning' had to come to an end:

> Death had become so ubiquitous and tragic, and grief so widespread and overwhelming, that even those remaining Victorian rituals – probably never effective even in the mid-nineteenth century – were now recognised as being inadequate, superfluous, and irrelevant.[114]

The excesses of death and funereal customs were then streamlined with the minimalist sweep of modernism, as Gothic cemeteries were overshadowed by mass burials, war memorials and the Tomb of the Unknown Soldier, the empty grave that came to signify all the bodies that were unrecoverable during World War I. Although Siegfried Sassoon condemned war memorials as 'a pile of peace complacent stone, a sepulchre of crime', the need for an underground space to stand in place of the absence of the dead was a substitution and a supplementation that expressed the excess of emptiness in a new era of mourning.[115] Despite the fact that the underground became reappropriated along the lines of nationalism and ideology, the symbolic space remained open to literary resurrections, as the grave continued to provide the silent but omnipresent energy behind many works of modernism, including T. S. Eliot's ghostly fragments in *The Waste Land* (1922), Virginia Woolf's subconscious streams in *Mrs. Dalloway* (1925) and James Joyce's haunted streets in *Ulysses* (1922). Although Chris Brooks argues that in the contemporary world '[d]eath had been emptied of meaning' and that the Victorian cemetery is 'a constant reminder of our own inarticulacy', writers have always found a way to articulate the void and the horror within textual layers that need to be disinterred and decoded in order to see the underlying corpse.[116] The 'buried life' continues to surface in a blurring of the living and the dead, as history and memory constantly rewrite subterranean spaces as a repository for all that is containable and uncontainable in modernity.

Notes

1. Ragon, *The Space of Death*, p. 36.
2. Foucault, 'Of Other Spaces', p. 25.
3. Curl, preface, p. xx.
4. Hallam, Hockey and Howarth (eds), *Beyond the Body*, p. 3.
5. See Rabaté, *The Ghosts of Modernity*.
6. Bown, Burdett and Thurschwell (eds), *The Victorian Supernatural*, p. 10.
7. See Freud, 'Mourning and Melancholia', pp. 237–58.
8. Douglas, *Purity and Danger*, p. 121.
9. See Noyes (ed.), *English Romantic Poetry and Prose*.
10. Percy Bysshe Shelley, *Adonaïs* (1821), cited in Curl, *The Victorian Celebration of Death*, p. 37.
11. Tennyson, *In Memoriam: Authoritative Text Criticism*, LIV, ll. 6–7.
12. Ibid. LV, ll. 5–8, 13–16.
13. Armstrong, *Victorian Poetry*, p. 254.
14. Kristeva, *Powers of Horror*, p. 4.
15. Thompson, *Cremation*, p. 20.
16. Kingsley, *Alton Locke*, vol. 2, p. 277.
17. Brooks, *Mortal Remains*, p. 35.
18. Walker, *Gatherings from Graveyards*, pp. 31–2. He was also the founder of the Metropolitan Association for the Abolition of Burials in Towns. His other reports included *Graveyards of London* (1841), *Interment and Disinterment* (1843) and *Burial-Ground Incendiarism* (1846).
19. Ibid. p. 32.
20. Edwin Chadwick, *A Supplementary Report on the Practice of Interment* (1843), cited in Curl, *The Victorian Celebration of Death*, p. 121.
21. Curl, *The Victorian Celebration of Death*, p. 39.
22. The direct service from Waterloo to Woking ran for 87 years, offering first-, second- and third-class travel for the dead as well as their mourners. See Clarke, *The Brookwood Necropolis Railway*. For a fictional evocation of the service, see Martin, *The Necropolis Railway*.
23. *The Builder* (Winter 1850), cited in Brooks, *Mortal Remains*, p. 47.
24. Cited in Arnold, *Necropolis*, pp. 172–3.
25. Holmes, *The London Burial Grounds*, p. 257.
26. Thompson, *Cremation*, pp. 9–10.
27. Curl, *The Victorian Celebration of Death*, p. 193.
28. Dickens, 'City of Absent', p. 16.
29. Cited in Ragon, *The Space of Death*, p. 39.
30. Cited in Arnold, *Necropolis*, p. 83.
31. Cataphiles have roamed the catacombs since the 1860s, and clandestine groups met to perform macabre music in a further dissemination of underground folklore and mythology. Situationists in the 1960s laid their claim to the underground with their slogan, 'The situationists are in the catacombs of known culture', and more recently, the Paris police discovered an underground cinema and restaurant built near the catacombs, maintained by cataphiles. For more see Jon Henley, 'In a Secret Paris Cavern . . .', *The Guardian*, 8 September 2004. <http://film.guard

ian.co.uk/News_Story/Guardian/0,4029,1299449,00.html> (accessed 15 May 2007).
32. Dickens, 'Travelling Abroad', (pp. 61–72), p. 64.
33. Mitchell, 'The Paris Morgue', pp. 588, 596.
34. Foucault, 'Of Other Spaces', p. 24.
35. Dickens, *Bleak House*, p. 180.
36. Bradley, *St. Pancras Station* (London: Profile, 2007), p. 6.
37. Thomas Hardy, 'In the Cemetery', in *The Collected Poems*, p. 382, ll. 7–14. Other poems that engage with the clearance of cemeteries are 'The Levelled Churchyard' and 'Ah, Are You Diggin on My Grave'. His later poetry, such as 'Neutral Tones', 'Dead Man Walking' and 'Rain on the Grave', takes on a much more sombre tone. See Armstrong, *Haunted Hardy*.
38. Loudon, *On the Laying Out*, p. 13.
39. *Report on a General Scheme for Extramural Sepulture* [1850], cited in Morley, *Death, Heaven, and the Victorians*, p. 70.
40. G. K. Chesterton, *The Rolling English Road* [1914], cited in Curl, *The Victorian Celebration of Death*, p. 68.
41. Maurice, *Theological Essays*, pp. 455, 473.
42. Gissing, *The Nether World*, p. 19.
43. Arnold, 'The Buried Life', in *Selected Poems and Prose,* ed. Allot, p. 85.
44. Dahl, 'The Victorian Wasteland', p. 39.
45. Thomson, *The City of Dreadful Night*, pp. 22, 27.
46. Ibid. p. 31.
47. Laqueur, 'Cemeteries', p. 2.
48. T. S. Eliot, 'Fiction, Fair and Foul', *Nineteenth Century* (June 1880), cited in Shelston, 'Dickens and the Burial of the Dead', p. 77.
49. Derrida, 'Marx, c'est quelqu'un', p. 23.
50. Wolfreys, *Victorian Hauntings*, p. x.
51. Cited in Wolfreys, *Deconstruction Derrida*, p. 140.
52. Norman Page in his introduction to Dickens, *The Old Curiosity Shop*, p. xv.
53. Dickens, *The Old Curiosity Shop*, p. 13.
54. Ibid. p. 136. Italics are my own.
55. Dickens, *The Old Curiosity Shop*, p. 136.
56. Ibid. p. 100.
57. Cited in Henson, 'Investigations and Fictions', pp. 44–63 (p. 44).
58. Dickens, 'The Haunted Man', p. 325.
59. The first indictment for bodysnatching was in 1777 in the churchyard of St George the Martyr in Southwark, but the trade had been well established in cities, most notably in Edinburgh and Dublin, since the mid century. The rise of grave robbery led to more class divisions even in death, as the wealthy were able to afford guards to watch over the graves or purchase inventions like 'Mortsafe' iron cages that added extra security. For more, see Adams, *Dead and Buried*.
60. Both poets contributed to the rise of Victorian sentimentalism concerning death; Arnold's poem was dedicated to his dachshund, reiterating the years that he was alive, while Wordsworth's lyric continued to acknowledge the dead as a member of the living.

61. Richardson, *Death, Dissection, and the Destitute*, p. 279. Julie-Marie Strange in *Death, Grief, and Poverty in Britain* argues against the myth that the working classes did not care about burials; rather, she notes that more cultural significance was given to the wake than the burial itself.
62. Dickens, *Martin Chuzzlewit*, p. 309.
63. Dickens, *A Tale of Two Cities*, p. 294.
64. Hutter, 'The Novelist as Resurrectionist', p. 21.
65. Dickens, *A Tale of Two Cities*, p. 360.
66. Ibid. pp. 360–1.
67. Stevenson, 'The Body Snatcher', p. 83.
68. For more on the trials, see Douglas, *Burke and Hare: The True Story*.
69. Stevenson, 'The Body Snatcher', p. 91.
70. Kincaid, 'Designing Gourmet Children or, KIDS FOR DINNER!' in *Victorian Gothic*, p. 3.
71. Castle, *The Female Thermometer*, p. 144.
72. Pike, *Subterranean Cities*, p. 103.
73. Cited in Bronfen, *Over Her Dead Body*, p. 65.
74. Freud, *Civilization and Its Discontents*, p. 77.
75. Ariès, *The Hour of Our Death*, p. 608.
76. Brontë, *Wuthering Heights*, p. 55.
77. See Freud, 'Mourning and Melancholia', pp. 237–58.
78. Brontë, *Wuthering Heights*, p. 165.
79. Bronfen, *Over Her Dead Body*, p. 314.
80. Le Fanu, 'Carmilla', in *In a Glass Darkly*, p. 317.
81. Ibid. p. 264.
82. Ibid. p. 312.
83. Ibid. p. 319.
84. For more, see Pykett, *The Sensation Novel*, p. 16.
85. Collins, *The Woman in White*, p. 50.
86. Ibid. p. 76.
87. Ibid. p. 119.
88. W. Fraser Rae, 'Lady Audley's Secret', in *The Times* (18 November 1862), p. 8.
89. Braddon, *Lady Audley's Secret*, pp. 5–6.
90. Ibid. p. 350.
91. Ibid. p. 379.
92. Robbins, *The Servant's Hand*, p. xii.
93. Dickens, 'Nurse's Stories', in *The Uncommerical Traveller*, p. 150.
94. Lynch, 'Spectral Politics', in Bown (ed.), *The Victorian Supernatural*, pp. 67–8.
95. Braddon, 'Ralph the Bailiff', p. 31. Her other works, such as *The Lady's Mile* (1866) and 'The Shadow in the Corner' (1879), also examined the haunted female terrain to articulate women's social and spectral dispossession. For a later example of a haunted female servant who comes to repossess the home, see Henry James, *The Turn of the Screw*.
96. Freud, 'Mourning and Melancholia', p. 248.
97. Ibid. p. 254.
98. Derrida, *Spectres of Marx*, p. 175.

99. Hardy, 'The Walk', in *The Collected Poems*, p. 309, ll. 14–16. All subsequent poems by Hardy are from this edition.
100. Hardy, 'Paying Calls', pp. 466–7, ll. 8, 14, 16.
101. Phelan, *Mourning Sex*, p. 12.
102. Hardy, 'The To-be-Forgotten', p. 128, l. 16. For an interesting Freudian case study of Hardy's mourning in which an artist finds an elegiac substitute for his lost love in her daughter and then her granddaughter, see Hardy, *The Well-Beloved*.
103. Macherey, 'Marx Dematerialized or the Spirit of Derrida', p. 18.
104. Schwenger, *The Tears of Things*, pp. 2–3. Cited in David Trotter, 'Household Clearances in Victorian Fiction', in *Interdisciplinary Studies in the Long Nineteenth Century*, 6 (2008) <www.19.bbk.ac.uk> (accessed 7 August 2009), p. 5. For more on Victorian materiality, see Freedgood, *The Ideas in Things*.
105. Chadwick, *The Practice of Internment in Towns*, cited in Brooks, p. 36.
106. *The Oxford Book of Death*, ed. Enright, p. 145.
107. James, 'The Altar of the Dead', p. 216.
108. Cadava, *Words of Light*, p. x.
109. For more on the role of photography in the literary imagination, see Groth, *Victorian Photography and Literary Nostalgia*.
110. Hardy, 'The Rival', p. 395, ll. 11–12.
111. Hardy, 'The Son's Portrait', pp. 799–800, l. 22.
112. Ariès, *Western Attitudes toward Death*, p. 67.
113. Arnold, *Necropolis*, p. 2.
114. Cannadine, 'War and Death', p. 218. For more comparative studies on the historical impact of defeat and mourning after World War I, see Schivelbusch, *Culture of Defeat*.
115. Sassoon, 'On Passing the New Menin Gate', p. 173, ll. 7, 14.
116. Brooks, preface, p. i.

Chapter 4

Underground Revolutions: Invisible Networks of Terror in *Fin-de-Siècle* London

It's pathological, it's always there – the subterranean world, where fantasies and violent urges every now and again come to the surface disguised as ideas.
Martin Amis, *The Independent* (29 January 2008)

As we have observed in previous chapters, the spaces underneath the city have always mapped ideological battles, from the class struggle in the bowels of the sewers to the redistribution of power through the construction of the underground railway. Although subterranean systems attempted to contain these agitations in the mid-nineteenth century, political discontent continued to foment and erupt on the surface of the city in more violent and explosive ways in the latter half of the century. Even the word 'underground' gained new currency, from a concrete, physical space to a more metaphorical representation of conspiratorial networks, extending its meaning to secret societies, crime syndicates and international political organisations. The *OED* maps this transformation from a concrete 'region below the earth' to a symbolic reference to all that is 'hidden, concealed, secret', tracing its political usage specifically to Sergei Kravchinsky's nihilist tract *Underground Russia* in 1883.[1] The underground's link to subversive activity was pervasive, most notably in connection with the Parisian sewers that housed the city's criminals and revolutionaries, as well as in the underground railway, which offered a transgressive space of class and sexual encounters. In this chapter, however, I wish to locate the underground as a tactical site of political insurgency, as explosions in underground trains and bombs found in crypts began to signal a closer alliance between 'underground' and 'terror' in a material and a metaphorical way. In his assessment of modern terror, Alex Houen, traces covert terrorism to the 'subversive militant tactics of the Russian Nihilists and the Irish "Fenians" in the 1860s and 1870s, along with developments in explosives and the advent of a mass media'.[2] The collusion of these scientific, political and media events is what Deaglán Ó Donghaile aptly terms the 'shock of modern-ism', as sensational headlines grabbed the popular imagination, and the dynamite attacks attacked both the 'power source and nervous system of the imperial establishment'.[3] Furthermore, the rapid proliferation of terrorism in the city had a profound impact on the meaning of the 'underground', complicating its spatial and conceptual significance in unsuspecting and far-reaching ways. Whereas the subterranean world before connoted secret networks underneath the city space, it began to extend its arms to international webs of intrigue and terror, from the anarchists in France and the nihilists in Russia, to the Fenians in Ireland and North America. Furthermore, the widespread coverage of revolu-tionary organisations in the press as well as the publication of under-ground pamphlets and journals divorced the term 'underground' from its material foundations to a more visible *and* invisible surface manifes-tation that permeated cultural and political discourse. In the contradic-tions that surfaced, the revolutionary underground also blurred the archetypal separation between the upper and lower classes, as masses in cities clamoured for change on the streets, while the educated and upper classes whispered words of revolution in salons and clandestine clubs. However, as a site of paradoxes and unknowability, the underground, as a physical space, begins to lose its signifying potential at the turn of the century in a new appropriation of the underground metaphor that diluted its meaning to any attempt to critique institutional forces and the *status quo*. In the pervasiveness of such sentiments, any genuine acts of underground resistance become impossible, as the invisible hands of conspiracy lie anywhere and everywhere in the expansive network of terror, as a part of, yet against, the very system under which it operates.

This chapter attempts to decipher the ways these underground revolu-tions surfaced in the literature and media of *fin-de-siècle* London and how inherent contradictions in their representation ultimately obfus-cated the objectives of underground organisations. I also look at the discrepancies in media and literary accounts to reveal the ways in which acts of terrorism were occluded in the literary imagination in favour of a more psychological portrayal of the underground revolutionary, who is often depicted as an anonymous individual with multiple allegiances and identities. The amorphousness of the revolutionary and his project, however, weakens the underground movement. As Adrian Wisnicki explains, throughout the Victorian period and beyond, 'conspiracy is *everywhere*, because it has grown to the extent of being *generalized*, potentially *indeterminate*, and even *beyond the conscious control or knowledge* of its conspirators'.[4] Although his conclusion alludes to the spectral insistence of underground revolutionary movements, I extend his argument to focus on the *absence* of concrete acts of terrorism in the novel to illustrate that conspiracy is merely a subtext and a subterfuge for the real terror within. Thus, I demonstrate a shift in the underground revolutionary landscape from an external act of defiance to an internal quest for knowledge and selfhood that eludes most characters in the novel.

In the interplay between historical accounts and what Henry James calls the 'imaginative realization' of the political landscape, there was much slippage in the conception of underground movements in the conflation of ideologies purposes and representation.[5] Socialists, Marxists, anarchists and nihilists all found revolutionary appeal in the subterranean metaphor and utilised its subversive potential to challenge existing systems of classification and control. Thus, what one observes in textual practice is the interchange of these groups, or a *heteroglossia* of language and ideologies, charged with violence, whether real or imagined, as the common denominator or detonator. In Joseph Conrad's *The Secret Agent* (1906), Stevie's drawings illustrate the entropic nature of this phenomenon in which organisations overlap one another like

> ... circles, circles, circles; innumerable circles, concentric, eccentric; a coruscating whirl of circles that by their tangled multitude of repeated curves, uniformity of form, and confusion of intersecting lines suggested a rendering of cosmic chaos, the symbolism of a mad art attempting the inconceivable.[6]

In the madness and tension of the new political climate, these overlapping circles also represented the amorphous nature of the struggle and underscored the ultimate futility of these revolutions. In the 'cosmic chaos', artists and writers also sought to articulate a vision that often oscillated between a utopian vision of society and a more dystopian portrait of the individual's place in it. By examining some of the key dynamite and revolutionary novels of Robert Louis Stevenson, Henry James, Joseph Conrad and G. K. Chesterton, as well as more popular fictions of W. H. Mallock, Edward Jenkins, and Donald McKay, I argue that the literary invention of underground terror was informed by, but departed dramatically from, the media's conception of the contagion sweeping Europe and the rest of the world. Although the more sensational novels warned of an external underground danger that threatened the empire, other novels of terrorism by more established authors raised psychological questions of identity and knowledge that departed from their original social and political context, while critiquing its own cultural production in face of a potential revolution. Anthony Kubiak, in his *Stages of Terror* proposes that '[t]errorism first appears in *culture* as a media event. The terrorist, consequently, does not exist before the media image, and only exists subsequently *as* a media image in culture'.[7] Although literature also took part in 'mediating' terror, creating its own breed of terrorist, the novel also self-reflexively pointed to its own limitations. From the deeply ironic portrayal of revolutionaries to caricatures of conspirators, authors engaged in both *mimesis* and *mimicry* of the events unfolding around them, reflecting and distorting the underground's potential for resistance. While imitating the actions and words of covert organisations, novels often participated in mocking their foundations, undercutting the symbolic power of terrorism to achieve its ideological aims.

'Infernal Machines' and Diabolical Plots

> A spectre is haunting Europe . . . the spectre of communism. All the powers of old Europe have entered into a holy alliance to exorcise the spectre: Pope and Czar, Metternich and Guizot, French Radical and German police spies.
> Karl Marx and Friedrich Engels, *The Communist Manifesto* (1848)

The 'spectre' that Marx refers to and the 'spectres' that Derrida revivify in *Specters of Marx* both contribute to a history of inheritance and the desire for justice in an increasingly untenable political situation. In the haunting of Marx's legacy, the spirit of a class revolution involved more than an exorcising of these ghosts – it precipitated a new atmosphere of violence and force to achieve these aims. A review of the political climate during this period of terrorism reveals the extent to which London became imbricated in the international web of terror and intrigue. The late nineteenth century was a dangerous time to be the head of state in Europe and North America. The emergence of subversive movements in many countries instilled great fear in the political leadership of major governments as bombs and assassinations became the (dis)order of the day. The assassination of Tsar Alexander II in 1881 triggered a wave of political violence, which culminated in the stabbing of President Marie Sadi Carnot in June 1894 in France, the assassination of the Spanish prime minister, Antonion Canovas in 1897, and the death of Empress Elizabeth of Austria in 1898. In the United States, President James Garfield's assassination in 1881 was followed by the death of President William McKinley in 1901, while in England, there was an attempt on Queen Victoria in 1872 by an Irishman and another failed attempt on her life in 1882. As Prince Metternich, the Austrian Chancellor, presaged in 1820:

> Kings have to calculate the chances of their very existence in the immediate future; passions are let loose, and league together to overthrow everything

which society represents as the basis of its existence; religion, public morality, laws, customs, rights and duties, all are attacked, confounded, overthrown, or called into question. The great mass of the people are tranquil spectators of these attacks and revolutions . . . A few are carried off by the torrent, but the wishes of an immense majority are to maintain a repose which exists no longer, and of which even the first elements seem to be lost . . .[8]

The fervour and passion with which the 'few' spread the revolutionary spirit to the 'masses' mirror previous associations with the underground as a conduit through which disease, disorder and new ideologies traversed the city like a contagion, its source indiscernible and its impact wide reaching. The submerged classes and political voices were no longer content to remain hidden in the depths, as they reappropriated the underground metaphor in a revolutionary movement to overturn and overthrow existing, and often oppressive, forms of government. The invisible network of terror spread throughout the world, as major cities became safe havens for dissidents who then continued to promote their cause in major metropolitan centres: Russian nihilists found willing ears in Paris and London, while Fenians sought refuge in New York and Boston, where they were able to raise the money and ammunition necessary for their overseas outrages. As revolutionaries circulated the globe, underground movements became a contagious phenomenon.

However, most of the violence in Europe was neither attributable to one single organisation, nor was it often attributed to the right organisation. According to Andrew Sinclair in his assessment of the prevalence of political activity 'hardly a capital in Europe was free from mob violence' during this period, while historian Sir Lewis Namier argues that 'revolutionaries were almost exclusively middle-class intellectuals, looking to take advantage of outbursts that initially began in overcrowded city slums'.[9] What is already apparent here is the complicated way in which underground protests were translated, from the actual event to the articulation of its intent. The question of the source behind the subversive activity crossed class lines and the political spectrum from Fenians to radical anarchists. The tendency of the press to confuse political groups due to biased reporting also contributed to the conflation of revolutionary sensibilities. Barbara Melchiori, in her historical study, emphasises that although Fenians were mostly responsible for the dynamite attacks in London, media and novelists elided the Irish Question in an attempt to 'canalise popular fear of explosions to build resistance to the whole socialist movement, which was rapidly growing at this time'.[10] External threat was then neutralised and displaced by internal strife, a more manageable representation of the problems at hand. Thus, the threat of terrorism from the outside was textually and psychologically buried in the press and literature, keeping foreign organisations relatively invisible and underground.

However, the English were riveted by the political upheaval abroad, especially in Russia, where the exploitations of the repressive regime made headlines in the popular press. In 1880, the assassination of Tsar Alexander II cast a spotlight on the nihilists, the largest and the most active underground organisation, whose overarching political philosophy later inspired socialists, anarchists and existentialists.[11] As the ultimate underground ideology in its negation of all surface capitalism, nihilism was defined first and foremost as an intellectual movement. As Sergei Kravchinsky (aka Stepniak) explains in his treatise, *Underground Russia* (1883):

> It was a struggle for the emancipation of the intelligence from every kind of dependence . . . It was the negation in the name of individual liberty, of all the obligations imposed upon the individual by society, by family life, and religion.[12]

To some degree, the emancipation from authority in the name of individual freedom was an extension of the nineteenth-century anti-hero in Russian literature, from Ivan Turgenev's deracinated character in *Diary of a Superfluous Man* (1850) to Fyodor Dostoevsky's disembodied voice in *Notes from Underground* (1864). Inspired by this lone, estranged figure during a time of severe persecution, nihilists developed the revolutionary ethos by which they would operate. Going underground for them meant a complete break from the upper world and a violent retaliation against the established order. Sergei Nechaev, the godfather of nihilism, defined the ideology and psychology further in his portrait of a political terrorist in *Catechism of a Revolutionary* (1869):

> The revolutionary is a doomed man. He has no personal interests, no affairs, sentiments, attachments, property, not even a name of his own. Everything in him is absorbed by one exclusive interest, one thought, one passion – the revolution . . .[13]

Such restless language appears in manifestoes and literary depictions of revolutionaries, as underground conspiracies hinged on men who were only known to each other by numbers or seasons. Such mysterious figures in Arthur and Mary Ropes's *On Peter's Island* (1901) and G. K. Chesterton's *The Man Who Was Thursday* (1908), both romanticised and caricatured the notion of an underground identity that lent a more dangerous anonymity on the city streets. Furthermore, London became a refuge for foreign nihilists and anarchists, inviting such high profile figures as Prince Peter Kropotkin, who expounded his ideals in town halls and private clubs. In some ways, what was underground was more aboveground than ever in London, as the subterranean revolutionary sensibility became more fashionable with each reappropriation. Zulaika and Douglass, in their theoretical work *Terror and Taboo*, claim that terrorism is a 'rhetorical product', and to an extent, 'a discursive practice'.[14] As information began to circulate through pamphlets, novels and mass journalism, fictionalisation and mythologisation of terror led to a consciousness of an all-pervasive spectre of communism on the brink of a bloody revolution.

Although the Russian nihilists and anarchists were perhaps the most prolific in the written promulgation of their political theories, the Fenians made the most palpable impact on London, attacking buildings that symbolised the authority of the state.[15] Fighting for Irish Home Rule, the Fenians were the first revolutionaries to attack the underground space, which became a psychological locus of fear, the nerve centre of British consciousness. Their calculated and deliberate bomb attacks on the underground railway, beginning with two explosions on Praed Street, between Charing Cross and Westminster, on 30 October 1883 marked the beginning of a new form of subterranean terror. Initially, the *Pall Mall Gazette* commented wryly, 'The explosions on the Underground Railway last evening, though fortunately attended with no loss of life, were very alarming and will add a new horror to an already disagreeable mode of locomotion.'[16] However, the underground bombings took on a more serious and deadly tone as machines and detonators proliferated during 1884–5, the 'year of the dynamitards'. There was a great explosion at Victoria Station on 25 February 1884, while bombs were found at Charing Cross, Paddington and Ludgate Hill, detonated to explode simultaneously. In the coverage of the explosions, the press eventually pointed to the Fenian hand behind the outrages:

> As reported yesterday, infernal machines were discovered at Charing-cross and Paddington Stations under circumstances which clearly prove that the explosion at Victoria Station was only part of a diabolical plan to destroy property and probably life . . . The whole thing is clearly of Irish American origin.[17]

The attack on London was relentless, as 'infernal machines' continued to appear in key urban sites, from Nelson's Column to London Bridge, exacerbating the fear and insecurity of Londoners while forcing the politicians to examine Gladstone's rather protracted proposal for a Home Rule Bill for Ireland. There was a further underground explosion on 2 January 1885 between Gower Street and King's Cross and a more audacious attempt at a simultaneous detonation in the Crypt of Westminster

Hall, the Houses of Parliament and the Tower of London. According to Houen, the randomness of the violence and the visual spectacle of the explosions terrorised the urban imagination:

> Dynamite's explosivity underscored the fact that instead of death and its significance being managed and contained within specific private and public spaces – such as the family home, the battleground, hospital, church, and cemetery – death could break into any space at any time.[18]

The bomb literally and figuratively exploded the most cherished notions of order and stability, while punctuating the map of the city with landmarks of violence. Zulaika and Douglass critically point to the significance of 'ritualization' in terror, which gains its power from 'repetitive and stereotyped forms'.[19] The subterranean space was a repetitive and ritualised target in the urban imagination, thereby imprinting the aura of terror onto all things associated with the explosions. Invisible connections between mysterious strangers, black paper bags in luggage compartments and hidden spaces beneath national buildings all came to be enmeshed in a web of intrigue and conspiracy. In the interchange of fact and fiction, media and literature, the discourse of terror also expanded into new narrative forms that struggled with the representation of a phenomenon that was supposed to remain silent, hidden and unseen.

'Fenian Fire': Unfolding the Revolutionary Plot

> The Irish cause requires skirmishers. It requires a little band of heroes who will initiate and keep up without intermission a guerrilla warfare – men who will fly over land and sea like invisible beings – now striking the enemy in Ireland, now in India, now in England itself, as occasion may present.
>
> *Irish World* (4 December 1875)

The recruitment of Fenian soldiers often demanded an invisibility and a ubiquity that reinforced their ghostly presence in the city. From oblique references to their organisational efficiency to a more direct indictment of their violent recourses, Fenians surfaced in contradictory ways in media and literature, as they waged their dynamite campaign from 1881–5. Although in essence they were a secret society, Fenianism mobilised itself as a mass movement that met openly in public spaces, while extending their branches to France and the US, from where they derived most of their tactical and financial ammunition. As a revolutionary organisation, Fenians embodied even more contradictions, as they publically operated their own dynamite press in the US, such as the *Irish World* and the *United Irishman*, which raised funds for their nationalist cause, while depicting England as an oppressive state, even offering a reward of $10,000 in one issue for the body of the Prince of Wales, 'dead or alive'.[20] However, on English soil, the Fenians were elided in the press and literature, often conflated with socialists and anarchists, which in turn kept them more underground than they may have intended. As discussed in Chapter 1, the Irishman was long associated with the social underworld, distinctly separate from the Englishman and the embodiment of 'other' in all his physical, moral and psychological manifestations. Matthew Arnold, in *Culture and Anarchy* (1869), focused on their alien and alienated status in his description of the Irish as a race apart:

> And then the difference between an Irish Fenian and an English rough is so immense, and the case, in dealing with the Fenian, so much more clear! He is so evidently desperate and dangerous, a man of a conquered race, a Papist, with centuries of ill-usage to inflame him against us, with an alien religion established in his country by us at his expense, with no admiration of our institutions, no love of our virtues, no talents for our business, no turn for our comfort! . . . Evidently, if we deal tenderly with a sentimentalist like this, it is out of pure philanthropy.[21]

The cultural disdain and colonising gaze are evident here, as anarchy is defined by the absence of culture, an argument that is circulated again later in the works of James and Chesterton. Furthermore, throughout the land war and the Home Rule Crisis of the 1880s, cartoonists regularly simianised Irish nationalists in the press that relegated them to a devolved species of the lower order, the same trope found in representations of Africans in McClintock's study of colonisation and purity.[22] However, the danger they posed to the seat of English power was felt everywhere.

In line with earlier depictions of the underground as a dangerous and unknowable space, the Fenians were also perceived as a major threat from below on multiple levels. Firstly, the constituency of the organisation were primarily from the working class of artisans, labourers and small farmers; secondly, they operated through invisible networks; and most importantly, they targeted underground infrastructure in random and unpredictable ways. Much of the earlier radical activity in the 1850s was attributable to the Irish Revolutionary Brotherhood (IRB), which later became the Irish Republican Brotherhood that advocated armed resistance against the British. Fenian leaders such as John Mitchel deployed a vertical metaphor to awaken nationalist sensibilities and to incite violence across the Channel:

> The earth is awakening from sleep: a flash of electric fire is passing through the dumb millions . . . Oh! My countrymen look up, look up! Arise from the

deathdust where you have long been lying, and let this light visit your eyes also, and touch your souls. Let your ears drink in the blessed words, 'Liberty! Fraternity! Equality!' which are soon to ring pole to pole . . . Above all, let the man amongst you who has no gun, sell his garment and buy one.[23]

Drawing on the French Revolution and other European insurgencies, the IRB reorganised itself as an oath-bound secret society, and although exact numbers are uncertain, there were purportedly 80,000 sworn members. Historian John Newsinger also remarks on the use of aliases and anonymous military units as effective and necessary tools in the new art of terror, further aligning the Irish nationalist movement with elusive subterranean tactics. Resembling Conrad's description of Stevie's drawings, the movement organised itself around overlapping spheres of command:

[The IRB was] organised into circles, each with some 800 members commanded by a centre or 'A'. Under each 'A' were nine 'B's' or captains, each commanding some 90 men, and under each 'B' were nine 'C's or sergeants, each commanding nine men. The intention was that each individual member of the organisation would only know his immediate comrades and his immediate superior. This, it was hoped, would prevent penetration by spies and informers.[24]

This very modern network of terror decentralised power and broke up the organisation into discrete cells that carried out clandestine operations independently in Glasgow, London and Liverpool. Borrowing the term 'Fianna', an ancient legendary Irish army, the term 'Fenians' then surfaced as the face of Irish militarism, associated with explosives and detonators discovered in public spaces, predominantly targeting utility and transport infrastructure that extended underground. In 1883, they targeted a gasometer in Glasgow that collapsed into flames and a coal shed at Buchanan Street Station of the Caledonian Railway. Shortly after, there was a discovery of the infamous 'bonnet box' on the aqueduct of Forth and Clyde Canal behind *The Times* publishing offices, a blatant message that mirrored the shocking headlines in the press. In order to protect the nation from 'Fenian Fire', another term for the highly inflammable liquid used in some explosions, a new secret service and the Special Irish Branch of Scotland Yard were created to take critical counter-terrorist measures. In London, even sewer workers were sworn in as Special Constables, as they joined teams of police in sweeping the passages under government offices. As *The Times* pointed out, 'the Houses of Parliament are searched as if continually on the eve of a GUY FAWKES plot'.[25] Furthermore, by co-ordinating explosions in the underground railway, London Bridge and the Crypt in the Houses of Parliament, the Fenians waged their guerrilla warfare, using subterranean targets to shake England's social and political foundations. The underground organisation, its invisibility, and its attack on subterranean infrastructure created the socio-spatial dialectic of fear and terror, as the fragility of the city and indeed the empire was magnified through Fenian attempts to explode the vertical hierarchy of the establishment.

As mentioned previously, a distinct aspect of this underground network was how it extended across national borders. In the popular literary imagination, another fear of an underground attack entered the Victorian psyche in the potential of underwater tactics from foreign invaders. As key Fenian leaders Jeremiah O'Donovan Rossa and John Devoy escaped to the US to garner support for their dynamite campaign, Gladstone was correct in his assessment that where 'Fenianism was concerned its root was in Ireland but its branches were in America'.[26] Anthony Trollope briefly alludes to this connection in his final, unfinished novel, *The Landleaguers* (1883), where his ambivalence towards the Irish cause is evident:

> A sweeter-tempered people than had existed there had been found nowhere; nor a people more ignorant, and possessing less of the comforts of civilization. But no evil was to be expected from them, no harm came from them . . . The tuition had come from America! That, no doubt, was true; but it had come by Irish hearts and Irish voices, by Irish longings and Irish ambition.[27]

Here, Trollope is almost trying to negotiate the fragmented nature of Irish identity, but fails to find a way to justify their terrorist activities. In England, the threat of a Fenian attack from abroad was envisaged in futuristic, apocalyptic narratives, particularly underwater fantasies, that portended another form of a subterranean technological invasion. Fred Burnaby's *Our Radicals: A Tale of Love and Politics* (1886) depicts an underwater tunnel, or a 'chunnel', connecting Ireland and England that would facilitate more dynamite attacks on English soil. Meanwhile, Donald MacKay's *The Dynamite Ship* (1888) also paints a technological fantasy where a phantom ship sails silently through the Thames 'like a spectre' and decimates London, thereby establishing Ireland as an independent state.[28] These 'sub-aqueous' plots also mirrored real scientific inventions, as the Fenians in the US attempted to build the first torpedo submarine to undercut England's naval might in the high seas.[29] Although drawings were made and experiments were carried out, the prototype, called Holland No. 1, was never to attack a British ship. However, it was to be the template of a generation of submarines launched in May 1897, heralding a new form of underwater terror.

Despite these popular forms of literature that alluded to the Irish movement, Fenianism was as spectral as an underwater torpedo during the dynamite war campaign, as many novelists alluded to Irish underground activities but avoided any overt political links to the organisation. Melchiori argues that the strategy was to divert attention from the Fenian cause to shift the emphasis to socialism in England, while Houen has linked the elision to the ways in which textuality and terrorism contributed to modernism. More recently, Ó Donghaile has conceptualised late nineteenth-century shocks as explosions that rocked the literary establishment and argues that dynamite and dynamite novels posed an equally destructive threat to the British consciousness. I would also add a psychological element to this argument to reveal that the experience of terror in literature remained embedded in the psyche, and thus the experience of the dynamite explosions was displaced onto detective and quest narratives that allowed for a more manageable apprehension of the fear at hand. Even after 9/11, authors initially struggled to articulate the terror, as the insufficiency of language in the Burkean sublime of destruction was beyond words, beyond action, and beyond comprehension. What I argue for, then, is an inward turning from the political to the philosophical, as many of the dynamite narratives shifted the underground focus from the revolutionary movements to the darker questions of *dasein* and consciousness of one's place in the world.

The popular narratives of this subconscious elision were more light-hearted and often turned an explosion into an exploration of urban identities. In Edward Jenkins's novel *A Week of Passion; or, The Dilemma of Mr. George Barton* (1884), which was published during the height of Fenian Fire, the narrative begins appropriately enough with an explosion at Regents Circus, mimicking the bombs that exploded in underground railway stations. However, rather than attributing the violence to an external political cause, Jenkins deftly subverts the conspiracy plot to a more predictable Holmesian detective mystery, as the traces lead to a firm of solicitors trying to destroy evidence of the company's malpractices. The genre of the detective novel then serves as the subterfuge for the real terror that confronts the city, diverting the attention away from the underground threat to a more concrete representation of the enemy that can be comprehended and apprehended.

The sensitivity surrounding the dynamite explosions and the lives that were lost offered another reason for the political evasion of Fenians in literary depictions. One of the more popular novels to address Fenian bombings was 'The Dynamiters' (1885) by Robert Louis Stevenson and his wife Fanny Van de Grift, but its intended publication date unfortunately coincided with a dynamite attack that delayed its release. When it was finally published, Stevenson added a foreword to commemorate the police who died in the bombing, thereby exempting himself from the criticism that would have accompanied his playful approach to terrorism. In the tale, Stevenson and Van de Grift dilute the terrorist plot to a comedic chase around London by three effete 'futiles' who decide to pursue a wanted terrorist for a monetary reward. What ensues is a game of charades, or more apropos of the title, Scheherazade, where three disparate narratives weave and intertwine in a constant unmasking of underground plots and identities. As one of the pursuants, Paul Somerset, remarks, 'Hark how, in this quiet corner, London roars like the noise of battle; four million destinies are here concentred; and in the strong panoply of one hundred pounds, payable to the bearer, I am about to plunge into that web.'[30] The cast of characters include a Mormon heroine, a Prince of Bohemia and a monomaniacal dynamiter named Zero, who all remain as caricatures and stereotypes of otherness, until veil by veil, they are all revealed to be a more local feature of the London landscape. Other than M'Guire, a bumbling accomplice who manages to kill himself with a bomb that detonates in the Thames with nothing but a minor splash, there are very few allusions to Irish dynamitards. Only the shadow of the terrorist Zero who leaves for Philadelphia at the end of the novel links the bomb to Irish-American sources. 'Mr. Jones' by day and the 'redoubted Zero' by night, he is the only compelling underground figure in the text, but he is ultimately a parody of Stevenson's own Dr Jekyll and Mr Hyde, a chemist who secretly hides in the back drawing room creating unknown concoctions of a highly destructive and self-destructive nature.

> If you love romance (as artists do), few lives are more romantic than that of the obscure individual now addressing you. Obscure yet famous. Mine is an anonymous, infernal glory. By infamous means, I work towards my bright purpose. I found the liberty and peace of a poor country, desperately abused; the future smiles upon that land; yet, in the meantime, I lead the existence of a hunted brute, work towards appalling ends, and practice hell's dexterities.[31]

In this ironically romantic and solipsistic assessment, traces of nihilism can be found in the putative justice he seeks, but Stevenson and Van de Grift subvert his madness into an exaggerated mimicry of a subterranean consciousness, nullifying any genuine intent in the text for a potential revolution. The terrorist's numerical moniker equates itself with the force he exerts in the narrative, as well as the sum of all the machinations of the characters in the text. In the end, when all is revealed, foreigners have either left the country or are revealed to have been English all along. Order is reinstated and any terrorist threat is neutralised to a case of mistaken identity. The underground here is merely a setting for domestic intrigue and an expression of the hidden elements in the city, which become decipherable through an unveiling of identities and narratives.

As the Fenian scare abated at the end of the 1880s and dynamite explosions in the city eventually ceased, another narrative form emerged to cast the underground organisation in a different light. Most notably, biographies and historical studies of Fenians were published that seemed to portend the end of their underground status. Once enough time had elapsed from the height of its terrorist threat, Fenianism surfaced textually that recast the movement in a different way. The hunted Fenians later became elevated heroes through such texts as John O'Leary's *Recollections of Fenians and Fenianism* (1896) and later, John Devoy's *Recollections of an Irish Rebel* (1929), which made Fenianism a popular literary phenomenon. In fact, some of the most frightening remnants of Fenianism in literature are captured in the modernist fragments of James Joyce's *Ulysses* (1922), in which oblique suggestions of the underground movement are embedded in the subconscious wanderings of the main protagonist, Leopold Bloom. In the section 'Cyclops', a Fenian, Martin Cunningham, encounters Leopold and berates him with anti-Semitic language, while in the 'Proteus' section, Stephen recalls his time in Paris with Kevin Egan, whose character is based on a Fenian dynamiter. The blue smoke curling around Egan's fingers reminds Stephens of a lit dynamite fuse, which has rich allusions to the bombings in London, but again, the evocation of a terrorist threat is more of a metaphor for a larger sense of violence in Leopold's dreamscape. Moreover, contemporary revisionist history such as Leon Ó Broin's *Revolutionary Underground* (1976) describes the organisation as anything but underground, while R. V. Comerford's *The Fenians in Context* (1985) presents the Fenian movement as more of a social activity for disillusioned youths that had 'deteriorated into a miscellany of purposeless gangs'.[32] In response, John Newsinger argued for a Marxist reading of the Fenian movement, noting the influence it exerted on the socialist movement in England, thereby adding another palimpsestic layer to the historical landscape of the elusive Fenians. Historian P. S. O'Hegarty is perhaps the most balanced in the importance he attaches to the IRB, emphasising the pervasiveness of the underground movement despite any concrete changes they may have made to the system in their failed uprisings.

> Parnell had crowded the I.R.B. out of the public mind, but it was there, underground all the time, small in numbers, very often divided, without effective leadership, and without any current policy save that of keeping the separatist spirit alive and maintaining the framework of a separatist organisation.[33]

The fragmentation of the organisation, yet the omnipresence of the revolutionary spirit, echoes what we have observed thus far in textual practice. Although the Fenian bombings served as the impetus and the basis for narratives about underground activity, they remained largely absent and 'out of the public mind' in literature and the press. Thus, the sense of undergroundedness in political movements can be seen as becoming more diffuse aboveground, a revolutionary spirit that haunts the city like the spectre of communism, disassociating itself from the material underground itself and melting into the air of modernity as a metaphor for dissension in a politically fragmented climate.

Middle-class Socialists and Anarchic Aristocrats

'Gestures! Gestures! Mere gestures of her class.'
Joseph Conrad, 'The Informer' (1908)

If representations of Fenian threat appeared fragmented and contra-dictory, the narratives of socialists and anarchists also maintained a strikingly paradoxical position, as novels focused on the upper levels of social hierarchy while depicting the struggles of those below. The social underground, commonly seen as the voice of the working classes, was primarily depicted in middle-class terms, especially in Gissing, who saw the failure of the socialist movement, while other authors, such as Walter Besant and George Bernard Shaw, reflected the potential for upward social movement through the education of the working classes. However, the greatest contradiction in the representation of under-ground movements came from that of the anarchists, whose plight was solely depicted in upper-class terms despite its constituency, which was primarily made up of working classes. Although anarchists wished to eradicate the entire class hierarchy, literature representing these factions often featured aristocrats and the gentry who wished to escape boredom while pursuing the loftier ideals of justice and democracy. In her exami-nation of class, Haia Shpayer-Makov traces real aristocrats who histori-cally joined the cause, from Prince Kropotkin to Italian scientist Errico Malatesta, whom she believes served as the basis for so many novels featuring upper, educated classes.[34] However, the delineation between upper and lower classes was more complicated, as underground and aboveground politics became enmeshed in the *fin-de-siècle* narrative. As it became more difficult to distinguish between competing political ideologies, a fluid, hybrid identity roamed the city streets, making the terrorist even less discernible in the ensuing crowd.

The figure of the *flâneur*, whom we have traced thus far from the sewers to the cemetery, also begins to embody the instability of his position in the face of conflicting revolutionary activities. We have observed various underground versions of the urban wanderer, from a by-product of waste in the sewers, a female passenger in the Underground Tube, to the spirit of the undead in cemeteries. Here, I want to pursue a final transformation of the underground *flâneur* as a *fin-de-siècle* terrorist whose aimless pursuit reflects the aimlessness of the political cause. Although a member of the leisured classes, the *flâneur*-terrorist could not have avoided the visual exchanges of mass meetings in Hyde Park, the Fenian detonations or the socialist demonstrations that were so pervasive in the 1880s. However, his detachment from, yet involvement in, the actual political cause is reflected in many novels of failed terrorist attempts. An example of this may be found in Henry James in his preface to *The Princess Casamassima*, where he confesses that he had gathered most of his anarchist material from newspapers, while culling his impressions of the working classes from 'nocturnal walks'. Critic Paul Hollywood emphasises James's technique of 'spectatorship' that allowed him to create the paradoxical and unstable figure of Hyacinth, who is both the observer and observed and a mixture of high and low classes.[35] In the hybrid figure of Hyacinth as a *flâneur*-terrorist, I hope to show how social boundaries ultimately collapse in the representation of the revolutionary subject in the concatenation of social hierarchies, undermining any attempt at a coherent representation of the socialist or anarchist movement. In his assessment of underground circles, Chesterton describes in his tale 'an outer ring and an inner ring . . . The outer ring – the main mass of their supporters are merely anarchists; that is, men who believe that rules and formulas have destroyed happiness'. Meanwhile, the inner ring is an elite corps, comprised of 'aristocrats' and even 'South African and American millionaires' who ostensibly control the inner ring.[36] Melchiori continues this metaphor by observing that, 'terrorists are often puppets dangling at the end of very long wires, wires so long that we lose sight of the hands that hold them'.[37] With invisible hands that bind, social differences become less discernible and ideological motivations even more fragmented as the underground pervades all arenas of life in a more fluid philosophical movement, rather than a political one. In the common dissent against social forces and political discontent, class warfare concedes to an intermingling and interbreeding of classes in a new revolutionary sensibility.

But first, it is important to keep in mind the roots of social activism in England that first established literature with the underground movement. In the mid-1800s, as outlined in Chapter 1, the underground was open to voyeuristic interpretation from the middle-class gaze that sought to expose the social injustices of the poor, while keeping the abject subject matter at arm's length. From Dickens's night walks to Henry Mayhew's spotlight on the 'skulking' masses, the Condition-of-England project exposed the social depths, but at the same time kept the underground safely underground. Other works, like Benjamin Disraeli's *Sybil, or The Two Nations* (1845), Charles Kingsley's *Alton Locke* (1850) and Mary Gaskell's *North and South* (1855), continued to map the class divide in vertical terms, with the poor firmly entrenched below ground and in slums that resembled a subterranean cavern. However, by the 1880s, the underground struggle merged with middle-class voices in a new expression of social protest as mass riots and protests flooded the streets. Predominantly fuelled by the difficulties of British industry and the subsequent economic downturn, vast unemployment led to widespread social unrest. Many of the socialist demonstrations were organised by the Social Democratic Federation (SDF) that was led by members of the middle or upper classes, including Henry Mayers Hyndman, William Morris and the Countess of Warwick. However, the translation of Marxist ideals into the activities of a socialist organisation was rife with contradictions, especially when it came to the objectives of the group, which ranged from a complete decimation of the existing capitalist order by the proletariat, to the education of the lower classes to offer greater social mobility within the existing system.

George Gissing's *Demos* (1886), which coincides with the height of this social struggle, exemplifies the conflicts within the movement in the conflation of purposes and ideologies. One of the reactionary characters, Hugh Eldon, shuts down a socialist project, citing differences between the continental underground movement and the English enterprise:

> Now in the revolutionary societies of the Continent there is something that appeals to the imagination. A Nihilist, with Siberia or death before him, fighting against a damnable tyranny – the best might sacrifice everything for that. But English Socialism! It is infused with the spirit of shop-keeping; it appeals to the vulgarest minds . . . it is stamped commonplace, like everything originating with the English lower classes. How does it differ from Radicalism, the most contemptible clap-trap of politics, except in wanting to hurry a little the rule of the mob?[38]

Gissing confers nobility upon the Russian nihilists but associates English revolutionary activity with baser motivations and the vulgarity of the lower classes, expressing his own disillusionment with socialism and its potential to liberate the uneducated classes. His later works move away from the lower classes to focus on the lower-middle classes in their struggle to negotiate a life in the city, a subtle shift that reflects his resignation with the socialist cause. Another novel of the same year, Walter Besant's *Children of Gibeon* (1886), offers a more optimistic view of class mobility, revealing how education as well as heredity can affect the development of class differences. A social experiment akin to George Bernard Shaw's *Pygmalion* (1916), two girls are raised in an aristocratic family, but one is told that she is the daughter of a smith and a washerwoman, while the other is an heiress. Ultimately, the novel goes on to disprove the hereditary argument that 'the daughter of a working class man and the daughter of a gentleman can ever stand upon the same level. Education can refine, but it cannot change base metal into gold.'[39] Once again, the dichotomy between high and low, base and refined is conjured up in an effort to sustain a division between classes; however, Besant's treatment of the two girls ultimately destabilises this vertical metaphor, revealing that in due course, no one is able to tell the difference between the two girls from radically different backgrounds. In this manner, he flattens out the social hierarchy in line with socialist ideals and reveals the potential for a more fluid horizontal movement between classes.

Although the upper classes are represented in socialist narratives, their participation is often tinged with irony, if not fear. In W. H. Mallock's *The Old Order Changes* (1886), a group of aristocrats gather in a French château to discuss the implications of socialism and invite socialist agitator Mr Foreman (a twist on H. M. Hyndman of the SDF), who proceeds to discuss the threat that would come from below:

> We come to Karl Marx's theorem as to the nature of profits or interest, or – to put the matter plainly – of the entire subsistence of the leisured and the propertied classes. This is the real dynamite that will shatter our existing civilization – this single economic discovery.[40]

Despite the dynamite metaphor that threatens to explode the entire social hierarchy, the lower classes are still depicted very much as an unruly mob, 'moving like a great volume of semi-liquid sewage, on the surface of which certain raised objects seemed to be floating, while the edges of it, in one place or another, were perpetually frothing against the sides of shops and houses'.[41] In reducing the entire socialist movement as an event to be observed with detachment from the château walls, Mallock reinforces the class divide while warning the upper class of their impending involvement in the mêlée.

Similarly, critics have also noted the detachment of the upper-class gaze in Henry James's *The Princess Casamassima*, which attempts to intermingle classes under the revolutionary cause. Mark Seltzer observes that in the novel, 'a relation between seeing and power becomes evident in the literature of the London underworld . . . not because the writer acknowledges the relation, but rather, because he works so carefully to disavow it'.[42] James self-consciously presents aristocrats who endeavour to align themselves with the underground cause, such as Lady Aurora, who is obsessively drawn to the slums, and, of course, Princess Casamassima herself, with her predilection for working-class men, from Hyacinth to Paul Muniment. However, both women are unable to sustain anything other than a voyeuristic relationship with the lower classes, as ultimately the revolutionary cause, embodied in Muniment, rejects them both. Despite James's attempts to confront issues of class, his depiction seems to elide the real social problems that Besant and Gissing sought to expose. As one critic notes, James 'vitiates the whole thesis of the book, by making the choice lie between terrorist assassination and aristocratic associations, instead of in the more actual problem on which Gissing had to make up his mind – working class revolt versus middle class culture'.[43] While the whole of the middle class is conspicuously absent from James's work, he displays the limitations of his own particular perspective by conflating so many issues, from socialism to continental anarchism, even though he was writing at the height of the Fenian bombings, of which he was acutely aware.

Although underground revolutionary ideas circulate freely through all classes, they fail to enact real changes to the overall social or political system. Rather, the idea of being underground becomes co-opted by the upper classes to pursue more personal ends, whether it is to escape a loveless marriage (as in the case of the Princess) or to find fulfilment in helping the poor (as in the endeavours of Lady Aurora). Beyond the personal, political motivations remain in the shadows of foreigners like Diedrich Hoffendahl, the man ostensibly behind the conspiracy with invisible ties to the continent. Thus, what remains of revolutionary impulses is the potential for violence that gives lower classes hope and the upper classes a frisson of danger and excitement in their otherwise dull and perfunctory existence.

Meanwhile, it is Hyacinth who epitomises the tension between classes and the contradictions within the revolution, as he attempts to negotiate his double life in the city. As the illegitimate son of an English duke and a French prostitute, he makes a living as 'bastard bookbinder', yet another interbreeding of high and low social and cultural elements. With Princess Casamassima as a patroness, he is able to experience a wealthier standard of life that he believes is a part of him through heredity, but one he must forfeit in service of the cause. In Paris, he is able to take on the role of the traditional *flâneur*, strolling through the city and visually consuming the architecture and culture; however, when he returns to London, he must assume the role of a reluctant terrorist who must destroy everything that represents status or hierarchy, including the arts. Reflecting on the excesses of England, James echoes the sentiments that are also passed on to Hyacinth regarding the impending violence stemming from the underworld:

> In England the Huns and Vandals will have to come *up* – from the black depths of the . . . enormous misery . . . At all events, much of English life is grossly materialistic and wants bloodletting.[44]

Despite such overt revolutionary inclinations, the only blood that is shed in the novel is that of Hyacinth, who kills himself in order to avoid destroying the entire establishment on which the arts and culture, and ultimately literature, so depend. Thus, Hyacinth begins to form the outline of the *flâneur*-terrorist, whose detachment allows him to detonate without remorse, but whose actions would paradoxically destroy the class differences on which his identity lies.

The class contradictions inherent in the *flâneur*-terrorist reveal the profound irony of most terrorist organisations, as Conrad reveals in his texts about radical anarchists. As revolutionary discourse became central to modern consciousness at the turn of the century, Conrad looks at the *poseurs* from lower and upper classes who engage in political discourse, only to find themselves in a web of deceit and lies. Historian Wm. M. Phillips suggests the interlocking fates of anarchists, as more people subscribed to its ideology:

> [T]he anarchist moves from the borders of mainstream understanding to the very middle of things . . . Each character attempts to be self-contained in her or his own simplified understanding of the world . . . and intersects with other characters only randomly; the overall effect of numerous simple shapes randomly related to each other, however, is not order but anarchy.[45]

Two short stories written by Conrad after the height of anarchism exhibit this anarchy in contrast to the violent, political threat it posed in the late 1880s.[46] 'An Anarchist' and 'The Informer' in Conrad's *A Set of Six* (1908) reveal the ubiquity of anarchist sentiments and the method by which the high and low oppositions that permeated social discourse ultimately become dismantled. In 'An Anarchist', a poor mechanic becomes an anarchist because others recognise him as one, while in 'The Informer', Mr X, a wealthy collector of bronzes and porcelains, proclaims himself to be an anarchist despite his distance from the centre of any revolutionary activity. Conrad builds on the dark irony he sustains throughout *The Secret Agent* and develops the ambiguity and ineffectuality of the anarchist movement. In 'An Anarchist', the mechanic resembles Stevie in his innocence and impulsiveness, as he is suddenly awakened to the inequities of the world and driven to destructive extremes.

> Gloomy ideas *des idées noires* – rushed into his head. All the world outside the café appeared to him as a dismal evil place where a multitude of poor wretches had to work and slave to the sole end that a few individuals should ride in carriages and live riotously in palaces. He became ashamed of his happiness ... There was only one way of dealing with the rotten state of society. Demolish the whole *sacrée boutique*.[47]

In a brief moment of epiphany, he aligns himself with the anarchist cause and sees violence as the only answer to social inequities. As Carol Hamilton observes, Conrad depicts the mechanic as a 'natural anarchist' by way of Cesare Lombroso and Max Nordau, who believed that anarchists had similar genetic tendencies to those of prostitutes, thieves and murderers.[48] Although the mechanic joins the anarchist group, he ultimately rejects them when he ends up in prison for being an accomplice to a bomb plot. In a prison mutiny, he manages to escape on a boat and finally ends up on an island in South America in a self-imposed exile, further distancing himself from the revolutionary movement and descending 'underground' in a physical and social sense. However, the manager and others continue to label him an anarchist as he descends into sleeplessness and madness, imputing a degenerative element to his overall psychological make-up. In this 'desperate tale', what is considered underground is ultimately categorised as a genetic defect by an outside observer, in this case a middle-class narrator, who remarks on the contagious nature of this 'disease':

> On the whole, my idea is that he was much more of an anarchist than he confessed to me or to himself; and that, the special features of his case apart, he was very much like many other anarchists. Warm heart and weak head – that is the word of the riddle; and it is a fact that the bitterest contradictions and the deadliest conflicts of the world are carried on in every individual breast capable of feeling and passion.[49]

In this tale, multiple undergrounds are explored, from the social to the psychological, but what is deemed to be 'anarchist' is a potentially degenerative trait that can traverse classes and countries, a quasi-medical assessment that attempts to categorise and isolate this contagion. Thus, anarchism even fuses with medical discourse in uncovering the layers of physiological and pathological impulses that produce the unsocial and anti-social figure of the terrorist capable of destruction who is usually a member of, but not limited to, the working class.

The contradictions in the comingling of class and underground sensibilities are also brought to surface in 'The Informer', where Conrad satirises a familiar tale of an anarchist from the upper-class. A story embedded in a story, as well as a conspiracy within a conspiracy, the anarchist and aristocrat Mr X is introduced to the narrator, a collector of fine *objets d'arts*, who then vicariously sees his life through the anarchist's romanticised underground existence.

> He is the greatest rebel (*révolté*) of modern times. The world knows him as a revolutionary writer whose savage irony has laid bare the rottenness of the most respectable institutions . . . And the world at large has never had an inkling of that fact! This accounts for him going about amongst us to this day, a veteran of many subterranean campaigns, standing aside now, safe within his reputation of merely the greatest destructive publicist that ever lived.[50]

Drawing on all the stereotypes of continental anarchists, Conrad posits Mr X as the anonymous figure behind the uprisings, coups and conspiracies, the mastermind who has 'sapped the vitality of at least one monarchy'.[51] Like Hoffendahl in *The Princess Casamassima*, his international connections remain dark and ominous, imitating the shadowy figure of the international conspirator infiltrating London through the upper classes. However, Conrad subverts this figure by casting him as an object of desire rather than a subject of intrigue, mimicking earlier works that characterised the anarchist spectrally as the invisible hand behind demonic acts of terrorism. Like a fine piece of china, the narrator appraises and admires the anarchist, and in exchange, the anarchist regales him with a conspiracy tale that has all the elements and trappings of a Victorian dynamite novel. In acknowledging this exchange, X remarks, 'What I have acquired has come to me through my writings; not from the millions of pamphlets distributed gratis to the hungry and the oppressed, but from the hundreds of thousands of copies sold to the well-fed bourgeois.'[52]

Thus, subversive pamphlets and oral narratives, not unlike Victorian tales of dynamite and conspiracy, all become part of the capitalist enterprise, their value appraised by the readership, confirming Conrad's view that a 'true anarchist is a millionaire'.[53] As X narrates the tale within the story, he introduces a double agent, Sevrin, who is involved in a conspiracy plot to bomb a great public building. Familiar figures like the professor reappear as an 'extreme revolutionist' who secretly makes bombs in a laboratory, only to perish by his own *métier* as one of the detonators prematurely explodes before reaching its destination. Meanwhile, a love plot unfolds involving Sevrin and an upper-class conspirator, Lady Amateur, who closely resembles Princess Casamassima in her role as an underground networker, revealing once again how multiple lives intersect at various points that allow revolutionary issues to circulate from the forefront of political activity to after-dinner conversations in upper-class salons. Mocking the revolutionary novel, the tale soon becomes a critique of the public who thrive on such sensationalism that allows them to emerge from the texts untouched by the real political struggle underneath. In the co-optation of the underground by the upper classes, all revolutionary ideals become surface, an artificial ruse that reinforces class hierarchies in which lower classes remain stagnant in the substratum, the middle-classes consume conspiracy narratives, and the upper classes control the grand narrative to their amusement.

Domesticating Terror

[The home] would be permeated from every direction by streams of energy which run in and out of it by every imaginable route.
                              Henri Lefebvre, *Production of Space* (1971)

If the representation of underground revolutions in the nineteenth and the early twentieth century was marked by contradictory images of terrorists and an absence of a coherent ideology, it was also beset by a lack of dynamite explosions and a clear spatial target. While in reality, the barrage of attacks on London signalled an external threat to the city, literary depictions often diverted such tactics to a more internal, domestic struggle that suggested the terror within. In spatial representations, the home became a contested site of political and psychological struggles, a Lefebvrian dialectic of outer and inner worlds. Often mirroring the abstract and inchoate struggle of political organisations, the domestic sphere revealed personal conflicts that threatened the fabric of the home, as well as society. Thus, the home became the new spatial underground of terrorist plots, where another form of explosion signalled a psychological break in the urban moral landscape.

In looking at space, it is useful to look at utopian and dystopian models of the underground as they privilege the political in the socio-spatial dialectic of the home. E. M. Forster's 'The Machine Stops' (1909) embraces some salient aspects of this relationship, while protesting against a prototypically revolutionary subterranean space. In response to the utopian novels of the late nineteenth century, which depicted the subterranean lair as a potential technological shelter, Forster depicts a dystopian futuristic world where civilisation has descended underground and individuals live in isolated cells, controlled by the invisible power of 'The Machine'. The underground habitat is an enclosed, hermetically sealed space, where one rebel, Kuno, seeks to reconnect with his mother and the outside world.

> This city, as you know, is built deep beneath the surface of the earth, with only the vomitories protruding . . . I could think of nothing but these ventilation shafts . . . If I came upon them anywhere, it would be in the railway tunnels of the topmost story. Everywhere else, all space was accounted for.[54]

In this representation, the underground home resembles more of a Heideggerian framework of space where '[m]an's relation to locations, and through locations to spaces, inheres in his dwelling. The relationship between man and space is none other than dwelling'.[55] This static notion of space, or the privileging of place over space, is what distinguishes science-fiction representations of the revolutionary underground. The concrete place one inhabits is part of the whole system against which one must rebel. Thus, to rise above one's dwelling/station and to rise above the surface of the earth is the vertical trajectory of the revolutionary impulse. Such forward and upward movement, or an uprising of sorts, becomes more complicated in later novels of resistance, where revolution no longer dwells underneath the earth's surface, but in more varied forms of discourse above and belowground.

In *The Princess Casamassima*, Henry James deals with this spatial incertitude by deftly avoiding the underground signifier and replacing it with politically discursive moments that shift around various domestic spheres. In the beginning, Hyacinth first paints London in subterranean overtones as a 'huge tragic city where unmeasured misery lurked beneath the dirty night, ominously, monstrously still', where the anarchist leader Muniment would

> surge through the sleeping world and gather the myriad miserable out of their slums and burrows, should roll into the selfish squares and lift a tremendous hungry voice and awaken the gorged indifferent to a terror that would bring them down.[56]

Influenced by the French Revolution and the French literary tradition, James echoes the impassioned cry of Hugo and the organic naturalism of Zola; however, beyond these exhortative words there is a desperate lack of action, commensurate with Hyacinth's outcries. Far from Heideggerian fixity, James uses a more fluid and psychological language, reminiscent of Bachelard's metaphysical approach to space, as he describes the socio-spatial separation that divides the 'haves' and the 'have-nots':

> Nothing of it appears above the surface; but there's an immense underworld peopled with a thousand forms of revolutionary passion and devotion . . .

And on top of it all society lives . . . and iniquities flourish, and the misery of half the world is prated about as a 'necessary evil', and generations rot away and starve in the midst of it . . . All that's one half of it; the other half is that everything's doomed! In silence, in darkness, but under the feet of each one of us, the revolution lives and works. It's a wonderful, immeasurable trap, on the lid of which society performs its antics. When once the machinery is complete there will be a great rehearsal.[57]

Again, there is a sense of foreboding and mystery, a promise of a *revolution* and a *revelation*, but in effect, neither comes to fruition. The silent underworld that threatens to explode all aspects of surface existence remains shut despite the machinations of international conspirators and domestic anarchists throughout the novel. Even the anarchist club, The Sun and Moon, the ostensible locus of underground political activity, is cursorily described in one chapter, but nothing actionable comes out of the meeting. The subterranean space is elided for what Eileen Sypher considers to be the 'foregrounding of domestic space', as gender relations predominate the development of the narrative and plot. 'Overwhelmingly, the space of the novel is taken up by the rooms of Pinnie, Mr. Vetch, the Poupins, the Muniments, the Princess, and Lady Aurora. Even though the characters discuss political matters in domestic spaces, the discussions are truncated.'[58] In shifting the focus, from 'weekend' anarchists to 'petticoat' anarchists, Sypher continues to assert that women are the actual terrorists or anarchists in the novel, while other feminist critics have noted that the eponymous heroine, the Princess, forms the absent centre of the narrative.[59] She may be the pervasive source of anarchist encounters, but like a Derridean 'spectre', she too flickers in and out of the novel like the accidental view of a puppeteer's hands. By keeping the real threat of terror at arm's length, James delays and displaces the underground's subversive potential and privileges aboveground spaces and relations among women that are the real sources of secrecy and terror.

The representation of female anarchists continued to proliferate in the popular fiction of the 1890s but in the bodies of Russian *femmes fatales* who suffered severe punishment for their transgressive ideals. Based on real Russian female nihilists who often forfeited their domestic lives to lead underground identities as a revolutionary and a spy, literary representations often stereotyped them as beautiful, but ultimately doomed women. In Oscar Wilde's melodramatic play, *Vera; or, The Nihilist* (1880), politics is diffused into a romantic subplot between a Russian spy and the future Tsar of Russia that ends in her suicide to save her love and the future of her country. Other sensational novels such as Joseph Hatton's *By Order of the Czar: The Tragic Story of Anna Klosstock,*

Queen of the Ghetto (1890) and L. T. Meade's *The Siren* (1898) feature women who are mutilated and tortured for their beliefs, leading David Trotter to comment that the narratives often descended into 'sado-masochism'.[60] However, these were all depictions of foreign subjects on foreign soil, which lent sufficient distance and intrigue to satiate the middle-class reading public who were fascinated with the events unfolding in Russia. On the home front, however, female figures were to have subtler subversive tendencies that led to darker, more sinister implications in the domestic and political spheres.

In Joseph Conrad's *The Secret Agent*, these two worlds collide against a more transgressive moral space as London becomes the centre of underground revolutionary activity. Conrad already casts a pall over the city, describing it as 'a cruel devourer of the world's light' and a virtual sewer of a town, 'slumbering monstrously on a carpet of mud under a veil of raw mist . . . where the dust of humanity settles inert and hopeless out of the stream of life'.[61] If, as Avrom Fleishman argues, the city is 'the spatial expression of its moral universe', then Conrad's picture of humanity is bleak indeed.[62] Each anarchist is holed up in his own underground hovel or individual cell, which resemble burial grounds more than homes. The lackadaisical Michaelis dwells 'in a damp and lightless cellar' in 'the sepulchral silence of the great blind pile of bricks near a river, sinister and ugly like a colossal mortuary for the socially drowned'.[63] The radical Professor lives alone in a room where he hoards his chemicals in a cupboard, waiting for the next moment of insurrection. However, it is the Verlocs' home that represents the complex intersection of social and political exchange. 'A square box of a place' that doubles as a shop of morally suspect merchandise, their domestic enterprise is a façade on multiple levels: their placid marriage belies the deep bitterness Winnie Verloc holds against her husband, the ostensible *agent provocateur*, while their shop is 'kept up on the wages of a secret industry eked out by the sale of more or less secret wares'.[64] To add another dimension to this dense space of undercover exchanges, the back parlour, which 'gave access to a passage and to a steep flight of stairs', leads to a private meeting area for 'evening visitors' who are plotting the next anarchist attack on London.[65] A transgressive space where a myriad of discourses feed in and out of the core, the home itself is really the bomb ready to explode, or implode.

In this networked, domestic space, it is Winnie who becomes the true subversive amidst the revolutionary plotting, the real bomb that explodes the treasured ideals of home and social order. When her innocent brother Stevie accidentally blows himself up in Greenwich Park, missing the mark of the Royal Observatory, the event itself becomes secondary to the real 'pyrotechnic display' to follow at the Verlocs'. The domestic space then becomes the real target of the terrorist plot. When violence and murder explosively erupt in the parlour room, Winnie is flung out onto the streets of London, 'the whole town of marvels and mud', where she finds herself 'at the bottom of a black abyss from which no unaided woman could hope to scramble out'.[66] In this spatial vertigo, Winnie mirrors the archetypal 'fallen woman' who has descended into the depths of moral impropriety, but she has gone much further than the typical heroine who has transgressed sexual boundaries; she has murdered her husband, thus representing a far greater anarchist threat than all the men who have penetrated her home with words and ideas. In this subversive manner, Conrad deftly explodes any line demarcating domestic and political spheres while connecting the labyrinthine underworld to everyone in its infinite web of treachery and lies, from which no one is immune or innocent. The underground space of protest thus becomes a space of terror embedded in the home, where female anarchy runs rampant, destroying men in its path.

Language of Rebellion/Performing Terror

I pondered all these things, and how men fight and lose the battle, and the thing that they fought for comes about in spite of their defeat, and when it comes turns out not to be what they meant, and other men have to fight for what they meant under another name . . .
William Morris, A Dream of John Ball (1888)

Hyacinth knew their vocabulary by heart, and could have said everything in the same words, that on any given occasion M. Poupin was likely to say. He knew that 'they,' in their phraseology, was a comprehensive allusion to every one in the world but their people – but who, exactly, the people were was less definitively established.
Henry James, The Princess Casamassima (1886)

As public and private distinctions collapsed in the representation of underground revolutions, the language of terror similarly broke down in conveying its moral and political imperative. What first appeared as a clear set of social demands by underground organisations was undercut by the growing sense that the revolution had become too diffuse, too widespread to articulate a clear course of action. The question of constituency was one such complication: separating the 'they' versus 'we', differentiating the socialists from the anarchists, all contributed to the breakdown of simple binary codes of classification. As revolutionary fervour proliferated, newspapers and literary texts often used the terms 'anarchism', 'socialism' and 'nihilism' interchangeably to convey any radical movement against the dominant culture and the established system of power. The ubiquity of such revolutionary sentiment is captured in *The Princess Casamassima*, where Hyacinth describes the underground movement as a miasmatic force of contagion:

> ... the sense, vividly kindled and never quenched, that the forces secretly arrayed against the present social order were pervasive and universal, in the air one breathed, in the ground one trod, in the hand of an acquaintance that one might touch or in the eye of a stranger that might rest for a moment on one's own. They were above, below, within, without, in every contact and combination of life; and it was no disproof of them to say it was too odd they should lurk in a particular form. To lurk in improbable forms was precisely their strength and they would doubtless have still clearer features to show ...[67]

In their 'improbable forms', the revolutionary forces surfaced as an intangible network on the surface of the city, implicating everyone in its conspiratorial path. The shapelessness of the revolution, however, was also its weakness, as the language of the mission became further neutralised in the surfeit of discourses surrounding the movement. As critic Hollywood notes, 'the known world was collapsing and dissolving under the pressure of forces beyond the senses ... beyond even the naming power, the existing linguistic range, of the ordinary individual'.[68] This *fin-de-siècle* malaise manifested itself textually in two separate but intertwining strands: in manifestoes, words substituted for 'bombs' in exploding the existing linguistic order, while in literature, fragmentation, incoherence and inarticulacy became the dominant motif in expressing the underground, gesturing towards modernist sensibilities. The tension between the two modes of representation then created a distorted reflection of actual historical events, further conflating the real and imagined threat of terror in the urban psyche.

On 18 February 1885, the Dynamite Revolutionary Section of the Irish Revolutionary Party issued a warning which the *Pall Mall Gazette* published under the title 'Fenian Manifesto to the British Cabinet': 'We are firmly resolved to assert the *lex talionis,* by availing ourselves of the resources of civilization.'[69] In their declaration of violent retribution, the Fenians were actually partaking in the language of an emerging genre of underground discourse: the manifesto. Its terse, demand-led approach attempted to break with the existing political jargon of empty promises pandering to the bourgeoisie. Taking its lead from Marx's *Communist Manifesto* (1848), which was a relatively peaceful harbinger of a proletarian revolution, manifestoes began to proliferate in the late nineteenth century in a more militant and threatening manner. Employing a more didactic and 'scientific' approach, the new language of politics and propaganda issued visionary statements and propagandistic slogans that were not too dissimilar, ironically enough, to advertising and newspaper headlines. For example, French anarchist Pierre-Joseph Proudhon published a well-known pamphlet, *What Is Property?* (1840), in which he boldly claimed, '"What is slavery?" "It is murder." "What is property?" "It is robbery."'[70] Cultural historian Janet Lyons astutely observes that although to write a manifesto 'is to participate symbolically in a history of struggle against dominant forces', it also 'promulgates the very discourses it critiques: it makes itself intelligible to the dominant order through a logic that presumes the efficacy of modern democratic ideals'.[71] In the repetition and anaphora of an almost evangelical political language, biblical allusions were not uncommon in exhorting the people to act. The founding father of anarchism, Mikhail Bakunin, participated in this religious allegory, paradoxically adopting the language of 'dominant forces' to articulate his stance against it.

> There must be anarchy, there must be – if the revolution is to become and remain alive, real, and powerful – the greatest possible awakening of all the local passions and aspirations, a tremendous awakening of spontaneous life everywhere . . . We must bring forth anarchy, and in the midst of the popular tempest, we must be the invisible pilots guiding the revolution, not by any kind of overt power but by collective dictatorship of our allies, a dictatorship without tricks, without official titles, without official rights, and therefore all the more powerful, as it does not carry the trappings of power.[72]

The promise of this great, spontaneous 'awakening', while echoing the coming of Christ, also places the anarchist leader in a God-like image, the *übermensch* of the people. Although Bakunin disdained any 'overt powers', his tactics and the strategies of other revolutionaries were anything but covert. The language of the underground spilled onto the surface of the city and permeated columns of newspapers, public hoardings and discussions in clubs. A poster of an anarchist talk with Peter Kropotkin, 'the Anarchist Prince', resembled an advertisement for a West End performance, alluding to the performativity of various speech acts of insurgency and revolution. The circulation of anarchist principles through such mainstream media only served to depoliticise revolutionary intentions and normalise the language to a more familiar and accessible mode of theatricality that appealed to the middle classes.[73]

Furthermore, the rise of another form of underground media, the anarchist journal, also contributed to the proliferation of revolutionary sentiments, especially in progressive middle-class circles. The international community of émigrés who were fleeing persecution joined forces with English radicals, congregating in such places as the Rose

Street Club in Soho, the Autonomie in Windmill Street and the Berners Street Club in Whitechapel.[74] The discourse of protest widened to reflect the polyphony of foreign voices in a new language of revolutionary appeal. The Rose Street Club published the English edition of *Freiheit*, a German anarchist journal, while Charles Bradlaugh, the owner of the *National Reformer,* began his paper, *The Anarchist*. Charlotte Wilson, a former member of the Fabian Society, made contact with Kropotkin during his exile and published the journal *Freedom*, while Olivia and Helen Rossetti published *The Torch*, containing articles by Bernard Shaw, Émile Zola and Ford Madox Brown. However, most of these journals had to shut down in the wake of bombings in the city that immediately stigmatised any organisation with anarchist affiliations in the late 1890s. The backlash against anarchism in London was evident in the press and the attack on anarchist clubs by the public; however, its legacy of counter-culture and revolutionary change remained very much alive as modernism adopted the ideals of anarchy in exploding existing art forms and challenging literary conventions.

In the early part of the twentieth century, the genre of leftist-leaning journals then shifted to a more radical aesthetic form when Wyndham Lewis, Ezra Pound and a consortium of international writers began the Vorticist movement, publishing the avant-garde periodical *Blast*, which used poetry as a weapon and a means of defence from the overriding forces of modernisation and mass production. *Blast*, according to Lewis, signified 'the blowing away of dead ideas and worn out notions', but implicit in the title was also the affinity to the more violent recourse to bombs.[75] Critic Renato Poggioli, further alludes to the terroristic nature of the Vorticist movement, describing it as 'an independent and isolated military unit, completely and sharply detached from the public, quick to act, not only to explore but also to battle, conquer and adventure on its own'.[76] Its polemical aesthetic was captured in the manifesto of the first issue of *Blast*, which included such visceral statements as 'Beyond Action and Reaction we would establish ourselves . . . We only want Tragedy if it can clench its side muscles like hands on its belly, and bring to the surface a laugh like a bomb.'[77] Fusing manifesto rhetoric with bombastic poetry, the short-lived magazine captured an explosive language emerging from the underground in an attempt to articulate the desire for change, a rupture from the everyday and a newfound medium for voices that moved from the margins to the centre of the international fray.

While revolutionary discourses circulated freely and abundantly in the city, literary treatment and fictionalised accounts of underground movements both mimicked yet strayed from the functional and propagandistic vocabulary of radical voices. In a self-conscious fashion, many writers chose to deflect the revolutionary impulse for a more personal, psychological longing for apprehending the world on the brink of cataclysmic change. In *The Princess Casamassima*, Hyacinth's revolutionary awakening sparks a deeper Oedipal yearning to know his murdered father: '[T]he first impulse he could have . . . and it lay far down, in the depths of the unspeakable – was a conjecture that it had something to do with his parentage on his father's side.'[78] Although the socialist leader Muniment speaks the language of revolutionaries, Hyacinth's vocabulary merely imitates Muniment's detached worldview, while his most passionate words are reserved for the high culture of Parisian art and architecture, which links him to a heightened sense of his own hybrid identity. The language that eludes him is not motivated by a utopian future, but a deeply personal and unknowable past. In his analysis of the rise of modernism, Carl Schorske writes of 'the turn from Marx to Freud' in which 'the search for and understanding of the ills that plague mankind tended to be translated from the public and sociological domain to the private and psychological one'.[79] This paradigmatic shift also becomes apparent in the silences and the ellipses of a new modernist aesthetic that features revolutions as an inward turning, rather than an external threat.

In *The Secret Agent*, there is a marked absence of communication, as well as an absence of spoken words in the Verloc household amidst all the subversive activity. Although Verloc may distribute incendiary pamphlets over the counter, his private life is a 'placid pool' of domesticity, underscored by 'prudent reserve without superfluous words, and sparing of signs'.[80] In place of the central anarchists in the novel, Winnie's stammering brother Stevie becomes the unwitting agent of action as a human detonator to blow up Greenwich Park. All he can comprehend from the activity around him is that it is a '[b]ad world for poor people', an oversimplified version of the socialist dogma.[81] Language further collapses when Stevie tragically and farcically blows himself up by accident, missing his target completely. The press reports of his death pitilessly dismember him into sound bite headlines, reflecting the inarticulacy of the event:

> Bomb in Greenwich Park . . . Half-past eleven. Foggy morning. Effects of explosion felt as far as Romney road and Park Place. Enormous hole in the ground under a tree filled with smashed roots and broken branches. All round fragments of a man's body blown to pieces.[82]

Unlike the fluency and exactitude of manifestoes and literary journals, words fail to articulate the confounding emptiness of this tragic event.

The actual bombing, which was based on a historical event, in which French anarchist Martial Bourdin attempted to blow up the Greenwich Observatory on 5 February 1894, further attests to the complicity between media and literature in dialectically creating and performing terror. Popular accounts of the outrage utilised sensational headlines and attempted to link the event to an international conspiracy. An article in *The Times* of the Bourdin funeral suggested:

> An elaborate scheme appears to have been drawn, showing the hand of persons seen in Paris or in Dublin, or in both, what an effect on the lowest of the people is produced by the long funereal procession of a revolutionist.[83]

By alluding to French anarchists and Fenians, the press transforms the event to a level of an international incident, pointing the finger at the foreign forces infiltrating the heart of London. However, Conrad's anarchists are all home-grown, and the greatest threat actually comes from the domestic troubles of the Verlocs. If, as Marx stated, 'all facts and personages of great importance in world history occur twice: the first time as tragedy, the second as farce', then Conrad's farce on the Greenwich outrage is a darker and more ironic inversionary act of defiance, where an individual can kill or be killed in the name of justice when what they are fighting for cannot even be properly articulated. [84]

From Individual Action to Existential Inertia

I am no man, I am dynamite.

Friedrich Nietzsche, Ecce Homo (1908)

Without a language, a cause or a home, the underground revolutionary in the late nineteenth century was riddled with contradictions. As spatial boundaries dissolved and language failed to signify a common ideology or purpose, the revolutionary in literature was mired in incertitude, indecision and ironically enough, inactivity. If dynamite represented all that was masculine and phallocentric, the number of narratives in which the bomb fails to detonate or explodes prematurely illustrates a form of emasculation or the indeterminacy of any action, violent or otherwise. Zulaika and Douglass assert that in descriptions of terrorism, '*activism* is quintessential to small militant groups. Action for action's sake becomes a credo'.[85] Likewise, Bakunin's famous anarchist call for a transition from 'Propaganda by Word' to 'Propaganda by Deed' had been a clarion call for most revolutionary groups. Although explosions and violence fuelled anxiety and fear on the city streets, the fictional accounts of those involved in terrorist activity were painted in comic and deeply ironic overtones. As the moral impulse behind their acts became ambiguous at best, the underground as a metaphor became less of a struggle against the world above and more of a self-imposed exile to meditate one's role in a society that moved inexorably on, despite all the protestations. In the ensuing paradoxes, the psychological aspects of subterranean consciousness became central to modern consciousness in the context of an even larger existentialistic question of how to exist in the absence of morality, faith and, ultimately, God.

Perhaps no voice defines the paradoxes of modern revolt more effectively than Fyodor Dostoevsky's nameless anti-hero in *Notes from Underground* (1864). Declaring 'consciousness is a disease', the Underground Man's inability to engage in any action, other than speak out against rationalism and the 'Crystal Palace of humanity', while constantly undercutting his own views, reveals the deadlock in the logic of underground rebellion. The famous opening lines, 'I am a sick man . . .' begin by inviting sympathy, but such sentiments are immediately undercut in the following self-assessment that seeks to evoke disgust, as he becomes all too aware of the reader's judgmental gaze. 'I am a spiteful man. I am an unattractive man. I think my liver is diseased'.[86] Unable to partake in the society above and trapped in his circular reasoning below, the Underground Man declares that:

> an intelligent man cannot become anything serious, and it is only the fool who becomes anything. Yes a man of the nineteenth century must and is morally obliged to be chiefly a characterless being; whereas a man with character, a man of action, is chiefly a limited being.[87]

However, it is this precise absence of action that relegates him to this morbid, solipsistic existence, in which he proclaims his free will by paradoxically taking away his freedom to act. As critic Robert Jackson observes, 'Malice is the "underground" protest of the humiliated individual against ineluctable abasement . . . Malice is no more than a last despairing effort of the individual to reject the consequences of his tragic position.'[88] Although the Underground Man represents the schizophrenic extremes of an individual who cannot extricate himself from the language and laws of the system he wishes to reject, other characters in English literature also exhibit this divided consciousness, though to a less frenzied and frenetic degree. In many of the revolutionary novels, the heroes also embark on a quest to change or understand the world around them, only to find themselves in the subterranean abyss of moral reflection and mired in inactivity.

This political paralysis afflicted turn-of-the-century sensibilities as concrete notions of freedom and action sublimated into anarchic entropy and existential inertia. The nihilist in the continental imagination was an alluring, invincible figure with a definitive revolutionary goal. 'He is noble, terrible, irresistibly fascinating, for he combines in himself the two sublimities of human grandeur: the martyr and the hero.'[89] Although the anarchist of the twentieth century held similar delusions of grandeur, he was neither martyr nor the hero in British literary representation. At a time when real anarchist activity was in decline, the role of the revolutionary in literature came to embody less an agent of social change, than a metaphor for the fallen human condition. Joseph Fradin focuses on the deep irony of Conrad's world, as he probes into the impossibility of action in *The Secret Agent*:

> Every human action reveals its ambiguity by being set in the context of the anarchy which Conrad exposes as the reality underlying the city-world; and no human action seems capable of stemming the inexorable movement of the community toward inertia and death.[90]

Although the leader, Mr Vladimir, constantly remarks on the anarchists' laziness, asserting, 'What we want now is activity – activity', the paradox of a revolution that must function within the paradigm of existing political discourse becomes evident. Another anarchist, Karl Yundt, elaborates on this contradiction:

> 'You revolutionists . . . are the slaves of the social convention, which is afraid of you; slaves of it as much as the very police that stands up in the defence of that convention. Clearly you are, since you want to revolutionize it. It governs your thought, of course, and your action, too, and thus neither your thought nor your action can ever be conclusive.'[91]

This paradox manifests itself most powerfully in the figure of the Professor, who carries a bomb with him at all times in case action becomes necessary; however, his bomb never goes off, gesturing at the impotence of his ideological stance. Echoing the nineteenth-century figure of the obsessive chemist, who spends most of his waking hours perfecting detonators, the Professor also concentrates his whole energy on his destructive mission. His will to power is exemplified in his denial of all value systems, declaring, 'No God, no master', but his freedom also ironically means having no connection to humanity, thereby eradicating his freedom to live, love or derive any pleasure from society.[92] The fact that the novel ends with the Professor walking along the streets of London, lost and disillusioned, further reinforces Conrad's critique of anarchist activity.

> And the incorruptible Professor walked, too, averting his eyes from the odious multitude of mankind . . . He walked frail, insignificant, shabby,

miserable – and terrible in the simplicity of the world. Nobody looked at him. He passed on unsuspected and deadly, like a pest in the street full of men.[93]

Like the Underground Man, the Professor is relegated to the status of an insect, undifferentiated in the anarchic horde, where anonymity and alienation become the new landscape of the urban psyche. He becomes the embodiment of the ineffectual *flâneur*-terrorist who wanders the streets of London, lamenting a world of lost ideals and, in essence, a city devoid of humanity.

The shift in revolutionary discourse from an external protest against the political system to an internal interrogation of one's existence is perhaps the most pronounced in G. K. Chesterton's underground thriller, *The Man Who Was Thursday*. Although the novel begins with a protracted argument about anarchy and order, the political discourse is merely a subtext for a more metaphysical detective story 'in which the criminal to be hunted and brought to bay is – God'.[94] In an intensely dreamlike sequence, poet and double agent Gabriel Syme infiltrates the Council of Anarchists and becomes elected to the Council of Days, comprised of seven men, each named after a day of the week. Parodying the anonymity and secret codes of international anarchist groups, the novel also intertwines anarchist dogma with religious discourse, comparing their common subterranean roots:

> For it is deep, deep under the earth that the persecuted are permitted to assemble, as the Christians assembled in the Catacombs. But if, by some incredible accident, there were here tonight a man who all his life had thus immensely misunderstood us, I would put this question to him: 'When those Christians met in those Catacombs, what sort of moral reputation had they in the streets above? What tales were told of their atrocities by one educated Roman to another? [S]uppose that we are only repeating that still mysterious paradox of history. Suppose we seem as shocking as the Christians because we are really as harmless as the Christians. Suppose we seem as mad as the Christians because we are really as meek.'[95]

Combining religious allusions and revolutionary ideals, the speech is in effect a parody of both, employing a cult-like language that mocks the foundations of all belief systems. The terrorists in the novel, however, do end up being 'meek' and 'harmless', as their search for the mastermind behind the conspiracy reveals each one to be a mimicry of an historical anarchist figure. In the continuous revelation of underground identities, each council member is exposed as an undercover agent, each in search of the elusive Sunday who deftly controls their actions and movements like pawns in an endless chess match. Mirroring Chesterton's own deep concerns about religion, there is little question that the search for Sunday is tantamount to a search for God, whose slippery identity constantly undercuts any attempt by the individual to gain a semblance of order or meaning in the universe.

> Each man of you finds Sunday quite different, yet each man of you can only find one thing to compare him to – the universe itself. Bull finds him like the earth in spring, Gogol like the sun at noonday. The Secretary is reminded of the shapeless protoplasm, and the Inspector of the carelessness of virgin forests. The Professor says he is like a changing landscape. This is queer, but it is queerer still that I also have had my odd notion about the President, and I also find that I think of Sunday as I think of the whole world.[96]

The fluidity and formlessness of Sunday then governs the world that is heading ever so swiftly towards anarchy and entropy. Thus, literary historian Wm. M. Phillips concludes that God is the 'ultimate anarchist' in the novel, who exposes the hubris behind both anarchy and human order, confounding humanity and challenging assumptions about order and knowledge in the universe.[97]

So where does that leave the individual in the constant oscillation between anarchy and order? When the secret agents finally corner Sunday, they demand to know the purpose of their existence in a litany of questions regarding his true identity. The only concrete reply from Sunday merely mocks their earnestness: 'Well, I will go so far as to rend the veil of one mystery. If you want to know what you are, you are a set of highly well-intentioned young jackasses.'[98] In the constant subversion of individual identity and pursuit of truth, Chesterton takes the anarchist discourse from a social and political sphere to a more sardonic and existential realm. As the frustrated Syme walks along the Embankment, his anger becomes the redness of the river and the sky, resembling 'a stream of literal fire winding under the vast caverns of a subterranean country'.[99] Cloaked in eternal mystery, London is set ablaze in a characteristically Dantean image; however, whether the flame destroys or redeems the individual remains inconclusive at best. From the interminable suffering of Dostoevsky's Underground Man to the alienated blackness of Conrad's London, the underground voice attempts to articulate the inarticulable, but in its failure, becomes the language of landscape and aura.

In a final wry dissection of the anarchist movement, Chesterton reveals all underground movements to be surface and false in his lesser-known piece, 'The Conversion of an Anarchist' (1919). Originally published in *The Touchstone* and *The American Art Student Magazine*, the story was never reprinted until its discovery by a secretary of the Chesterton Society in 1982; however, the dormancy of the text is the only underground element of this tale, as it lifts anarchy from its shadowy, political sphere to a superficial world of upper-class frivolity. Reflecting the familiar trope of upper-class anarchists, Lady Joan Garnet marries Anthony Home, a professor and anarchist, and tries to introduce him to Liberty Hall, a private club of wealthy intellectuals with a penchant for radical, anarchist ideals. With his trademark humour, Chesterton introduces Lady Garnet as a woman of a 'restless and enterprising temper' who did not take long 'to find a man wrong enough to marry' and concludes that Home 'was a perfectly serious Anarchist'.[100] Unlike the mad, monomaniacal professor of previous dynamite and conspiracy novels, Home is a sedate, rational man whose motivations are neither political nor revolutionary, but personal and philosophical:

> He had a complete philosophic scheme of negations. He looked at Nothing from every possible point of view; he divided Nothing into sections and then recombined it into systems; he distinguished one kind of Nothing from another kind of Nothing, and then proved that the difference amounted to Nothing after all.[101]

In negating nothingness, Chesterton mocks nihilism, even existentialism to a degree, in a world where anything can be rationalised and reduced to insignificance. After exposing the hypocrisy behind such ideologies, Home proceeds to offend every member of Liberty Hall, thereby forfeiting any chance of membership, which was never his original intention. His disgust at the so-called anarchists he meets at the club is expressed emphatically as leaves the club:

> I have found the limit of anarchy. Anarchists will endure everything except one thing – sense. They will tolerate a hundred heresies – they will not tolerate orthodoxy. There is one thing that is sure to be right; the thing that is most hated. There is one thing that is most hated. Respectability![102]

In a radical departure from its original underground intent, anarchy is redefined as a mindless revolt against, yet a part of, the establishment, a paradox that Chesterton delights in exposing through the fashionable anarchist set. As Home leaves the club, he notices the 'Man of the Street', a reminder of the working classes with whom the socialist and anarchist movement initially resided:

> 'Think of him, and then think of those people in Liberty Hall Club' – A surge of disgust went over him like an earthquake – 'those foxes have holes, and those vultures of the air have nests; but man has nowhere to lay his head.'[103]

Likewise, the anarchist movement never manages to find a 'home' and thus, like a commodity, its ideals are doled out and traded in wealthy circles until it goes out of vogue in the beginning of the twentieth century. The physical underground as a metaphor for the poor, oppressed and the disenfranchised also begins to lose its force, as modernity and its attending modernism seeks to flatten representation in favour of a more horizontal map of interrelations between classes, as well as a collapsing of high and low art forms. The question of class and social mobility becomes a pervasive yet accepted facet of modern life, while socialism and anarchism give way to more immediate concerns regarding danger- ous ideologies that would ultimately shift the international balance of power and lead to the Great War. The subterranean vision would then go through one more metamorphosis that would align itself with the physical underground of trench warfare and the ensuing psychological trauma that would afflict post-war consciousness in the new century.

After the 'Revolution'...

A sincere man owes it to himself to expose the frightful barbarity which still prevails in the hidden depths of a society so outwardly well-ordered. Below the London of fashion is a London accursed, a London whose only food are dust stained fragments, whose only garments are filthy rags, and whose only dwellings are fetid dens . . . Others may turn their eyes away from these horrors, we socialists look them full in the face and seek out their causes.

Elisée Reclus, *Contemporary Review* (May 1884)

As the anarchist geographer Elisée Reclus suggests, the socialist and anarchist movement continued the mapping project of early Condition- of-England writers in exposing the lower depths, while taking stronger, more militant measures to bring social issues to the forefront of urban consciousness. Taking its cues from French, Russian and other interna- tional revolutionaries, the English underground movement attempted to delineate its own spatial and political discourse, a language com- mensurate with continental manifestoes and exhortative propaganda. However, as subterranean impulses emerged on the surface of the city, the idea of the 'underground' as a politically viable and sustainable alter- native began to lose its lustre in the way various writers appropriated the concept to point to its own futility and absurdity. Despite media coverage of riots, demonstrations and dynamite explosions that were linked to various Fenian and anarchist sources, literature mediated underground revolutionary activity in dark parodies, grotesque caricatures and apoca- lyptic narratives. Writers such as Stevenson, Conrad and Chesterton engaged in mimesis and mimicry, divorcing the political aspect from their terrorist novels and opting for a more psychological depiction of subver- sion that often satirised the revolutionary movement. The shift in empha- sis in underground representation from the social depths of Marx to the subconscious layers of Freud also contributed to a more internal characterisation of the struggle, blurring the distinction between the public and the private, and privileging a domestic spatial realisation of the terroristic impulse. Chesterton in particular expanded the anarchic vision to a more personal metaphor for all that lies beyond human control, embodying nihilism and the entropic nature of modern life: '[T]here is your precious order, that lean, iron lamp, ugly and barren; and there is anarchy, rich, living, reproducing itself – there is anarchy, splendid in green and gold.'[104] The blurring of the distinction between the political and the personal, the conflation of revolutionary groups and the intermingling of classes in the appropriation of the underground metaphor all contributed to the violence and messiness of a new modernity.

The proliferation of meaning and meaninglessness in the subterranean space was setting the stage for the turn-of-the-century reappropriation of the word to signify the emptiness of the struggle, or the resistance to signification in a world where the underground can only express loss, lack and a longing for more concrete definitions of defiance. As Stephen Kern elucidates:

> The beasts of nineteenth-century novels were generally tangible – forces of nature, vices, machines, institutions. There was prostitution, alcoholism, and gambling; there were railroads, factories, and coal mines; and there was materialism, capitalism, and the big city. As terrifying and overwhelming as these things seemed, they could at least be named. But the beasts of the twentieth century would be far less identifiable, living in the mysterious realm of negativity we find in Conrad, James, and Strindberg. For them the void supplies the focus. Their characters seek meaning outside of themselves – in a jungle, in a cemetery, behind a door – and find only the horror of nothingness within.[105]

This existentialistic crisis manifests itself in the terrorist literature of the period, paving the way for future conspiracy novels and postmodern conspiracy theories that maintain a more paranoid stance to all actions and consequences in the city. The materiality of the underground as a space of dissent then permeates everyday discourse as a more symbolic, sinister presence that becomes a projection of subconscious fears and frustrations in a hyper-mediated world where there is nowhere to hide. The spatial and linguistic power of the underground then collapses into a world of surfaces where suspicion and intrigue become the new order of an unrealisable and unrecognisable totality.

Notes

1. *Oxford English Dictionary*, available at <http://dictionary.oed.com> (last accessed 29 September 2008).

2. Houen, *Terrorism and Modern Literature*, p. 20. For more modern definitions of 'terrorism', see Laqueur, *The Age of Terrorism*, and Wardlaw, *Political Terrorism*.
3. Ó Donghaile, *Blasted Literature*, p. 4.
4. Wisnicki, *Conspiracy, Revolution, and Terrorism*. Wisnicki's emphases.
5. Henry James acknowledged getting most of his information on European politics from the press for his novel. See Hollywood, 'The Artist as Anarchist', pp. 277–312.
6. Conrad, *The Secret Agent*, p. 45.
7. Kubiak, *Stages of Terror*, p. i. Kubiak's emphasis.
8. Cited in Miller, *Mastering Modern European History*, p. 53.
9. Cited in Sinclair, *The Anatomy of Terror*, p. 80.
10. Melchiori, *Terrorism in the Late Victorian Novel*, p. 9.
11. See Ford, *Political Murder*.
12. Kravchinsky, aka 'Stepniak', *Underground Russia*, p. 4.
13. Sergei Nechayev, *Catechism of a Revolutionary* (1866). Cited in Sinclair, *The Anatomy of Terror*, p. 132.
14. Zulaika and Douglass, *Terror and Taboo*, p. 23.
15. See Pollard, *The Secret Societies of Ireland*.
16. *Pall Mall Gazette*, 3 October 1883.
17. *Pall Mall Gazette*, 29 February 1884.
18. Houen, *Terrorism and Modern Literature*, p. 25.
19. Zulaika and Douglass, *Terror and Taboo*, p. 84.
20. *United Irishman*, 11 February 1885, cited in Short, *The Dynamite War*, p. 216.
21. Arnold, *Culture and Anarchy*, p. 87.
22. For more, see Curtis, *Apes and Angels*.
23. Cited in Newsinger, *Fenianism in Mid-Victorian Britain*, p. 11.
24. Ibid. p. 25.
25. *The Times*, 19 March 1883. Cited in Short, *The Dynamite War*, p. 102.
26. Ibid. p. 17.
27. Trollope, *The Landleaguers*, p. 229.
28. Burnaby, *Our Radicals* and MacKay, *The Dynamite Ship*.
29. See Cyprian Bridge, 'Sub-Aqueous Warfare', *Frasers Magazine*, 98 (October 1878), p. 463. Also, Lesesne's *Torpedoes* illustrates how torpedoes and submarines would bring about effective social and political change.
30. Stevenson and Stevenson, *More New Arabian Nights*, p. 8.
31. Ibid. p. 115.
32. Comerford, *The Fenians in Context*, p. 243. Furthermore, Lyons, in *Culture and Anarchy in Ireland*, argues that the fragmented nature of the Irish nationalist movement ultimately led to their downfall.
33. O'Hegarty, *A History of Ireland under the Union*, p. 633.
34. Shpayer-Makov, 'A Traitor to His Class', pp. 299–325.
35. Hollywood, 'The Artist as Anarchist', p. 288.
36. Chesterton, *The Man Who Was Thursday*, p. 47.
37. Melchiori, *Terrorism in the Late Victorian Novel*, p, viii.
38. Gissing, *Demos*, p. 102.
39. Besant, *Children of Gibeon*, p. 45. The figure that is able to move

between classes then becomes a popular motif in such works as Shaw's *An Unsocial Socialist* and Meredith's *A Girl Among the Anarchists*. The latter was co-authored by Olivia and Helen Rossetti under a pseudonym that detailed their revolutionary experiences running the anarchist journal *The Torch*.

40. Mallock, *The Old Order Changes*, vol. 2, p. 63.
41. Ibid. 3, pp. 31–2.
42. Seltzer, *Henry James and the Art of Power*, p. 29. Irving Howe criticised James's clichéd politics as 'melodramatic journalism' in *Politics and the Novel*, p. 146.
43. Cited in Scanlan, 'Terrorism and the Realistic Novel', p. 393.
44. James, 'Letters', p. 146.
45. Phillips, *Nightmares of Anarchy*, pp. 188, 193.
46. Critics have often downplayed the political role of anarchy in England. Lionel Trilling concluded that the anarchist movement 'never established itself firmly in England', while Eric Hobsbawm conceded that 'there was no anarchist movement of significance'. See Hobsbawm, *Revolutionaries*.
47. Conrad, 'An Anarchist', p. 157.
48. For more, see Hamilton, 'Revolution from Within', pp. 31–48.
49. Ibid. p. 172.
50. Conrad, 'The Informer', in *A Set of Six* (London: Methuen, 1908), pp. 79–109, p. 80.
51. Ibid. p. 82.
52. Ibid. p. 84.
53. Cited in Shpayer-Makov, 'A Traitor to His Class', p. 304.
54. Forster, 'The Machine Stops', p. 101.
55. Heidegger, 'Building, Dwelling, Thinking', in *Poetry, Language, and Thought*, p. 147.
56. James, *The Princess Casamassima*, p. 358.
57. Ibid. p. 276.
58. Sypher, 'Anarchism and Gender', p. 7.
59. See Miller, 'The Inward Revolution'. Also, for a compelling queer reading of the text, see Graham, 'Henry James's Subterranean Blues'. The term 'petticoat anarchists' was coined by Cunningham in *The New Woman and the Victorian Novel*, p. 18. 'Weekend anarchists' referred to James's imaginary and ineffectual revolutionaries in Rowe, *The Theoretical Dimensions of Henry James*, p. 175.
60. Houen, *Terrorism and Modern Literature*, p. 66.
61. Conrad, *The Secret Agent*, p. 300.
62. Fleishman, 'The Symbolic World of *The Secret Agent*', p. 212.
63. Conrad, *The Secret Agent*, p. 44.
64. Ibid. p. 258.
65. Ibid. pp. 258, 5.
66. Ibid. pp. 270–1.
67. James, *The Princess Casamassima*, p. 415.
68. Hollywood, 'The Artist as Anarchist', p. 281.
69. *Pall Mall Gazette*, 20 February 1885.
70. Proudhon, *What Is Property?*, pp. 3–4.
71. Lyon, *Manifestoes*, pp. 3, 4.

72. Cited in Schulkind, *The Paris Commune of 1871*, p. 28.
73. For more on terrorism and drama, see Orr, *Terrorism and Modern Drama*.
74. See Thomas, *Anarchist Ideas and Counter-Cultures in Britain*.
75. Wyndham Lewis in an interview with *Daily News*, 7 April 1914.
76. Poggioli, *The Theory of the Avant-Garde*, p. 10.
77. Wyndham Lewis (ed.), *Blast 1*, 20 June 1914, p. 30.
78. James, *The Princess Casamassima* p. 185.
79. Schorske, *Fin-de-Siècle Vienna*, p. xxiv.
80. Conrad, *The Secret Agent*, p. 264.
81. Ibid. p. 171.
82. Ibid. p. 70.
83. *The Times*, 21 February 1894, p. 9, cited in Mulry, 'Popular Accounts of the Greenwich Bombing', p. 47. For more press details of the Greenwich explosion, see Bugoyne, 'Conrad Among the Anarchists', pp. 147–85.
84. Marx, *The Eighteenth Brumaire of Louis Bonaparte*, p. 141.
85. Zulaika and Douglass, *Terror and Taboo*, p. 75.
86. Dostoevsky, *Notes from Underground*, p. 3.
87. Ibid. p. 4.
88. Jackson, *Dostoevsky's Underground Man*, p. 34.
89. Stepniak, *Underground Russia,* p. 44.
90. Fradin, 'Anarchist, Detective, and Saint', p. 1414.
91. Conrad, *The Secret Agent*, pp. 22, 69.
92. Ibid. p. x.
93. Ibid. p. 311.
94. Chesterton, *G. K. Chesterton*, pp. 210–11.
95. Chesterton, *The Man Who Was Thursday*, p. 134.
96. Ibid. p. 149.
97. Phillips, *Nightmares of Anarchy*, p. 214.
98. Ibid. p. 160.
99. Ibid. p. 36.
100. 'The Conversion of an Anarchist', *The Chesterton Review*, 8 (Feb 1982), pp. 1–9 (p. 1).
101. Ibid. p. 2.
102. Ibid. p. 9.
103. Ibid. p. 9.
104. Chesterton, *The Man Who Was Thursday*, p. 13.
105. Kern, *The Culture of Time and Space, 1880–1918*, p. 170.

Conclusion

Are you really sure that a floor can't also be a ceiling?

M. C. Escher, *On Being a Graphic Artist* (1981)

In many ways, this book attempts to uncover the paradoxes of the underground that complicated its spatial, linguistic and metaphorical representations in the modern metropolis. While the overarching significance of subterranean infrastructure and its impact on the city cannot be overemphasised, the unseen, invisible aspects of the space and the tensions this absence signified also attest to its ghostly presence in the urban literary landscape. In examining the subterranean space through various frameworks, from a Foucauldian and Freudian to a Marxist and Derridean lens, the ultimate picture of the underground that emerges is a fragmented one, a spatial heuristic through which critical discourses of the time were reflected and refracted. Although newspapers and journals often mapped a teleological journey of engineering triumph, literary endeavours elided the space for a more oblique and disjointed response to the vast changes occurring underfoot. If the ultimate goal of the sewers, underground railways and cemeteries was to be a civilising agent in the goal towards creating a New Jerusalem, the undercurrent of degeneration and devolution also flowed along the same lines to articulate a Modern Babylon.

As an alternative space for the poor, women and the dispossessed, the underground appeared as a shadowy but powerful backdrop for illicit and transgressive moments that correlated with a powerful awakening of feelings and memories beyond individual consciousness. The Thames that snakes like a sewer through London, both defiling and purifying people in its path, evokes a sinister subterranean aura that lingers over the entire city. The passing glimpses into the underground train connect individual itineraries into a larger network of social relations that often threatens to shatter the surface of everyday lives. Cemeteries and graveyards, in their attempt to contain the dead, actually become a site of more ghostly encounters and spectral guises that return to haunt the living. Meanwhile, underground revolutionary groups, with no spatial fixity, become a pervasively violent force in the city, with tentacles reaching beyond national borders but without any coherent ideology. In this maelstrom of underground representations, it is possible to see why a single English novel or literary work that confronts these subterranean networks in a sustained manner does not exist. As Antonio Gramsci maintains in his study of social structures that lie beyond hegemonic institutions, 'The history of subaltern social groups is necessarily fragmented and episodic.'[1] As a space of otherness, the underground could not be articulated as a coherent structure in the way it stood outside the existing systems of signs and language. Thus, how we place the fragments under a larger umbrella of urban discourses reveals the significance of the underground in expressing the liminal layers of the city.

Although the physical underground space appears sporadically throughout nineteenth-century literature, *fin-de-siècle* representations begin to embrace the world below ground, as the networks became absorbed by the middle classes and were integrated into the capitalist structure of the expanding metropolis. At the same time, however, we witness what can be considered a 'de-ghosting' of subterranean spaces, as the underground becomes more of a platform for political contestations in the technocratic race for the future. By 'de-ghosting', there is a marked absence of 'return' or other forms of Gothic interference that imbued the underground space with such powerful, symbolic significance. Gone were the Dickensian mud-caked streets and cesspit alleys that gave rise to spirits past, or Gissing's underground train encounters that lent an illicit aura to the space. In a more rationalised, technological context, the material underground structures re-emerges as an abstract, inorganic subterranean space in utopian and apocalyptic revisions, beginning with H. G. Wells and inherited by such visionaries as Aldous Huxley and Yevgeny Zamyatin. Thus, the underground becomes a repository for the past as well as the battleground for the future. What these representations attest to is the extent to which the underground becomes a more visible, popular medium through which surface struggles are magnified and integrated into the image of the city. The conclusions of the chapters offered a glimpse into this futuristic space. Here, I suggest some of the ways the underground transforms itself in the latter part of the twentieth century and the millennium to articulate an alternative space of dissension even after the space has become a familiar trope in the ideological landscape of the city.

As Chapter 4 on the underground revolutions argued, the symbolic potential of the underground space was waning at the turn of the century, when political contestations relegated the term 'underground' to any form of revolt against the existing system or government. This was a decisive break from the physical materiality of the underground, as the term no longer relied on the images of sewers, underground railways and graves from which it derived its original subversive identity. In its departure from the physical loci of repressed fears and ghostly encounters, underground movements and revolutions manifested themselves on the surface of the city in the lead-up to the outbreak of World War I. During this time, subterranean representations remained relatively dormant at a time when the sheer violence and incomprehensibility of war could only conjure up underground trenches where soldiers were dying every day. Futurists, utopian ideals and the technological future all perished in the frontlines. Similarly during World War II, the most haunting images of the underground were the sketches by Henry Moore and photographs of Tube shelters by Bill Brandt that conveyed the underground as more of a tomb than a space for the living, an incubatory moment before the release of another wave of underground images. In the stark and terrifying reality of war, the underground lost its signifying potential during the wars, with the only redemptive image embodied in Harry Beck's abstract Tube map that merged the concrete necessity of creating a legible map and the desire to reimagine a dream-like, ordered city recreated from the chaos of war.

However, the underground space did not remain dormant for long. In a re-emergence of the subterranean metaphor, post-war depictions, especially in film, reinvigorated the underground networks to express the split political consciousness in a new fragmented urban climate. Many of these representations relied on Victorian imagery, as traces of class conflict, political aporia and glaring inequities in the world above still resonated in the tunnels below. In Vienna, the sewers in Carol Reed's *The Third Man* (1949) become more than a simple backdrop of a chase scene through visually arresting passages, as the underground also seeks to reconcile the double identity of Harry Lime, whose identity is further fractured in a city torn into four national factions in the aftermath of World War II. Again, the underground represents a space where questions of selfhood and national identity are contested but never fully resolved. Andrzej Wajda's film *Kanal* (1956) also politicises the sewers as the last refuge for the communist resistance, but they unfortunately lead the revolutionaries straight into the hands of Germans in an impasse of the human spirit in post-war Warsaw. Such bleak and existential modes of representation echo the sealed-off enclaves of poverty in Victorian London, but the material sewers here are foregrounded and depicted as an extension of the repressive regime above that closed off possibilities of escape or exile. The visual plenitude of the underground then paradoxically signals the lack of symbolic spaces of resistance in a demystification of subterranean passages. They were patrolled, closed off and regulated by the order above in a systematic integration into a hermetically sealed, vertically policed and politically repressed ideological totality.

In the global proliferation of underground images in the latter part of the twentieth century, New York City gained mythic status in its inculcation of subterranean sensibilities. With the sweeping rise of the metropolis, the skyscrapers of the city often contended with the residuum of capitalist exploitations, tracing back the underground's foundations in the Marxist notion of the invisible underclass upon which the achievements of the upper classes rest. However, in the US, class divisions in the 1940s were often compounded by racial strife in the increasing social unrest that swept through the nation. In 'The Man Who Lived Underground' (1944), Richard Wright suggests that the only escape for a black man wrongly accused of a crime is to flee into the sewers, completely cut off from the inequities of the justice system above. Meanwhile, in *Invisible Man* (1952), Ralph Ellison articulates the existentialistic fate of the black man who is invisible both above and below ground. Unable to participate fully in society, the main protagonist's descent marks the illusion of free will, reminiscent of Dostoevsky's Underground Man, but the protest falls on deaf ears, as he is trapped in a prison of his own making. In the 1980s, the intersection of class and race relations reached a crescendo in the underground when a white middle-class American, Bernard Goetz, shot four black teenagers intent on mugging him in the subway, sparking one of the most heated debates about race and crime in the metropolis. The ensuing court case and media coverage merely exacerbated the tensions and fears running through the city, and the growing hostility between blacks and whites was to be the basis for more racial explosions and riots in America in the 1990s.

Such images of a socially and politically disenfranchised underworld were reinforced by the discovery of 'mole people' living under Grand Central Station and in the tunnels of New York City, who developed their own principles and strategies of survival. In her investigative account, Jennifer Toth descends underneath the city to shed light on how and why people choose to live in the tunnels, but her sympathetic observations often turn into voyeuristic gazes into their appalling living conditions, echoing Mayhew's anthropological forays into Victorian slums.[2] However, New York was not the only city to house the city's dispossessed. More recently, a community living under Las Vegas storm sewers was discovered who survived on coins left in casino slot machines, while in the Russian city of Kazan, an Islamist sect built an eight-level labyrinth where they lived without heat or sunlight for a decade.[3] They exemplify the extent to which underground passages still represent threshold spaces, the forgotten 'in-between' cracks of modernity through which society's most disenfranchised and self-exiled descend. Mudlarks, Morlocks and toshers still live amongst us today. The fear and fascination that compelled Victorians to shed light on marginalised communities still drive subterranean representations in the modern cultural imagination. More explicitly than ever, the under-ground passageways have become synonymous not with refuse, but with refuge and shelter, a far cry from utopian ideals of a technologi-cally sustained society. As a disturbing reminder of the lack of spatial alternatives in the globalised postmodern metropolis, the underground serves as a return to an almost pre-modern civilisation in which survival becomes the prime objective.

In the final analysis, there are two opposing trends in underground representation that underscore the continuing tension in the appropria-tion of subterranean space. The contradictory visions of creation and destruction, utopian impulses and apocalyptic nightmares, still persist in creating the dialectic that fuels the underground imagination. Visions of destruction and violence still underpin the spatial metaphor, but in more elusive ways. For example, the secrets of the past, conspiracy theo-ries and the wastefulness of modern life in Don DeLillo's *Underworld* (1997) cast a pall over the entire city, as if perennially under a dark subterranean influence. Other historical moments of real violence in the underground parallel the Dickensian terror of the railways in the psychological ruptures they bring to urban consciousness. From the sarin gas attacks in the Tokyo subway in 1995 by the cult members of Aum Shinrikyo, to the 7/7 terrorist attacks that targeted the vertical spectrum from buses aboveground to the London Tube in 2005, subter-ranean conduits have become targets against capitalism and Western ideals in a contentious battle for ideological control. War is no longer fought along national borders, but in invisible networks of undercover terrorists whose random acts of violence shake the very foundations of the city, both spatially and metaphorically. However, what is more terrorising than an explosion underground is an explosion aboveground that lays bare what lies beneath. In the vertical decimation of the World Trade Center in the 9/11 bombings, the vast pit of rubble and broken infrastructure below expressed the inchoate nature of the event and reimagined New York as a city of ruins, an overturned cemetery that finally portended the end of civilisation. Such an apocalyptic outcome is not far from what nineteenth-century revolutionaries and terrorists declared in their manifestoes and in their attack on symbols of the ruling state. Even their methodologies of developing global networks of independent 'cells' are replicated in the structure of contemporary terrorist organisations. However, the invisibility and the 'undergroundedness' of such networks are complicated by the development of terrorism along another subterranean plane: cyberspace. In the miles of fibre optic cables that run underneath cities, information is coded, passed and accessed at a speed that poses the greatest challenge to surveillance and scrutiny. It is this anonymous space that will most certainly be the next arena for underground contestations. The ability to offer freedom and knowledge to its users makes cyberspace the ideal platform for egalitarianism and democracy; however, the disseminating power and the control for information flows threaten personal, national and global security, as the recent furore with WikiLeaks attests. As an infrastructure and a conceptual space, the internet then offers every individual a chance at an underground existence, and what this new community of underground dwellers seek remains to be (un)seen.

So is there a redemptive future for the underground? As a physical structure, the underground has also attracted a number of artists and adventure seekers as they attempt to uncover the infinite discursive potential of the space. The ghosts of Marx, Lefebvre and de Certeau still wander through the passages, seeking a *détournement* to the designated usage of public areas. Organisations such as Space Hijackers are using the internet to organise covert activities in the underground, from a moving disco on the Circle Line to an all-night 'Pirate Party' in the Greenwich Foot Tunnel. Armed with a manifesto and dedicated to 'battling the constant oppressive encroachment onto public spaces of institutions, corporations and urban planners', space hijackers have been reclaiming underground and aboveground spaces in the celebratory manner of revellers.[4] Meanwhile, in Paris, 'cataphiles' continue to elude the police as they convene in disused tunnels and use them as art spaces, bars and even a cinema. In *Parisian Art Underground* (2003), Caroline Archer and Alexandre Parré celebrate the etchings, sculpture and graffiti that remain in the underground passages, while in New York, arts organisations such as Ars Subterranea support 'art installations, history-based scavenger hunts, unusual preservation campaigns and much more'.[5] Finally, in Tokyo, a group of young artists went under Shinjuku station and offered to paint cardboard box homes for the homeless, resulting in an exhibition of provocative images that shed light on a growing social issue that the government was all too willing to ignore. In addition, in *Imperial City Tokyo: Secret of a Hidden Underground Network* (2002), Shun Akiba, a former foreign reporter, questions the thousands of kilometres of underground space unaccounted for underneath the metropolis and imagines their potential usage, though such classified information is well guarded by the government.[6] So perhaps the new millennium does not presage a disappearance of the underground, but a more difficult barrier to entry, as subterranean inhabitants, recreationists and artists bury themselves more inventively in an attempt to evade institutional control or the all-seeing 'eye'. After all, once it is in print, it is no longer underground.

Notes

1. Gramsci, *Selections from the Prison Notebooks*, p. 55.
2. See Toth, *The Mole People*.
3. See O'Brien, *Beneath the Neon*. Also see Associated Press, 'Russian Islamist sect kept children underground for a decade' in *The Guardian*, 9 August 2012 <http://www.guardian.co.uk/world/2012/aug/09/russian-islamist-sect-children-underground?INTCMP=SRCH> (accessed 24 September 2012).
4. See <http://www.spacehijackers.co.uk> (accessed 1 August 2009).
5. Archer and Parré, *Parisian Art Underground*. For more details on the New York underground art scene, see *Ars Subterranea* <http://arssubterranea.org> (accessed 20 October 2009). The organisation's founder and her photojournalistic work can also be found in Solis, *New York Underground*.
6. Akiba, *Imperial City Tokyo*.

Bibliography

Historic Journals, Magazines, Reports, and Papers

Blast
Frasers Magazine
Household Words
Illustration
Pall Mall Gazette
Parliamentary Papers
Privy Council Papers
Punch
The Builder
The Illustrated London News
The Illustrated Times
The Journal of Public Health and Sanitary Review
The Lancet
The Quarterly Review
The Times

Web Sources

Ars Subterranea <http://arssubterranea.org> (accessed 20 October 2009).
Associated Press, 'Russian Islamist sect kept children underground for a decade' in *The Guardian*, 9 August 2012 <http://www.guardian.co.uk/world/2012/aug/09/russian-islamist-sect-children-underground?INTCMP=SRCH> (accessed 24 September 2012).
Henley, John, 'In a Secret Paris Cavern, the Real Underground Cinema', *The Guardian*, 8 Sept 2004 <http://www.guardian.co.uk> (accessed 15 May 2007).
Oxford English Dictionary <http://dictionary/oed.com> (accessed 29 September 2008).
Space Hijackers <http://www.spacehijackers.co.uk> (accessed 1 August 2009).
Subterranea Britannica <http://www.subbrit.org.uk> (accessed 10 September 2007).
Trotter, David, 'Household Clearances in Victorian Fiction', 2008,

Interdisciplinary Studies in the Long Nineteenth Century <http://www.19.bbk.ac.uk.> (accessed 7 August 2009).

Williams, Hywell, *Underground History* <http://www.underground-history.co.uk> (accessed 1 September 2012).

Films

Lang, Fritz (dir.), *Metropolis*. Germany: Universum Film, 1927.

Menzies, William Cameron (dir.), *Things to Come*. UK: London Film Productions, 1936.

Reed, Carol (dir.), *The Third Man*. UK: British Lion Film Corporation, 1951.

Wajda Andrzej (dir.), *Kanal*. Poland: Zespól Filmowy, 1957.

Works Cited

Ackroyd, Peter, *Dickens* (London: Minerva, 1991).

—, *London Under* (London: Chatto &Windus, 2011).

Acton, William, *Prostitution Considered in Its Moral, Social, and Sanitary Aspects* (London: Frank Cass, 1972).

Adams, Norman, *Dead and Buried: The Horrible History of Body Snatching* (Aberdeen: University Press, 1972).

Akiba, Shun, *Imperial City Tokyo: Secret of a Hidden Underground Network* (Tokyo: Yoshenda, 2002).

Altick, Robert, *The Presence of the Present: Topics of the Day in the Victorian Novel* (Columbus: Ohio University Press, 1991).

Aquinas, Thomas, *On Faith Summa Theologiae*, trans. Mark D. Jordan (Notre Dame: University of Notre Dame Press, 1990).

Archer, Caroline and Alexandre Parré, *Parisian Art Underground* (New York: Mark Batty, 2003).

Ariès, Philippe, *Western Attitudes toward Death: From the Middle Ages to the Present*, trans. Patricia M. Ranum (London: Marion Boyers, 1976).

—, *The Hour of Our Death*, trans. Helen Weaver (London: Allen Lane, 1981).

Armstrong, Isobel, *Victorian Poetry: Poetry, Poetics, and Politics* (London: Routledge, 2002).

Armstrong, Tim, *Haunted Hardy: Poetry, History, Memory* (Basingstoke: Palgrave, 2000).

Arnold, Catherine, *Necropolis: London and Its Dead* (London: Simon & Schuster, 2006).

Arnold, Matthew, 'The Buried Life', in *Selected Poems and Prose*, ed. Miriam Allot (London: Everyman, 1978), pp. 85–6.

—, *Culture and Anarchy and Other Writings* (Cambridge: Cambridge University Press, 1993).

Augé, Mark, *In the Metro*, trans. Tom Conley (Minneapolis: University of Minnesota Press, 2002).

Bakhtin, Mikhail, 'Forms of Time and of the Chronotope in the Novel', trans. Caryl Emerson and Michael Holquist, in *The Dialogic Imagination: Four Essays* (Austin: University of Texas Press, 1982), pp. 84–258.

—, *Rabelais and His World*, trans. Hélène Iswolsky (Bloomington: Indiana University Press, 1984).

Banton, Eric, 'Underground Travelling London', in George R. Sims (ed.), *Living London* (London: Cassell, 1903).

Barker, T. C., and Michael Robbins, *A History of London Transport: Passenger Travel and the Development of the Metropolis* (London: Allen & Unwin, 1974).

Barringer, Tim, *Men at Work: Art and Labour in Victorian Britain* (New Haven: Yale University Press, 2005).

Barthes, Roland, *Mythologies*, trans. Annette Lavers (London: Paladin Grafton, 1989).

Baudelaire, Charles, 'Hygiene Projects', trans. C. Isherwood, in *Intimate Journals* (San Francisco: City Light Books, 1983).

Beard, George M., *American Nervousness* (New York: G. P. Putnam's Sons, 1881).

Bell, Shannon, *Reading, Writing, and Re-Writing the Prostitute Body* (Bloomington: Indiana University Press, 1994).

Benjamin, Walter, 'On Some Motifs on Baudelaire', trans. Harry Zohn, in Hannah Arendt (ed.), *Illuminations* (New York: Schocken, 1969), pp. 155–200.

—, 'Paris: Capital of the Nineteenth Century', trans. Edmund Jephcott, in *Reflections* (New York: Harcourt Brace Jovanovich, 1978), pp. 146–62.

—, *Charles Baudelaire: A Lyric Poet in the Era of High Capitalism*, trans. Harry Zohn (London: Verso, 1983).

Berthet, Elie, *Les Catacombes de Paris* (Milton Keynes: Lightning Source UK, 2012).

Besant, Walter, *Children of Gibeon* (London: Chatto & Windus, 1886).

Blumenthal, R. D., *R. D. B.'s Diary, 1887–1914* (London: William Heinemann, 1930).

Boucicault, Dion, *After Dark: A Tale of London* (London: Edward Ashman, 1868).

Bourke, John, *Scatalogic Rites of All Nations* (Washington, DC: W. H Lowdermilk, 1891).

Bowlby, Rachel, *Just Looking: Consumer Culture in Dreiser, Gissing, and Zola* (London: Methuen, 1985).

Bown, Nicola, Carolyn Burdett, and Pamela Thurschwell (eds), *The Victorian Supernatural* (Cambridge: Cambridge University Press, 2004).

Braddon, Mary Elizabeth, 'Ralph the Bailiff", in *Ralph the Bailiff and Other Stories* (London: Ward, Lock & Tyler, 1867).

—, *Lady Audley's Secret* (Oxford: Oxford University Press, 1998).

Bradley, Simon, *St. Pancras Station* (London: Profile, 2007).

Briggs, Asa, *Victorian Cities* (Berkeley: University of California Press, 1993).

Brock, Thomas D., *Robert Koch: A Life in Medicine and Bacteriology* (Madison: Science Tech Publishers, 1988).

Bronfen, Elizabeth, *Over Her Dead Body: Death, Femininity, and the Aesthetic* (New York: Routledge, 1992)

Brontë, Emily, *Wuthering Heights* (Harmondsworth: Penguin, 1965).

Brooks, Chris, *Mortal Remains: The History and Present State of the Victorian and Edwardian Cemetery* (Devon: Wheaton, 1989).

Brown, Norman O., *Life Against Death: The Psychoanalytical Meaning of History* (New York: Vintage, 1959).

Budd, William, *Typhoid Fever, Its Nature, Mode of Spreading and Prevention* (New York: American Public Health Association, 1931).

Burgoyne, Mary, 'Conrad Among the Anarchists: Documents on Martial Bourdin and the Greenwich Bombing', in Allan H. Simmons and J. H. Stape (eds), *The Secret Agent: Centennial Essays*, 32 (Spring 2007), pp. 147–85.

Bulwer-Lytton, Edward, *Vril: The Power of the Coming Race* (New York: Rudolph Steiner Publications, 1972).

Burke, Edmund, *A Philosophical Enquiry into the Origin of Our Ideas of the Sublime and Beautiful* (Oxford: Basil Blackwell, 1987).

Burnaby, Fred, *Our Radicals: A Tale of Love and Politics* (London: R. Bentley and Son, 1886).

Cadava, Eduardo, *Words of Light: Theses on the Philosophy of History* (Princeton: Princeton University Press, 1988).

Cannadine, David, 'War and Death, Grief and Mourning in Modern Britain', in Joachim Whaley (ed.), *Mirrors of Mortality: Studies in the Social History of Death* (London: Europa, 1981), pp. 187–242.

Carpenter, William Benjamin, *Principles of Mental Physiology* [1874] (Whitefish: Kessinger, 2004).

Castle, Terry, *The Female Thermometer: Eighteenth-Century Culture and the Invention of the Uncanny* (Oxford: Oxford University Press, 1995).

Chadwick, Edwin, *Report on the Sanitary Conditions of the Labouring Population of Great Britain* (London: W. Clowes, 1842).

—, *Parliamentary Papers* [1846], vol. 10, p. 651.

Chesterton, Cecil, *G. K. Chesterton: A Criticism* (Seattle: Inkling Books, 2007).

Chesterton, G. K., 'The Conversion of an Anarchist', *The Chesterton Review*, 8 (February 1982), pp. 1–9.

—, *The Man Who Was Thursday* (Oxford: Oxford University Press, 1996).

Cheyette, Bryan, *Constructions of the Jew in English Literature and Society* (Cambridge: Cambridge University Press, 1995).

Christianson, Rupert, *Tales of the New Babylon: Paris 1869–1875* (London: Sinclair Stevenson, 1994).

Clark, T. J., *The Painting of Modern Life: Paris in the Art of Manet and His Followers* (London: Thames & Hudson, 1985).

Clarke, John M., *The Brookwood Necropolis Railway* (Oxford: Oakwood Press, 1988).

Cohen, William A., and Ryan Johnson (eds), *Filth: Dirt, Disgust, and Modern Life* (Minneapolis: University of Minnesota Press, 2005).

Collins, Wilkie, *The Woman in White* (Harmondsworth: Penguin, 1974).

Comerford, R. V., *The Fenians in Context: Irish Politics and Society 1848–82* (Dublin: Wolfhound Press, 1985).

Conrad, Joseph, 'An Anarchist', in *A Set of Six* (London: Methuen, 1908), pp. 145–73.

—, 'The Informer', in *A Set of Six*, (London: Methuen, 1908), pp. 79–109.

—, *The Secret Agent* (Oxford: Oxford University Press, 1983).

Corbin, Alain, *The Foul and the Fragrant: Odor and the French Social Imagination*, trans. Miriam L. Kochan (Cambridge, MA: Harvard University Press, 1988).

—, *Women for Hire: Prostitution and Sexuality in France after 1850* (Cambridge, MA: Harvard University Press, 1990).

Cox, Edward William, *The Principles of Punishment* (London: The Law Times Office, 1877).

Croome, Desmond F., *The Circle Line: An Illustrated History* (London: Capital Transport Publishing, 2003).

Crosland, T. W. H., *The Suburbans* (London: John Long, 1905).

Cunningham, Gail, *The New Woman and the Victorian Novel* (London: Macmillan, 1978).

Curl, James Stevens, *The Victorian Celebration of Death* (Stroud: Sutton Publishing, 2000).

Curtis Jr., L. Perry, *Anglo-Saxons and Celts: A Study of Anti-Irish Prejudice in Victorian England* (Bridgeport: University of Bridgeport, 1968).

—, *Apes and Angels: The Irishman in Victorian Caricature* (Washington: Smithsonian Institute, 1997).

Dahl, Curtis, 'The Victorian Wasteland', in Austin Wright (ed.), *Victorian Literature: Modern Essays in Criticism* (New York: Oxford University Press, 1961), pp. 32-40.

Dallas, E. S., *The Gay Science* (London: Chapman & Hall, 1866).

Daly, Nicholas, 'Blood on the Tracks: Sensation Drama, the Railway, and the Dark Force of Modernity', *Victorian Studies,* 42 (Winter 1998–1999), pp. 47–76.

Davies, Colin, *Haunted Subject: Deconstruction, Psychoanalysis, and the Return of the Dead* (London: Palgrave, 2007).

Davies, Sir J., *Discovery of the True Causes Why Ireland Was Never Entirely Subdued* (Washington, DC: Catholic University of America Press, 1989).

De Amicis, Edmondo, *Jottings about London* (Boston: Alfred Mudge & Son, 1883).

De Certeau, Michel, *The Practice of Everyday Life*, trans. Steven Rendall (Berkeley: University of California Press, 1984).

De la Carrera, Rosalina, 'History's Unconscious in Victor Hugo's *Les Misérables*', *MLN,* 96 (1981), pp. 839–55.

DeLillo, Don, *Underworld* (New York: Scribner, 1997).

Derrida, Jacques, *Of Grammatology*, trans. Gayatri Chakravorty Spivak (Baltimore: Johns Hopkins University, 1976).

—, *Specters of Marx: State of the Debt, the Work of Mourning, and the New International*, trans. Peggy Kamuf (New York: Routledge, 1994).

—, 'Marx, c'est quelqu'un', in Jacques Derrida, Marc Guillaume and Jean-Pierre Vincent (eds), *Marx en jeu*, ed. (Paris: Descartes & Cie, 1997), pp. 9–28.

—, 'Interview with Bernard Stiegler' [1993], *Echographies of Television: Filmed Interviews*, trans. Jennifer Bajorek (Cambridge: Polity Press, 2002).

Devoy, John, *Recollections of an Irish Rebel* (Shannon: Irish University Press, 1969).

Dickens, Charles, 'An Unsettled Neighbourhood' in *The Railway through Dickens's World: Texts from Household Words and All the Year Round*, ed. Ewald Mengel (Frankfurt: Verlag Peter Lang, 1989).

—, *A Tale of Two Cities*, ed. Andrew Sanders, (Oxford: Oxford University Press, 1999).

—, *Bleak House* (London: Penguin, 2003).

—, 'City of Absent', in *The Uncommercial Traveller and Reprinted Pieces* (Oxford: Oxford University Press, 1997), pp. 233–40.

—, *David Copperfield* (Oxford: Oxford University Press, 1999).

—, *Dombey and Son* (Harmondsworth: Penguin, 1970).

—, *Little Dorrit*, ed. H. P. Sucksmith (Oxford: Clarendon Press, 1979).

—, *Martin Chuzzlewit* (London: Penguin, 2000).

—, 'Mugby Junction', in *Christmas Stories* (Oxford: Oxford University Press, 1956), pp. 473–536.

—, *Nicholas Nickleby* (London: Penguin, 2003).

—, 'Nurse's Stories', in *The Uncommerical Traveller and Reprinted Pieces* (Oxford: Oxford University Press, 1997), pp. 148–58.

—, *Oliver Twist* (Oxford: Oxford University Press, 1994).

—, *Our Mutual Friend* (London: J. M. Dent, 2000).

—, 'The Haunted Man', in Robert Douglas-Fairhurst (ed.), *A Christmas Carol and Other Christmas Books* (Oxford: Oxford University Press, 2006), pp. 323–408.

—, *The Mystery of Edwin Drood* (London: Mandarin, 1991).

—, *The Old Curiosity Shop* (London: Penguin, 2000).

—, *The Pickwick Papers* (London: J. M. Dent, 1945).

—, 'The Signalman', in *The Signalman and Other Ghost Stories* (Gloucester: Alan Sutton, 1984), pp. 2–11.

—, 'Travelling Abroad', in *The Uncommerical Traveller and Reprinted Pieces* (Oxford: Oxford University Press, 1997), pp. 233-40.

Disraeli, Benjamin, *Sybil, or The Two Nations* [1845] (Oxford: Oxford University Press, 1926).

Ditmore, Melissa Hope, *Encyclopedia of Prostitutes and Sex Work* (Westport: Greenwood Press, 2006).

Dobraszczyk, Paul, 'Sewers, Wood Engraving and the Sublime: Picturing London's Main Drainage System in the *Illustrated London News*, 1859–62', *Victorian Periodicals Review*, 38 (Winter 2005), pp. 349–78.

—, *Into the Belly of the Beast: Exploring London's Victorian Sewers* (Reading: Spire, 2009).

Dostoevsky, Fyodor, *Notes from Underground*, trans. Michael R. Katz (New York: W. W. Norton, 2001).

Douglas, Hugh, *The Underground Story* (London: Robert Hale Limited, 1963).

—, *Burke and Hare: The True Story* (London: R. Hale, 1973).

Douglas, Mary, *Purity and Danger: An Analysis of Concept of Pollution and Taboo* (London: Routledge, 2002).

Doxat, John, *The Living Thames, the Restoration of a Great Tidal River* (London: Hutchinson Benham, 1977).

Doyle, Arthur Conan, *A Study in Scarlet* (London: Wordsworth, 2001).

—, 'The Bruce-Partington Plans' in *The Complete Sherlock Holmes* (Hare: Wordsworth, 2008), pp. 1146–68.

Drinka, George F., *The Birth of Neurosis: Myth, Malady, and the Victorians* (New York: Simon & Schuster, 1984).

Dumas, Alexandre, *The Mohicans of Paris*, trans. John Latey (London: George Routledge & Sons, 1875).

Du Maurier, George, *Trilby* (Oxford: Oxford World Classics, 2009).

Durkheim, Émile, *The Elementary Forms of Religious Life: A Study in Religious*

Sociology, trans. Joseph Ward Swain (London: George Allen and Unwin, 1915).

Dyos, H. J., *Exploring the Urban Past*, ed. David Cannadine and David Reader (Cambridge: Cambridge University Press, 1982).

Dyos, H. J., and Michael Wolff (eds), *The Victorian City: Images and Realities* (London, Boston: Routledge and Kegan Paul, 1973).

Eagleton, Terry, *Heathcliff and the Great Hunger: Studied in Irish Culture* (London: Verso, 1995).

Edwards, Dennis, and Ron Pigram, *The Romance of Metroland* (London: Baton Transport, 1986).

Eliot, T. S., *The Waste Land and Other Poems* (London: Faber & Faber, 2002).

Ellison, Ralph, *Invisible Man* (London: Penguin, 2005).

Engels, Friedrich, *The Condition of the Working Class in England*, trans. W. O. Henderson (Oxford: Blackwell, 1971).

Enright, D. J. (ed.), *The Oxford Book of Death* (Oxford: Oxford University Press, 1983).

Erichsen, John, *On Railway and Other Injuries of the Nervous System* (London: Walton & Maberly, 1866).

Fleishman, Avrom, 'The Symbolic World of *The Secret Agent*', *English Literary History*, 32 (1965), pp. 196–219.

Flint, Kate, *The Victorian Novelist: Social Problems and Social Change* (London: Croom Helm, 1987).

Ford, Ford Madox, 'Antwerp', in Peter Jones (ed.), *Imagist Poetry* (Harmondsworth: Penguin, 1972), pp. 81–2.

—, *The Soul of London: A Survey of a Modern City*, ed. Alan G. Hill (J. M. Dent, 1995).

Ford, Franklin L., *Political Murder: From Tyrannicide to Terrorism* (Cambridge, MA: Harvard University Press, 1985).

Forster, E. M., 'The Machine Stops', in Rod Mengham (ed.), *The Machine Stops and Other Stories* (London: Andre Deutsch, 1997).

—, *Howard's End* (London: Penguin 2000).

Forster, John, *The Life of Charles Dickens* (London: J. W. T. Ley, 1928).

Foucault, Michel, *Discipline and Punish: The Birth of the Prison*, trans. Alan Sheridan (New York: Random House, 1979).

—, 'Of Other Spaces', trans. Jay Miskowiec, *Diacritics*, 17 (Spring 1986), pp. 22–7.

—, *The History of Sexuality: An Introduction, Volume 1*, trans. Robert Hurley (London: Vintage, 2000).

Fradin, Joseph I., 'Anarchist, Detective, and Saint: The Possibilities of Action in *The Secret Agent*', *PMLA*, 83 (October 1968), pp. 1414–22.

Freegood, Elaine, *The Ideas in Thing: Fugitive Meaning in the Victorian Novel* (London: University of Chicago Press, 2006).

Freeman, Michael, and Derek Aldcroft (eds), *Transport in Victorian Britain* (Manchester: Manchester University Press, 1988).

Freud, Sigmund, *Civilization and Its Discontents*, trans. James Strachey (New York: W. W. Norton, 1961).

—, 'Character and Anal Eroticism' [1908], trans. and ed. James Strachey, in *Standard Edition of the Complete Psychological Works of Sigmund Freud*, 9 (London: Hogarth, 1974), pp. 167–75.

—, 'Mourning and Melancholia', trans. and ed. James Strachey, in *The Standard Edition of the Complete Psychological Works of Sigmund Freud*, 14 (London: Hogarth, 1974), pp. 237–58.

—, 'Notes upon a case of obsessional neurosis', trans. and ed. James Strachey, in *Standard Edition of the Complete Psychological Works of Sigmund Freud*, 10 (London: Hogarth, 1974), pp. 151–318.

—, 'On Transformations of Instinct as Exemplified by Anal Eroticism' [1917], trans. and ed. James Strachey, in *Standard Edition of the Complete Psychological Works of Sigmund Freud*, 17 (London: Hogarth, 1974), pp. 127–33.

—, 'Studies on Hysteria (1835–95)', trans. and ed. James Strachey, in *Standard Edition of the Complete Psychological Works of Sigmund Freud*, 2 (London: Hogarth, 1974), pp. 1–323.

—, *The Complete Letters of Sigmund Freud to Wilhelm Fliess 1887–1904*, trans. Jeffrey Moussaieff Masson (Cambridge, MA: Harvard University Press, 1985).

Gaskell, Elizabeth Cleghorn, *Mary Barton* (London: Cassell & Co., 1890).

—, *North and South* (London: Penguin, 2003).

Gissing, George, *Demos: A Story of English Socialism* (London: Smith, Elder, & Co., 1886).

—, *The Whirlpool* (London: Hogarth Press, 1984).

—, *In the Year of Jubilee* (London: Hogarth Press, 1987).

—, *The Nether World* (Oxford: Oxford University Press, 1992).

—, *The Odd Women* (Oxford: Oxford University Press, 2008).

Graham, Wendy, 'Henry James's Subterranean Blues: A Rereading of *The Princess Casamassima*', *Modern Fiction Studies*, 40 (Spring 1994), pp. 51–84.

Gramsci, Antonio, *Selections from the Prison Notebooks*, ed. and trans. Quintin Hore and Geoffrey Nowell-Smith (London: Lawrence & Wishart, 1971).

Green, Oliver, *Underground Art: London Transport Posters, 1908 to the Present* (London: Studio Vista, 1989).

Greenblatt, Stephen, 'Filthy Rites', *Daedalus*, 3 (1982), pp. 1–16.

Greenhow, Edward Headlam, *Second Report of the Medical Officer of the Privy Council, 1858* (1859), *Privy Council Papers*.

Groth, Helen, *Victorian Photography and Literary Nostalgia* (Oxford: Oxford University Press, 2004).

Hall, Radclyffe, *The Well of Loneliness* (London: Hutchinson, 1986).

Hallam, Elizabeth, Jenny Hockey, and Glennys Howarth (eds), *Beyond the Body: Death and Social Identity* (London: Routledge, 1999).

Halliday, Stephen, *The Great Stink of London: Sir Joseph Bazalgette and the Cleansing of the Victorian Metropolis* (Stroud: Sutton Publishing, 1999).

—, *Underground to Everywhere: London's Underground Railway in the Life of the Capital* (Stroud: The History Press, 2001).

Hamilton, Carol Vanderveer, 'Revolution from Within: Conrad's Natural Anarchists', *The Conradian*, 18 (Autumn 1994), pp. 31–48.

Handy, Ellen, 'Dust Piles and Damp Pavements: Excrement, Repression, and the Victorian City in Photography and Literature', in Carol T. Christ and John O. Jordan (eds), *Victorian Literature and the Victorian Visual Imagination* (Berkeley: University of California Press, 1995), pp. 111–33.

Haraway, Donna, *Primate Visions: Gender, Race, and Nature in the World of Modern Science* (London: Routledge, 1989).

Hardy, Thomas, *The Well-Beloved* [1897] (London: Wordsworth, 2000).

—, *The Collected Poems of Thomas Hardy* (Ware: Wordsworth Editions, 2006).

Harrington, Ralph, 'The Neuroses of the Railway', *History Today,* 44 (July 1994), pp. 15–21.

Hartley, Jenny, *Charles Dickens and the House of Fallen Women* (London: Methuen, 2008).

Hatton, Joseph, *By Order of the Czar: The Tragic Story of Anna Klosstock, Queen of the Ghetto* (London: Hutchinson & Co., 1890).

Heidegger, Martin, *Poetry, Language, and Thought*, trans. Albert Hofstadter (New York: New Directions, 1971).

Henson, Louise, 'Investigations and Fictions: Charles Dickens and Ghosts', in Nicola Bown, Carolyn Burdett and Pamela Thurschwell (eds), *The Victorian Supernatural* (Cambridge: Cambridge University Press, 2004).

Hibbert, Christopher, *The French Revolution* (New York: Penguin, 1982).

Himmelfarb, Gertrude, *The Idea of Poverty: England in the Early Industrial Age* (New York: Knopf, 1984).

Hipple Jr., Walter John, *The Beautiful, the Sublime, and the Picturesque in Eighteenth-Century British Aesthetic Theory* (Carbondale: Southern Illinois University Press, 1957).

Hobsbawm, Eric, *Behind the Times: The Decline and Fall of the Twentieth Century Avant-Gardes* (New York: Thames and Hudson, 1999).

—, *Revolutionaries: Contemporary Essays* (New York: The New Press, 2001).

Hollingshead, John, *Ragged in London in 1861* (London and Melbourne: Dent, 1986).

Hollywood, Paul, 'The Artist as Anarchist: Henry James's *The Princess Casamassima* and the Prospect of Revolution', in Keith Carabine and Owen Knowles (eds), *Conrad, James, and Other Relations* (New York: Columbia University Press, 1998), pp. 277–312.

Holmes, Basil Isabella, *The London Burial Grounds: Notes on Their History from the Earliest Times to the Present Day* (London: T. Fisher Unwin, 1896).

Hood, Thomas, 'The Bridge of Sighs', in Arthur Quiller-Couch (ed.), *The Oxford Book of English Verse: 1250–1900* (Oxford: Clarendon, 1919).

Horn, Pamela, *The Rise and Fall of the Victorian Servant* (Stroud: The History Press, 2004).

Houen, Alex, *Terrorism and Modern Literature, from Joseph Conrad to Ciaran Carson* (Oxford: Oxford University Press, 2002).

Howe, Irving, *Politics and the Novel* (New York: Horizon, 1957).

Hugo, Victor, *Les Misérables*, trans. Norman Denny (London: Penguin, 1982).

Hutter, Albert D., 'The Novelist as Resurrectionist: Dickens and the Dilemma of Death', *Dickens Studies Annual,* 12 (1983), pp. 1–39.

Jackson, Robert Louis, *Dostoevsky's Underground Man in Russian Literature* (The Hague: Mourton & Co., 1958).

James, Henry, 'The Altar of the Dead', in *Terminations* (New York: Harper and Brothers, 1895), pp. 185–242.

—, *The Turn of the Screw: An Authoritative Text and Background and Sources: Essays in Criticism* [1898], ed. Robert Kimbrough (New York: Norton, 1966).

—, 'Letters', ed. Léon Edel, vol. 3, 1883–1895 (London: Macmillan, 1981).

—, *The Princess Casamassima* (London: Penguin, 1987).

—, *The Wings of the Dove* (London: Penguin Classics, 2003).

Jenkins, Edward, *A Week of Passion; Or, The Dilemma of Mr. George Barton the Younger* [1884] (London: Bliss, Sands & Co., 1897).

Joyce, James, *Ulysses* (Ware: Wordsworth, 2010).

Keating, P. J., *The Working Classes in Victorian Fiction* (London: Routledge and Kegan Paul, 1971).

Kellett, John R., *The Impact of Railways on Victorian Cities* (London: Routledge Kegan Paul, 1969).

Kern, Stephen, *The Culture of Time and Space, 1880–1918* (Cambridge, MA: Harvard University Press, 2003).

Kestner, Joseph, *Sherlock's Men: Masculinity, Conan Doyle, and Cultural History* (Aldershot: Ashgate, 1997).

Kincaid, James R., 'Designing Gourmet Children or, KIDS FOR DINNER!' in Ruth Robbins and Julian Wolfreys (eds), *Victorian Gothic: Literary and Cultural Manifestations in the Nineteenth Century* (Basingstoke: Palgrave, 2000).

Kingsley, Charles, *Charles Kingsley: His Letters and Memories of His Life*, ed. Frances E. Kingsley (London: Henry S. King & Co., 1877).

—, *Alton Locke: Tailor and Poet. An Autobiography*, vol. 2 (London: Macmillan & Co., 1881).

Klingender, Francis D., *Art and the Industrial Revolution*, ed. Arthur Elton (New York: Schocken, 1970).

Koch, Robert, 'The Etiology of Cholera', trans. George Lockwood Laycock, in W. Watson Cheyne (ed.), *Recent Essays by Various Authors on Bacteria in Relation to Disease* (London: New Sydenham Society, 1888), pp. 327–69.

Kravchinsky, Sergei, *Underground Russia* (London: Smith & Elder, 1883).

Kristeva, Julia, *Powers of Horror: An Essay on Abjection* (New York: Columbia University Press, 1992).

Kropotkin, Petr Alekseevich, *Kropotkin's Revolutionary Pamphlets* (Whitefish: Kessinger, 2005).

Kubiak, Anthony, *Stages of Terror: Terrorism, Ideology, and Coercion as Theatre History* (Bloomington: Indiana University Press, 1991).

Laporte, Dominique, *History of Shit* (Cambridge, MA: MIT Press, 2002).

Laqueur, Thomas W., 'Cemeteries, Religion and the Culture of Capitalism' in Colin Matthews and Jane Garnet (eds), *Revival and Religion since 1700* (London: The Hambledon Press, 1993), p. 200.

Laqueur, Walter, *The Age of Terrorism* (Boston: Little, Brown, 1987).

Le Fanu, Sheridan, 'Carmilla', in *In a Glass Darkly* (Oxford: Oxford University Press, 1993), pp. 243–319.

Ledger, Sally, *The New Woman: Fiction and Feminism at the Fin-de-Siècle* (Manchester: Manchester University Press, 1997).

Lefebvre, Henri, *The Production of Space*, trans. Donald Nicholson-Smith (Oxford: Blackwell, 1991).

Léonard, Jacques, *Les Médecins de l'Ouest au XIX Siècle* (Paris: Librairie Honoré, 1978).

Lesesne, Mary Richardson, *Torpedoes; or Dynamite in Society* (Galveston: Shaw & Blaylock, 1883).

Lesser, Wendy, *The Life Below Ground: A Study of the Subterranean in Literature and History* (Boston, London: Faber & Faber, 1987).

Lévi-Strauss, Claude, *Tristes Tropiques*, trans. John and Dorren Weightman (New York: Penguin, 1992).

Lewis, R. A., *Edwin Chadwick and the Public Health Movement 1832–1854* (London: Longmans, Green, 1952).

Loudon, John Claudius, *On the Laying Out, Planting, and Managing of Cemeteries and On the Improvement of Churchyards* (London: Longman, Brown, Green & Longmans, 1843).

Lynch, Eve M., 'Spectral Politics: The Victorian Ghost Story and the Domestic Servant', in Nicola Bown, Carolyn Burdett and Pamela Thurschwell (eds), *The Victorian Supernatural* (Cambridge: Cambridge University Press, 2004), pp. 67–87.

Lyon, Janet, *Manifestoes: Provocations of the Modern* (Ithaca: Cornell University Press, 1999).

Lyons, F. S., *Culture and Anarchy in Ireland: 1890–1939* (Oxford: Clarendon Press, 1979).

Macherey, Pierre, 'Marx Dematerialized or the Spirit of Derrida', in Michael Sprinker (ed.), *Ghostly Demarcations: A Symposium on Jacques Derrida's Spectres of Marx* (London: Verso, 1999), pp. 17–25.

MacKay, Donald, *The Dynamite Ship* (London: Page, Pratt, & Turner, 1888).

Mallock, W. H., *The Old Order Changes*, 2 (London: Bentley & Son, 1886).

Marcus, Steven, 'Reading the Illegible', in H. J. Dyos and Michael Wolff (eds), *The Victorian City: Images and Realities* (London, Boston: Routledge and Kegan Paul, 1973), pp. 257–76

Marinetti, Filippo Tommaso, 'The Founding and Manifesto of Futurism', ed. Umbro Apollonio in *Futurist Manifestoes* (New York: Viking, 1973), pp. 19–24.

Martin, Andrew, *The Necropolis Railway* (London: Faber & Faber, 2005).

Marx, Karl, *Capital: A Critique of Political Economy*, trans. Ben Fowkes (London: Penguin, 1976).

—, *The Eighteenth Brumaire of Louis Bonaparte* (New York: International Publishers, 1994).

Marx, Leo, *The Machine in the Garden: Technology and Pastoral Ideal in America* (Oxford: Oxford University Press, 1999).

Matthews, Samantha, *Poetical Remains: Poets' Graves, Bodies, and Books in the Nineteenth Century* (Oxford: Oxford University Press, 2004).

Matus, Jill L., 'Trauma, Memory, and Railway Disaster: The Dickensian Connection', *Victorian Studies*, 43 (Spring 2001), pp. 413–36.

Maurice, Frederick Denison, *Theological Essays* (Cambridge: Cambridge University Press, 1853).

Maxwell, Richard, *The Mysteries of Paris and London* (Charlottesville, London: University Press of Virginia, 1992).

Mayhew, Henry, *Shops and Companies of London and the Trades and Manufactories of Great Britain*, 1 (London: Strand, 1865).

—, *London Labour and the London Poor* [1851], 4 vols (New York: Cosimo, 2009).

McClintock, Anne, *Imperial Leather: Race, Gender, and Sexuality in the Colonial Contest* (New York: Routledge, 1995).

McLaughlin, Terence, *Coprophilia; or, a Peck of Dirt* (London: Cassell, 1971).

Meade, L. T., *The Siren* (London: F. V. White & Co., 1898).

Melchiori, Barbara Arnett, *Terrorism in the Late Victorian London Novel* (London: Croom Helm, 1985).

Melosi, Martin V., *The Sanitary City: Urban Infrastructure in America from Colonial Times to the Present* (Baltimore: Johns Hopkins University, 2000).

Menninghaus, Winfried, 'Walter Benjamin's Theory of Myth', in Gary Smith (ed.), *On Walter Benjamin* (Cambridge, MA: MIT Press, 1988).

—, *Disgust: The Theory and History of a Strong Sensation* (Albany: SUNY Press, 2003).

Meredith, Isabel, *A Girl Among the Anarchists* (London: Duckworth Press, 1903).

Milbank, Alison, 'Powers Old and New: Stoker's Alliances with Anglo-Irish Gothic', in William Hughes and Andrew Smith (eds), *Bram Stoker: History, Psychoanalysis, and Gothic* (Basingstoke: Macmillan, 1998), pp. 12–28.

Miller, Elizabeth Carolyn, 'The Inward Revolution: Sexual Terrorism in *The Princess Casamassima*', *The Henry James Review*, 24 (Spring 2003), pp. 146–67.

Miller, Stuart, *Mastering Modern European History* (London: Macmillan, 1980).

Miller, William Ian, *The Anatomy of Disgust* (Cambridge, MA: Harvard University Press, 1998).

Minkowski, Eugène, *Lived Time* (Evanston: Northwestern University Press, 1970).

Mitchell, Allan, 'The Paris Morgue as a Social Institution in the Nineteenth Century', *Francia*, 4 (1976), pp. 581–96.

Morley, John, *Death, Heaven, and the Victorians* (London: Studio Vista, 1971).

Morris, Edward, 'Advertising and the Acquisition of Contemporary Art', *Journal of the History of Collections*, 4 (1992), pp. 195–200.

Morris, William, *New from Nowhere* (London: Lawrence and Wishart, 1968).

Mulry, David, 'Popular Accounts of the Greenwich Bombing and Conrad's *The Secret Agent*', *Rocky Mountain Review of Language and Literature*, 54 (2000), pp. 43–64.

Mumford, Lewis, *Technics and Civilization* (New York: Harcourt Brace, 1934).

Murakami, Haruki, *Underground*, trans. Alfred Birnbaum and Philip Gabriel (London: Harvill Press, 2001).

Nead, Lynda, *Myths of Sexuality: Representations of Women in Victorian Britain* (London: Wiley-Blackwell, 1988).

—, *Victorian Babylon: People, Streets, and Images in Nineteenth-Century London* (New Haven: Yale University Press, 2000).

Newsinger, John, *Fenianism in Mid-Victorian Britain* (London: Pluto, 1994).

Nord, Deborah Epstein, 'The Urban Perpipatetic: Spectator, Streetwalker, Woman Writer', *Nineteenth Century Literature*, 46 (1991), pp. 351–75.

—, *Walking the Victorian Streets: Women, Representation, and the City* (Ithaca: Cornell University Press, 1995).

Nordau, Max, *Degeneration* [1895] (London: William Heinemann, 1920).

Noyes, Russell (ed.), *English Romantic Poetry and Prose* (New York: Oxford University Press, 1956).

O'Brien, Matthew, *Beneath the Neon: Life and Death in the Tunnels of Las Vegas* (Las Vegas: Huntington Press, 2007).

Ó Broin, Leon, *Revolutionary Underground* (Dublin: Gill & MacMillan, 1976).

O'Connor, Erin, *Raw Material: Producing Pathology in Victorian Culture* (Durham: Duke University Press, 2000).

Ó Donghaile, Deaglán, *Blasted Literature: Victorian Political Fiction and the Shock of Modernism* (Edinburgh: Edinburgh University Press, 2011).

O'Hegarty, Patrick Sarsfield, *A History of Ireland under the Union* (London: Methuen, 1952).

O'Leary, John, *Recollections of Fenians and Fenianism* (London: Downey & Co., 1896).

Oliver, Hermia, *The International Anarchist Movement in Late Victorian London* (London: Croom Helm, 1983).

Orczy, Baroness Emmuska, 'The Mysterious Death on the Underground Railway', in Glen and Karen Bledsoe (eds), *Classic Mysteries II* (Los Angeles: Lowell House, 1999), pp. 8–18

Orr, John, *Terrorism and Modern Drama* (Edinburgh: Edinburgh University Press, 1980).

Orwell, George, *Down and Out in Paris and London* (London: Secker & Warburg, 1986).

Oxenham, John, 'A Mystery of the Underground', in *Murder on the Railways*, ed. Peter Haining (London: Orion, 1996), pp. 270–7.

Paolozzi, Eduardo, *Eduardo Paolozzi Underground*, ed. Richard Cork (London: Royal Academy of the Arts, 1986).

Parent-Duchâtelet, Alexandre J., *On Prostitution*, 2nd edn (London: T. Burgess, 1840).

Parsons, Deborah L., *Streetwalking the Metropolis: Women, the City, and Modernity* (Oxford: Oxford University Press, 2000).

Pelling, Margaret, *Cholera, Fever, and English Medicine* (London: Oxford University Press, 1978).

Phelan, Peggy, *Mourning Sex: Performing Public Memories* (London: Routledge, 1997).

Phillips, Wm. M., *Nightmares of Anarchy: Language and Cultural Change: 1870–1914* (Lewisburg: Bucknell, 2003).

Pike, David L., 'Underground Theater: Subterranean Spaces on the London Stage', *Nineteenth Century Studies*, 13 (1999), pp. 102–38.

—, 'Modernist Space and the Transformation of Underground London', in Pamela K. Gilbert (ed.), *Imagined Londons* (Albany: State of University of New York Press, 2002), pp. 101–16.

—, *Subterranean Cities: The World beneath Paris and London 1800–1945* (Ithaca: Cornell University Press, 2005).

—, *Metropolis on the Styx: The Underworlds of Modern Urban Culture, 1800–2001* (Ithaca: Cornell University Press, 2007).

Pittard, Christopher, *Purity and Contamination in Late Victorian Detective Fiction* (Farnham: Ashgate, 2011).

Poe, Edgar Allen, 'The Philosophy of Composition', in *Poetry, Tales, and Selected Essays* (New York: Library of America Press, 1996), pp. 1373–85.

Poggioli, Renato, *The Theory of the Avant-Garde*, trans. Gerald Fitzgerald (Cambridge, MA: Harvard University Press, 1968).

Pollard, H. B. C., *The Secret Societies of Ireland: Their Rise and Progress* (London: Kessinger Publishing, 2003).

Pound, Ezra, 'In a Station of the Metro', in Peter Jones (ed.), *Imagist Poetry* (Harmondsworth: Penguin, 1972), p. 33.

Prashad, Vijay, 'Native Dirt/Imperial Ordure: The Cholera of 1832 and the Morbid Resolutions of Modernity', *Journal of Historical Sociology*, 7 (1994), pp. 243–60.

Prendergast, Christopher, *Paris and the Nineteenth Century* (Oxford: Blackwell, 1992).

Proudhon, Pierre-Joseph, *What is Property?*, ed. Donald R. Kelley and Bonnie G. Smith (Cambridge: Cambridge University Press, 1994).

Pykett, Lyn, *The Sensation Novel: From The Woman in White to The Moonstone* (Plymouth: Northcote, 1994), pp. 15–22.

Quail, John, *The Slow Burning Fuse: The Lost Movement in Late Victorian London* (London: Paladin, 1978).

Rabaté, Jean-Michel, *The Ghosts of Modernity* (Gainesville: University of Florida Press, 1996).

Ragon, Michel, *The Space of Death: A Study of Funerary Architecture, Decoration, and Urbanism*, trans. Alan Sheridan (Charlottesville: University Press of Virginia, 1983).

Rappaport, Erika Diane, *Shopping for Pleasure: Women in the Making of London's West End* (Princeton: Princeton University Press, 2002).

Read, Alan, *Theatre and Everyday Life: An Ethics of Performance* (London and New York: Routledge, 1993).

Reid, Donald, *Paris Sewers and Sewermen: Realities and Representations* (Cambridge, MA: Harvard University Press, 1991).

Richards, Jeffrey, and John M. MacKenzie, *The Railway Station: A Social History* (Oxford: Oxford University Press, 1988).

Richardson, Angelique, *Love and Eugenics in the Late Nineteenth Century: Rational Reproduction and the New Woman* (Oxford: Oxford University Press, 2003).

Richardson, Ruth, *Death, Dissection, and the Destitute* (London: Penguin, 1988).

Robbins, Bruce, *The Servant's Hand: English Fiction from Below* (Durham, London: Duke University Press, 1993).

Robinson, Mary S., 'Zola and Manet: The Poetry of the Railway', *Journal of Modern Literature*, 10 (March 1983), pp. 55–70.

Ropes, Arthur and Mary, *On Peter's Island* (London: John Murray, 1901).

Rosen, George, 'Disease, Debility, and Death', in H. J. Dyos and Michael Wolff (eds), *The Victorian City: Images and Realities* (London, Boston: Routledge and Kegan Paul, 1973), pp. 625–68.

Rotandaro, Anna, *Women at Work on London Transport* (Stroud: The History Press, 2004).

Rowe, John Carlos, *The Theoretical Dimension of Henry James* (Madison: University of Wisconsin Press, 1984).

Sadler, Simon, *The Situationist City* (Cambridge, MA: MIT Press, 1999).

Said, Edward, *Orientalism* (New York: Vintage, 1979).

Saler, Michael T., *The Avant-Garde in Interwar England: Medieval Modernism and the London Underground* (Oxford: Oxford University Press, 1999).

Sanders, Andrew, *Charles Dickens Resurrectionist* (New York: St. Martins Press, 1982).

Sant'Elia, Antonio, and Filippo Tommaso Marinetti, 'The Futurist Manifesto of Architecture', in Ulrich Conrads (ed.), *Programmes and Manifestoes on Twentieth Century Architecture* (London: Lund Humphries, 1964), pp. 34–8.

Sartre, Jean-Paul, *Being and Nothingness*, trans. Hazel E. Barnes (New York: Washington Square Press, 1973).

Sassoon, Siegfried, *Collected Poems 1908–1956* (London: Faber & Faber, 1984).

Scanlan, Margaret, 'Terrorism and the Realistic Novel: Henry James and *The Princess Casamassima*', *Texas Studies in Literature and Language,* 34 (Fall 1992), pp. 380–402.

Schivelbusch, Wolfgang, 'Railroad Space and Railroad Time', *New German Critique,* 14 (Spring 1978), pp. 31–40.

—, *The Railway Journey: The Industrialization of Time and Space in the Nineteenth Century*, trans. Anselm Hollo (Berkeley: University of California Press, 1986).

—, *Culture of Defeat: On National Trauma, Mourning, and Recovery* (New York: Metropolitan, 2003).

Schorske, Carl, *Fin-de-Siècle Vienna: Politics and Culture* (New York: Vintage, 1981).

Schreiner, Olive, *Women and Labour* (London: T. Fisher Unwin, 1911).

Schulkind, Eugene, *The Paris Commune of 1871: The View from the Left* (London: Cape, 1972).

Schwenger, Peter, *The Tears of Things: Melancholy and Physical Objects* (Minneapolis: University of Minnesota Press, 2006).

Seed, David, 'Mystery in Everyday Things: Charles Dickens's "Signalman"', *Criticism,* 23 (Spring 1981), pp. 42–57.

Seltzer, Mark, *Henry James and the Art of Power* (Ithaca: Cornell University Press, 1984).

Shaw, G. B., *An Unsocial Socialist* [1884] (London: Virago, 1980).

Shelston, Alan, 'Dickens and the Burial of the Dead', in Valeria Tinkler-Villani (ed.), *Babylon or New Jerusalem? Perceptions of the City in Literature* (Amsterdam, New York: Roldopi, 2005), pp. 77–92.

Short, K. R. M., *The Dynamite War: Irish American Bombers in Victorian Britain* (Atlantic Heights: Humanities Press, 1979).

Shpayer-Makov, Haia, 'A Traitor to His Class: The Anarchist in British Fiction', *Journal of European Studies,* 26 (September 1996), pp. 299–325.

Simmel, Georg, 'The Metropolis and Mental Life', in Kurt H. Wolff (ed.), *The Sociology of Georg Simmel* (Glencoe: Free Press, 1950), pp. 409–24.

Simmons, Jack, *The Railway in Town and Country, 1830–1914* (Newton Abbot: David & Charles, 1986).

—, *The Victorian Railway* (London: Thames & Hudson, 1991).

Sinclair, Andrew, *The Anatomy of Terror: A History of Terrorism* (London: Macmillan, 2003).

Smith, Stephen, *Underground London: Travels Beneath the Streets* (London: Little, Brown, 2004).

Solis, Julia, *New York Underground: The Anatomy of a City* (New York, London: Routledge, 2005).

Spongberg, Mary, *Feminizing Venereal Disease: The Body of the Prostitute in Nineteenth-Century Medical Discourse* (New York: New York University Press, 1997).

Stallybrass, Peter, and Allon White, *The Politics and Poetics of Transgression* (London: Methuen, 1986), pp. 125–8.

Steig, Michael, 'Dickens's Excremental Vision', *Victorian Studies*, 13 (1970), pp. 339–54.

Stevenson, Robert Louis, and Fanny Van de Grift Stevenson, *More New Arabian Nights: The Dynamiter* (London: Longmans, Green, & Co., 1885).

—, 'The Body Snatcher', in *The Strange Case of Dr. Jekyll and Mr. Hyde and Other Tales of Terror*, (London: Penguin, 2002), pp. 71–92.

Stoker, Bram, 'The Burial of the Rats', in *Dracula's Guest*, (Dingle: Brandon Books, 1990), pp. 104–31.

—, *The Lair of the White Worm* (Dingle: Brandon Books, 1991)

—, *Dracula* (Oxford: Oxford University Press, 1998).

Strange, Julie-Marie, *Death, Grief, and Poverty in Britain, 1870–1914* (Cambridge: Cambridge University Press, 2005).

Sutherland, John, 'Dickens's War on Filth', *The Guardian* (20 October 2005), p. 16.

Sypher, Eileen, 'Anarchism and Gender: James's *The Princess Casamassima* and Conrad's *The Secret Agent*', *The Henry James Review*, 9 (Winter 1988), pp. 1–16.

Taylor, Lawrence J., and Maeve Hickey, *Tunnel Kids* (Tucson: University of Arizona Press, 2001).

Tennyson, Alfred, *In Memoriam: Authoritative Text Criticism*, ed. Erik Irving Gray (New York: W. W. Norton, 2003).

Thacker, Andrew, *Moving through Modernity: Space and Geography in Modernism* (Manchester: Manchester University Press, 2003).

Thomas, Donald, *Victorian Underworld* (London: John Murray, 1998).

Thomas, Matthew, *Anarchist Ideas and Counter-Cultures in Britain, 1880–1914: Revolutions in Everyday Life* (Aldershot: Ashgate, 2005).

Thomas, Ronald, *Detective Fiction and the Rise of Forensic Science* (Cambridge: Cambridge University Press, 1999).

Thompson, E. P., 'Time, Work-discipline, and Industrial Capitalism', *Past and Present*, 38 (1967), pp. 56–92.

Thompson, Henry, *Cremation: The Treatment of the Body after Death* (London: Smith, Elder, & Co., 1884).

Thomson, James, *The City of Dreadful Night* (London: Methuen, 1932).

Tilley, Elizabeth, 'Stoker, Paris, and the Crisis of Identity', *Literature and History*, 10 (2001), pp. 26–42.

Toth, Jennifer, *The Mole People: Life in the Tunnels beneath New York City* (Chicago: Chicago Review Press, 1993).

Trench, Richard, and Ellis Hillman, *London under London: A Subterranean Guide* (London: John Murray, [1984] 1993).

Trollope, Anthony, *The Landleaguers* (London: Chatto & Windus, 1883).

—, *The Eustace Diamonds* (London: Oxford University Press, 1973).

—, *The Claverings* (New York: Dover Publications, 1977).

—, *The Way We Live Now* (Oxford: Oxford University Press, 1982).

—, *The Prime Minister* (Oxford: Oxford University Press, 1983).

Trollope, Thomas Adolphus, *What I Remember*, ed. Herber van Thal (London: William Kimber, 1973).

Trotter, David, *Cooking with Mud: The Idea of Mess in Nineteenth-Century Fiction and Art* (Oxford: Oxford University Press, 2000).

Turgenev, Ivan, *Diary of a Superfluous Man*, trans. David Patterson (New York: Norton, 1999).

Turner, Mark W., 'Periodical Time in the Nineteenth Century', *Media History*, 8 (2002), pp. 183–96.

—, *Backward Glances: Cruising the Queer Streets of New York and London* (London: Reaktion Books, 2003).

Vadillo, Ana Parejo, *Women Poets and Urban Aestheticism: Passengers of Modernity* (London: Palgrave, 2005).

Vigarello, Georges, *Concepts of Cleanliness: Changing Attitudes in France since the Middle Ages* (Cambridge: Cambridge University Press, 2008).

Walker, George Alfred, *Gatherings from Graveyards* (London: Longmans, 1839).

Walkowitz, Judith R., *Prostitution and Victorian Society* (Cambridge: Cambridge University Press, 1980).

—, *City of Dreadful Delight: Narratives of Sexual Danger in Late-Victorian London* (Chicago: University of Chicago Press, 1992).

Ward, F. O., *Circulation or Stagnation* (London: Cassell, 1889).

Wardlaw, Grant, *Political Terrorism: Theory, Tactics, and Counter-Measures* (Cambridge: Cambridge University Press, 1989).

Weber, Samuel, *Mass Mediauras: Form, Technics, Media* (Stanford: Stanford University Press, 1996).

Wells, H. G., *Anticipations of the Reaction of Mechanical and Scientific Progress upon Human Life and Thought* (London: Chapman & Hall, 1902).

—, *The Sleeper Awakes* (London: Sphere, 1980).

—, *The First Men in the Moon* (London: Gollancz, 2001).

—, *The Shape of Things to Come* (London: Penguin, 2006).

—, *The Time Machine* (London: Penguin, 2005).

—, *The War of the Worlds* (London: Penguin, 2005).

Welsh, David, *Underground Writing: The London Tube from George Gissing to Virginia Woolf* (Liverpool: Liverpool University Press, 2010).

Wheeler, Michael, *Heaven, Hell, and the Victorians* (Cambridge: Cambridge University Press, 1994).

Whistler, James McNeill, 'The Ten O'Clock Lecture' in *Symbolist Art Theories: A Critical Anthology*, ed. Henri Dorra, pp. 65–70.

Wilde, Oscar, *Vera; or, The Nihilist*, ed. Frances Miriam Reed (Lewiston: Edwin Mellen Press, 1989).

—, *The Importance of Being Earnest* (Clayton: Prestwick House, 2005).

Wilkins, W. H., *The Alien Invasion* (London: Methuen, 1892).

Williams, Rosalind, *Notes on the Underground: An Essay on Technology, Society, and the Imagination* (Cambridge, MA: MIT Press, 1990).

Wilson, Elizabeth, *The Sphinx in the City: Urban Life, the Control of Disorder, and Women* (Berkeley: University of California Press, 1991).

—, 'The Invisible Flâneur', *New Left Review*, 191 (Jan/Feb 1992), pp. 90–110.

Winslow, C. E. A., *The Conquest of Epidemic Disease: A Chapter in the History of Ideas* (Princeton: Princeton University Press, 1943).

Winter, James, *London's Teeming Streets 1830–1914* (London and New York: Routledge, 1993).

Wisnicki, Adrian, *Conspiracy, Revolution, and Terrorism from Victorian Fiction to the Modern Novel*, ed. William E. Cain (New York, London: Routledge, 2008).

Wohl, Anthony S., *Endangered Lives: Public Health in Victorian Britain* (London: J. M. Dent & Sons, 1983).

Wolff, Janet, 'The Invisible Flâneuse: Women and the Literature of Modernity', *Theory, Culture, and Society*, 2 (1985), pp. 37–46.

Wolfreys, Julian, *Deconstruction, Derrida* (New York: St. Martins Press, 1998).

—, *Victorian Hauntings: Spectrality, Gothic, the Uncanny and Literature* (Basingstoke: Palgrave, 2002).

—, *Writing London: Materiality, Memory, Spectrality*, 2 (Basingstoke and New York: Palgrave Macmillan, 2004).

Wolmar, Christian, *The Subterranean Railway: How the London Underground Was Built and How It Changed the City Forever* (London: Atlantic, 2005).

Woolf, Virginia, 'The Mark on the Wall' in *Two Stories* (Richmond: Hogarth Press, 1917).

—, *Mrs. Dalloway* (London: Grafton Books, 1976).

—, *To the Lighthouse* (Basingstoke: Macmillan, 1987).

—, *The Waves* (London: Vintage, 2000).

Wright, Lawrence, *Clean and Decent: The Fascinating History of the Bathroom and Water Closet* (New York: Viking, 1960).

Wright, Richard, 'The Man Who Lived Underground' in Abraham Chapman (ed.), *An Anthology of African-American Literature* (New York: Penguin, 2001), pp. 114–60.

Zola, Émile, 'Courrier de Paris', *Illustration*, vol. 77 (29 January 1881), p. 66.

—, *Nana*, trans. George Holden (Harmondsworth: Penguin, 1970).

—, *Germinal*, trans. Peter Collier (Oxford and New York: Oxford University Press, 1993).

—, *La Bête Humaine*, trans. Roger Pearson (Oxford: Oxford University Press, 2009).

Zulaika, Joseba, and William A. Douglass, *Terror and Taboo: The Follies, Fables, and Faces of Terrorism* (New York, London: Routledge, 1996).

Index

Page numbers in *italic* denote illustrations; *n* = endnote.